THE COMPLETE GUIDE TO LEARNING CENTERS

By Susan S. Petreshene

PENDRAGON HOUSE

The Complete Guide to Learning Centers

BY SUSAN S. PETRESHENE

*Illustrations by Anne Drummond
and Victor Petreshene*

PENDRAGON HOUSE, PALO ALTO
California

THE COMPLETE GUIDE
TO LEARNING CENTERS

First published 1978
by Pendragon House, Inc.
2595 E. Bayshore Drive
Palo Alto, CA 94303
U.S.A.

First Printing: January 1978
Second Printing: September 1978
Third Printing: July 1979
Typesetting: Lehmann Graphics
Printing: The George Banta Co., Inc.
MANUFACTURED IN THE U.S.A.

ISBN No. 0-916988-08-2
Library of Congress
Catalog Card No. 76-49794

Library of Congress Cataloging in Publication Data

Petreshene, Susan S.
   The complete guide to learning centers.

   1. Individualized instruction.   2. Open plan schools.   I. Title.
LB1031.P43   371.39'4   76-49794
ISBN 0-916988-08-2

TABLE OF CONTENTS

Introduction

Teachers are accustomed to dealing with the reality of many children with many different academic and emotional needs in the same classroom. So, it is not surprising that it was classroom teachers who evolved the concept of learning centers as a practical method for dealing with the special needs of children. Nor is it surprising that this unique book, *Complete Guide to Learning Centers*, is written by a classroom teacher for practicing classroom teachers.

Unlike some sources which list a variety of activities and material for use in a learning center, Mrs. Petreshene not only presents a wealth of activities in the basic skill subjects, but also deals with the mechanics of operating learning centers within the regular classroom. It is not merely a series of activities in the classroom which constitutes an individualized program. The activities in themselves are only a stimulus to learning. The teacher must understand both the needs of the individual child and the sequential nature of the skills to be learned. The important and key factor of this book is that it shows the teacher how to develop a sequential individualized curriculum.

This is a working book for classroom teachers. The beginning teacher will find the "how to do it" approach particularly valuable. In careful detail, the author has dealt with the problems which must be resolved in establishing an effective individualized approach to teaching. With samples of each activity, any teacher following this *Guide* would be well-launched on an individualized program. The experienced teacher may want to adapt many of these activities and suggestions to her or his own particular situation or classroom needs. But whether the teacher is a novice or an experienced professional, this book offers guidance and ideas certain to enhance learning in any classroom. The wealth of activities in the basic skill subjects listed in this book are not listed in a vacuum, nor are they enumerated in and for themselves. Instead, they are incorporated as a part of a total sequence and total classroom program. This unique method of presentation enhances the value of the book beyond that of being just another good book. It provides the teacher with an indispensible guide for an individualized program.

Acceptance of the philosophy of individualization of instruction came many years before attempts were made to apply this philosophy to classroom instructional practices. Initial attempts, unfortunately, often resulted in patterns of grouping which categorized children and, in a classic demonstration of the self-fulfilling prophecy, resulted in high achievers continuing to achieve at a high level, average students achieving at an average level, and poorer students slipping progressively further and further behind. Research clearly indicates that individualization of instruction, if done correctly, has far-reaching and long range effects. There is a growing trend throughout the country for state programs to mandate individualized instruction. This book is a practical way to implement the concepts of these programs.

Two distinct changes in classroom practices are apparent in today's schools. The traditional three-group approach to classroom learning has become suspect; at the same time, "mainstreaming" of students with special learning problems is more widespread. In too many instances, these changes have created new problems for the classroom teacher to solve in whatever manner she or he can devise.

In this book, basic considerations such as "Where to Begin?" and "Time Schedules" are preceded by a brief but convincing discussion of the philosophical basis for learning centers. Teachers are urged to avoid the temptation to skip over this section in their haste to get to practical ideas which can be implemented tomorrow. Because there is still sufficient opposition to the concept of individualizing instruction, it is wise to be forearmed with a sound rationale for the learning center approach.

The current attention to greater emphasis on basics is nationwide. A return to large group instruction of isolated skills as a way of achieving this goal can only result in tragic consequences. A denial of individual differences in an effort to "return to basics" would frustrate teachers and children alike. The learning center approach, as proposed in this *Guide*, is a means by which individual differences can be provided for, as emphasis is placed upon mastery of basic skills.

WALTER B. BARBE
The Ohio State University
Adjunct Professor
HIGHLIGHTS FOR CHILDREN
Editor-in-Chief

Acknowledgements

I shall be eternally grateful to my husband, Vic, for his encouragement, support and help, and to my children Kathy and Steve for their patience and understanding.

I am much indebted to Dr. Mary E. Collins who started me on the road to individualization; to my former principal, Thomas H. Smith, and to the many parents at West Novato School who supported my efforts to individualize and humanize my classroom; to Anne Drummond and my husband, who transformed a multitude of rough sketches into illustrations; to Annette Conklin who edited the manuscript and made many invaluable suggestions; and to the many children and teachers who will never know how much they personally contributed to this book.

Preface

The ideas presented in this book were originally used in my own classroom. Later, when the methods and materials were shared and tested with teachers in my college classes, workshops, and consultant work, their overwhelming reaction was that roadblocks barring the individualization of instruction had been removed.

Many teachers talked about their previous frustrations with learning centers and individualization of instruction. They discussed having been faced with a multitude of books and articles describing learning centers, open classrooms, integrated days, and numerous other programs, many of which promised instant success in the individualization of a program.

With hopes high, some teachers had followed recipes for "short-term" learning centers. Weeks had been spent constructing materials needed for the learning centers, only to have them quickly consumed by the students. The perennial question, "What do I do now?" was the result.

Other teachers who had accumulated a large number of varied materials tried the "games and gimmicks" approach to learning centers. Despite the seeming abundance, they found they were unable to plan a program which met the needs of children over the long haul. The numbers game in materials quickly deteriorated into busy work. Little time could be devoted to sequential skill development. In addition, keeping track of the movement of thirty or more children and maintaining accurate records on their skills in a variety of subject areas, became overwhelming.

The purpose of this book is to help teachers deal with these problems. It is intended for teachers who want to individualize their classroom while retaining a sense of structure and organization, with an emphasis on basic skills.

The process of structuring "on-going" centers is described in detail. These are centers which enable teachers to prepare materials that remain in continuous use throughout the year. This eliminates the "What do I do now?" obstacle.

A step-by-step approach, on how to prepare sequential materials for individualized instruction in each major subject area, is presented. Methods of determining the needs of each student and prescribing for those needs are incorporated. Record-keeping systems which do not require hours of paper work, yet provide helpful information for the teacher, are detailed.

Classroom environment, grouping children, developing independence, and the use of volunteer and paid aides, are discussed.

The heart of this book is the necessary "how to" information to help teachers feel competent in organizing and operating learning centers in mathematics, creative writing, handwriting, and individualized spelling, and in constructing an environment in which each student is working on materials at an appropriate level, reflecting personal needs, interests and abilities.

Susan S. Petreshene

CHAPTER I

Learning Centers and Individualization

Why Individualize?—A Personal Appraisal

Teachers decide to individualize instruction within their classrooms for a variety of reasons. In my case I gradually became aware of factors which made me stop and evaluate what I was doing. My classroom was traditional and quiet. A large portion of the day was spent at the front of the room with the children intently listening and watching (or at least so I thought!). The students were given identical assignments. As they completed their work, they were allowed to go to the back of the room and select a book or some "fun" activity to keep them occupied while they waited for me to introduce the next lesson.

As I analyzed the classroom, I realized that certain students, who worked the hardest, just managed to finish an assignment before we started the next subject. Their re-ward was a smile or encouraging word. But there was never time for them to choose any of the "fun" activities. Instead it was a continuous push and struggle, since they were being asked to do work which was too difficult for them. I began wondering if, inadvertently, I might not be creating some of our future discipline problems.

The so-called bright students in the classroom fared no better. They certainly were not being challenged. They were able to complete the assignments practically before the words were out of my mouth. Yet they were being continuously rewarded—and for what? For having the ability to complete assignments quickly, which were far below their capacity.

I kept thinking, "If I'm supposed to be instilling good study habits, this is a strange way to go about it: rewarding those who put forth little effort, and penalizing those who work the hardest!''

I also realized that the number of students being ''reached'' when I stood at the front of the classroom explaining an assignment, were few. For the majority, the assignment was either too easy or too hard. More guilt feelings!

Obviously the time had come to make some changes. But what and how? I kept thinking, ''I need to find out the deficits and strengths of each of these children, and develop a program for them. But there are thirty of them and only one of me! How am I ever going to accomplish individualization and still maintain my sanity!''

Further compounding my problem was the fact that during this time *Summerhill* (1) was in vogue. The prevailing attitude indicated a teacher should sit back and let the children unfold like flowers. Otherwise, the classroom would not truly be individualized. Despite this advice, I finally came to the conclusion that my classroom had to be comfortable for me, if I were to do my best for the students.

Others might be comfortable in an unstructured classroom, allowing the students to decide when and if they wanted to do various tasks. But I needed structure, a sense of organization, and a feeling of confidence about each student's growth in the basic skills. Yet I didn't want the students to become ''computers,'' continuously taking tests, completing material, and taking more tests. (Programmed learning and criterion reference tests were also in vogue at that time.) Nor did I want a situation where ''everyone did his or her own thing'' all day, with no regard for anyone else.

At this point I attempted to discover what changes would be necessary if I were to try to meet the needs of individual students.

Children almost always completed their assignments in my classroom. Yet when the last child handed in the assignment, there was not a feeling of success. Instead it was a sense of relief—''Thank heavens I made it!'' Success and relief are two different emotions!

It became apparent that, if the students were to feel successful, it would be necessary to provide a variety of materials covering a wide span of abilities and interests. Materials of this type would enable each child to proceed at the special rate right for an individual, not a standardized robot. The child would not have to wait patiently (or otherwise) for everyone to understand a concept, nor have to struggle in an attempt to keep up with others. However, it would also be necessary for me to structure the environment in such a way that I would know what each of the children was doing in order to be able to guide the students, provide instruction, and keep track of their progress.

Too many children were waiting to be told what to do, how to do it, when to do it, and where to put it when they were finished. Then they waited for the next set of what, how, when, and where directions. If the students were to learn a sense of responsibility, they would need to be given choices, and to bear the consequences (both positive and negative) of their decisions. These experiences then could provide the foundation for other choices and responsibilities in the future.

I was convinced that the child who did not learn to get along with his or her peers was not a happy child, and quite possibly, would not be a happy adult. Therefore peer interaction would be necessary so students could discover the give and take of human relationships.

Certain criteria emerged from this analysis as being of utmost importance. I wanted a classroom where children would (1) feel successful, (2) learn a sense of responsibility, (3) learn to get along with others, and (4) grow academically at a rate in accordance with their abilities.

Now at least I had established the requirements for myself and my students. The program based on this foundation is what this book is about. A description of the resulting classroom and a typical day follows.

Overview

The classroom is arranged in four learning centers. Each of these centers consists of a large table, or a group of desks or small tables pushed together. A learning center seats approximately eight students, and accommodates the materials the students will need as they work in one subject area.

The basic learning centers are Writing, Computational Mathematics, Individualized Spelling, and Discovery (manipulative mathematics or science). Art, cooking, additional language-arts experiences, and independent centers are interspersed throughout the week. Writing and computational mathematics are included on a daily basis.

The day begins with everyone together. This time is set aside for students to talk about what is important in their lives. The emphasis is on discussing topics of genuine interest to the students (often related to crafts, sports, science, social studies, and other topics of current interest). This is different from traditional "show and tell" when a child talks about *anything,* regardless of how boring it is to everyone else! I am convinced that what we often teach children in "show and tell" periods is to tune out, but look alert—teacher included!

After the children have had a time for discussion, the teacher explains the learning centers for that day and provides any instruction or information the children will need.

Three or four heterogeneous groups have been formed in order to enable the teacher to work with students individually and to keep track of their progress.

The groups rotate through three or four of the centers during the next 1½ to 2½ hours (25-40 minutes at each center). Time is provided later in the day for total group activities such as story time, music, physical education, movies, discussions, and Glasser "circle meetings" (2).

The majority of work at the centers is "on-going." For example, at the Creative Writing Center, the child begins writing a story, and spends as many days as necessary to finish it. The emphasis is on quality and doing the best job possible. The student writes as much as possible on the first day and continues the following day or days. One project flows into the next one. (This eliminates the problems of daily assignments which have clear-cut completion points. With this type of deadline assignment, the child rushes to finish it, and then asks what to do next!)

Since materials are frequently changed at the Creative Writing Center, there are always many stimulating ideas available.

Many language-arts skills (punctuation, capitalization, grammar, sentence structure, dictionary skills, etc.), are taught by using the child's own writings. The children's stories are made into illustrated books. The class often cooperates in making class booklets. Creative Writing becomes so exciting to children that they often continue to write stories during recess and during their independent time.

Work on the mechanics of printing or cursive handwriting is included as part of the Writing Center. Assignments are planned to meet each individual child's needs. After a brief diagnosis, the teacher determines which letters the child needs to practice further. Assignments are then given which provide drill on those specific letters. When the student has mastered the basic letter formations, "copy work" is used for reinforcement. The materials parallel each child's reading level, so students are never asked to copy something which they cannot read. High-interest material is used for "copy work." The student has a selection of topics: poems, riddles, tongue twisters, selections from the *Guinness Book of World Records,* autograph verses, science experiments, information about animals, etc.

Each child's copy work is written in a book format. As the student finishes each topic, the booklet becomes a prize to bear home as it contains information which was interesting in a very personal sense.

I have had children come back, years later, with a somewhat tattered copy-work book and say, "Do you remember when I wrote this?" It obviously has been well used as an important part of a home library.

There is a tremendous difference between a child's handwriting if you compare a copied page from the handwriting textbook, versus the animated writing in a copy work book when the young writer has chosen the topic!

At the Math Center there is a range of materials of varying difficulty. After a brief diagnostic inventory, the child's strengths and deficits are determined. Accordingly, each student is placed in appropriate "ongoing" material. The child then proceeds at a purely personal pace, receiving "check-ups" at the conclusion of work on each skill in order to determine whether the current skill or any of the previous skills need additional reinforcement. Manipulative materials are used whenever a child is learning a new concept. These materials remain available for the student's use, as needed.

The Individualized Spelling Program is designed to work upon the specific skill deficits of each child. The teacher administers a non-threatening diagnostic inventory to a small group of children to determine which skills a child needs to perfect. One child may be working on short vowel three-letter phonetic words. The child in the next seat is working on long vowels, blends, and digraphs. Still another child is studying "spelling demons," all in the same group. Because the student is working at an appropriate level, success and positive attitudes are assured. Yet, within a predetermined framework, each student can select a "personal" group of words and work toward their mastery.

During the week the students practice their own spelling words, choosing from twenty or more different ways to practice them. They are given a weekly spelling test. Any words spelled incorrectly are automatically forwarded to each child's list for the following week. The emphasis is on working at an appropriate level, and on mastering words and spelling concepts.

The Discovery Center consists of manipulative math activities. These employ such materials as balance scales, measurement devices, geoboards, attribute blocks, and three-dimensional materials, as well as science projects. The focus at this center is on discovery. The students learn by doing, and then record their findings. They often work as partners, resulting in cooperation and verbal communication.

At each of the above centers there are daily minimum requirements which vary according to individual children.

The Independent Center allows a child to choose activities in which to become involved. Choices include returning to any of the previously described centers, provided that there is "room for one more"; art projects, painting, reading, library "privileges"; or any of the activities which used to be on the "free-time fun shelf"—games, puzzles, animals and blocks.

The latter type of learning experiences are often confined to the kindergarteners. But anyone who has ever taught kindergarten knows that the students who most want to hold the animals, build with the blocks, etc., are the upper-grade children. A steady flow of older children want to know if the animals' cages need cleaning, or if some of the children need help building with blocks. What they are saying is, "May I please become involved in these activities?" Perhaps intuitively they know they will learn something. As Jacob Bronowski said, "You could not get a being to build anything unless the child had put together a set of bricks. That is the beginning of the Parthenon and the Taj Mahal, of the dome at Sultaniyeh. . . . and the Pentagon" (3).

The Independent Center allows the teacher to provide these kinds of choices. Now instead of only the "smartest" or fastest-working children having a choice, all children are entitled to an independent choice, provided that they have used other class time effectively.

Sometimes an Independent Center is used daily. In other circumstances it may be used only once a week. But regardless of frequency, it is an important time when children have the opportunity to choose for themselves.

It is always interesting to notice the number of children who return to an "academic" center to continue writing a story, or to work some additional math problems during their Independent Center time. Interesting and exciting things happen when children's needs are being met, and they are involved in their work!

What does this type of program accomplish? (1) It enables the teacher to deal with many levels because of the small group at each center. (2) It facilitates working with children in a warm and personal way. (3) It permits the teacher to provide for individual differences. It also eliminates the situation of the child who continually has free time owing to an ability to finish the work quickly, as well as the problem of the child who seldom can complete the assignment and never has free time. The tasks and expectations correspond to the individual child's needs and abilities. (4) It enables the children to become quite independent, further freeing the teacher to teach. (5) Children become excited about school, gain academically and— most important—are happy and successful.

Reading has not been mentioned as one of the centers. I prefer to schedule it separately rather than try to incorporate it as part of the learning centers time-block. (See Chapter XIV, "Planning the Reading Program in a Centers Environment.") I have found that if reading is included as a center, I am continuously frustrated. If I work at the Reading Center, I wonder how things are progressing at the other centers. I become concerned because I cannot follow through on skills I introduced the previous day. However, if I spend my time at the Writing or Math Center, I become concerned about the Reading Center! So for my classroom, it is much better to save reading *instructions* for a separate time period. This enables me to work daily with students in this area. However, every effort is made to integrate reading skills into the other centers. This is a personal choice. Other teachers may prefer to incorporate reading during their centers timeblock. The decision needs to be determined by what works best for you.

Although there is no "one right way," the learning centers environment described in this book has proven to be a successful system for organizing and operating an individualized classroom. It provides sufficient structure to enable both the teacher and students to feel confident that they know what they are doing. The organization is such that, once the teacher has made the necessary materials, the basic program, including diagnosis, planning for individual students, and evaluation is set for the entire year. To this basic structure the teacher can periodically add short-term learning centers, instructional games, etc., without having the entire program disintegrate when these materials are withdrawn.

As you become more familiar with learning centers and the on-going materials and experiences described in the book, you will want to make changes, additions, and deletions. The result, as it well should be, will be a successful individualized program which reflects you.

Will This Meet Your Needs?

The materials and methods described in this book can be incorporated into many different environments and are suitable for many different teaching styles. You can adopt the whole, or cull parts and pieces, taking into consideration what is comfortable for you and your students, your school and community.

Notes

1. A. S. Neill, *Summerhill,* Hart Publishing Company, New York, 1960.
2. William Glasser, *Schools Without Failure,* Harper and Row, New York, 1969.
3. Jacob Bronowski, *The Ascent of Man,* Little, Brown, and Company, Boston, 1973, p. 416.

CHAPTER II

Basic Considerations

Learning Centers, With And Without Teacher Aides

Volunteer or para-professional aides can be a great asset to an individualized program. They can be used at centers daily to provide the one-to-one, or small group relationships, which are important in this type of environment. (See Chapter VII, "Recruiting and Training Teacher Aides.") The program, however, can be run without the use of aides; I have done it in my own classroom, as have many teachers who have taken courses from me. The classroom organization described in this book can be structured to enable the learning-centers program to function with or without aides, by adapting it to the specific set of circumstances. (Detailed instruction on planning daily centers are given in Chapter XVI, "Developing Your Own Basic Learning Centers Lesson-Plan.")

The ideal situation is one teacher aide, either volunteer or para-professional, assisting the teacher during centers time. This enables both the Language Arts Center and the Computational Mathematics Center to be supervised. It is then easy to plan activities for the other centers which require minimal teacher supervision or assistance. (See Chapter XIII.)

If you have no teacher aides, it becomes necessary for you to balance your time between the two major centers. One plan which allows for this balance is for the teacher to alternate days, one day at the Math Center, the following day at the Writing Center. The activities planned for the other two or three centers must function with a minimum of teacher direction. (See Chapter XIII, "Centers Which Require Minimal Teacher Supervision.")

*Day 1: Writing Center: Assignment on punc-
tuation and capitali-
zation*
    Independent Center
    Math Center: Instruction with teacher
    *Discovery: Working with fractions,
using manipulative mate-
rials*
*Day 2: Writing Center: Creative writing;
teacher supervises
and assists*
    Independent Center
    Math Center: Review problems
    *Discovery: Continuation of work with
fractions, using manipula-
tive materials*

This schedule can also be adapted so that you can spend the day at one of the centers, to introduce, for example, a series of new science experiments. In this case, activities planned at the Math and Writing Centers are those which students can manage independently.

*Writing Center: Copy work on basic mechanics
of printing or cursive*
Independent
Math: Review problems
*Discovery: Introduction of new science unit
and materials with teacher*

Another possible schedule, which facilitates the use of centers without teacher

aides, consists of a "total group" math period. During this total group time-block, the math program can be (1) non-individualized, (2) individualized and self-pacing, or (3) ability-grouped. (Specifics are detailed on pages 223-227.)

Although in the above plan, math is covered during a specific time block, learning centers are not ruled out. They can be operated during a different daily time period.

MATH: TOTAL GROUP MATH PERIOD
*Total group instruction, ability groups,
individualized, or self-pacing format*
SEPARATE CENTERS TIME BLOCK
    *Writing Center: Creative writing;
teacher supervises
and assists*
    Independent
    *Discovery: Linear-measurement as-
signments*

The importance of adapting to varying circumstances will be discussed throughout the book, and specific suggestions made. Remember though that successful individualization can occur with or without teacher aides.

Where to Begin?

It would be impossible to make, all at one time, sufficient materials to individualize mathematics, writing mechanics, creative writing, and spelling, not to mention constructing materials for manipulative math and science! For some reason many teachers feel they should individualize everything at once. Then they end up feeling guilty when they are unable to live up to this goal.

The best way is to proceed slowly and gradually build in change. It is much better to individualize *one subject* successfully, than to attempt to individualize three or four subjects. Invariably this will result in you becoming overwhelmed and frustrated.

Although you may not initially individualize all subjects, it is extremely important that you provide for an instructional program which assures continued growth in each basic subject.

An outline of a sound beginner's learning-center environment follows.

Three centers are set up. The Language Arts Center is individualized. Math is not. Instead there are daily "class assignments" to be completed when the students are at the Math Center. The third center is a structured Independent Center.

At the beginning of the day the teacher explains the math assignment for that day. (There is only one.) The children all work on the same page and then hand in the assignment. If any time remains (the centers last approximately 30 minutes), students can stay at the Math Center and use flash cards. Or they can play any of the math-reinforcement games which are arranged on a nearby shelf. Or they can move to the next station, which is a structured Independent Center.

This center should be arranged with sufficient chairs and table space to accommodate extra children. Although it consists of a variety of activities, it is considered structured since the teacher has predetermined and limited the choices. These consist of art projects, designing flannel board or puppet stories and plays (presented to the entire class when they are perfected), a listening post and tapes, and geography jig-saw puzzles. The structured Independent Center is also used to provide reinforcement activities for specific children. For instance, children who are having difficulty learning to tell time are asked to play *Time Bingo* when they come to the Independent Center.

Generally you should spend a short time helping the students get settled at the Independent Center at each rotation, making suggestions or asking challenging questions. You can then move to the Creative Writing Center, where you would spend most of your time. Here the children write stories, rewrite them in book formats with illustrations, and work on writing mechanics.

At the end of creative writing, many children stay an extra 10 or 15 minutes where chairs and desks have been added.

Many of the students discover that a full 30 minutes is not necessary in order to complete the math assignment. Therefore they time it so that they arrive at the Math Center with just enough time to complete the assignment, and can then move to the Independent Center.

The students, however, should leave Independent at the completion of the time alloted to their group, in order to make room for the next group.

This is the first big step along the path to individualization. Though you may want to individualize the Math Center initially, not everything can be done at once. It is better to wait until you feel more secure with the learning centers structure. You may of course choose math as the first subject to be individualized. In that case, language-arts assignments would be given the total group.

The diagram below indicates the arrangement of the furniture.

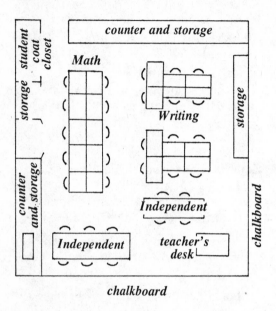

Room diagram for three centers

To Rotate or Not to Rotate

The next step is to decide whether to rotate students from center to center. Chapter
III details the procedures for grouping children and the rotation process. The primary
advantages of this system are the availability
of materials at the center or nearby; knowing
where students are (or are supposed to be);
and being able to remain at one center for the
entire day to observe and work with each
student on a one-to-one basis, or in a small
group in a specific subject.

There are some circumstances, however,
when a teacher may feel it is better to have
the students remain at their own desks, and
bring the materials to their desks. This occurs more often with upper-grade students
who have always had a desk, and feel a need
for a place which is their very own. This can
become an important ''need'' to pre-
adolescent youngsters. It is extremely important not to push students into a classroom
structure which is uncomfortable for them. If
individual desks are of importance to the
class, the student's desks can be grouped
into four centers. They can follow the same
time schedule as if they were rotating to a
new center every 30-40 minutes. But, instead
of rotating, they bring the needed material to
their desks. This system still results in four
different activities at any given time.

Start here
→*Math* . . . . *Group 1*
  ↓
  Spelling . . . . *Group 2*
  ↓
  Writing . . . . *Group 3*
  ↓
└*Science* . . . . *Group 4*

If the class were following the above diagram, Group 1 would spend the first half
hour on math, the next half hour on spelling,
etc. Group 4 would begin with science, and
after a half an hour work on math, etc.

The teacher, to insure working closely
with the students in a specific subject area
every day, moves to each cluster of desks as
a new group begins that subject. If you have
decided to work with them on science, you
would begin by working with Group 4. At
the end of the 30-40 minutes, the materials
would be put away, and you would move on
to Group 3.

One teacher I know kept the specific materials, needed for the individual centers, packed in four boxes. At the end of each block of time, the students were responsible for packing up the material and taking the box to the next group that would be using it. In this case the boxes of materials rotated!

Other teachers group the desks into four centers and assign a desk to each student as "home base." This is where the students start the day and where they go for any total group activities. In addition, they keep their own materials inside their desks. During centers time they go in turn to the four different centers. This means they are now sitting in each other's desks, rather than at their own desks. It works relatively well except when a student wants to get materials out of his or her desk, or to put something away. Invariably a squabble will result. The person who is involved in an activity at that center resents being disrupted. This problem can be solved by having cubby holes, made from gallon ice-cream cartons (see page 44), for storage of the individual student's materials and personal belongings. However, keep in mind that often one of the main attractions of "my own desk" is the concealed storage space the desk provides!

The final decision will be determined by what is comfortable for you and your students. Often you can start with one classroom structure; and, by holding periodic discussions with the students about the advantages and disadvantages of the current system, and possible adaptations of that system, changes can be effected which make the classroom structure more functional for all.

My own preference is to have the students work and move from center to center, without assigned desks. Their belongings are kept in ice cream carton cubby-holes. The materials needed are available at each of the centers. If privacy of stored belongings is important, the student can attach a piece of fabric to the cubby-hole top. It can then be flopped down to conceal the contents of the cubby hole!

Time Schedules

Before grouping your students, you will need to decide on the number of daily centers. Generally the school's schedule dictates your centers schedule.

The following two schedules provide for either four centers or two centers daily.

SCHEDULE I

8:30-9:15 .... "Early Bird" reading
(half the class)
Recess
9:30-9:45 .... "Together Time"
9:45-10:15 ... Center 1
Recess
10:25-10:55 .. Center 2
Lunch
11:50-12:20 .. Center 3
12:20-12:50 .. Center 4
Recess
1:05-1:45 .... Total group activities:
Music, physical education, films, discussions, introduction to science and social studies concepts, story time, choral reading, plays . . .
Recess
1:55-2:45 .... "Late Bird" reading

```
         SCHEDULE II

8:30-9:25 .... "Early Bird" reading
Recess
9:30-9:45 .... "Together Time"
9:45-10:15 ... Center 1
Recess
10:25-11:00 .. Center 2
Lunch
11:50-1:45 ....Total group activities
                (Music, physical edu-
                cation, science, social
                studies . . .)
1:55-2:45 .... "Late Bird" reading
```

The above schedules incorporate "split-reading" sessions, during which only half the students are in the classroom for the first and last hours of the day. In situations where there is not a split reading session, an hour and a half to two hours need to be allotted for teaching reading and related skills. (See Chapter XIV, "Scheduling a Reading Program in a Centers Environment.") The following schedules facilitate this type of program.

```
        SCHEDULE III

8:30-9:25 .... Reading and related skills
Recess
9:30-10:15 ... Continuation of reading
                and related skills
10:25-10:40 .. "Together Time"
10:40-11:00 .. First part of Center 1
Lunch
11:50-12:05 .. Completion of Center 1
12:05-12:35 .. Center 2
12:35-12:50 .. Total group activities
```

```
Recess
1:05-1:45 .... Continuation of total
                group activities
```

```
         SCHEDULE IV

8:30-8:45 .... "Together Time"
8:45-9:25 .... Reading and related skills
Recess
9:30-10:15 ... Continuation of reading
                and related skills
Recess
10:25-10:40 .. Introduction to centers
                for the day
10:40-11:00 .. First part of Center 1
Lunch
11:50-12:05 .. Completion of Center 1
12:05-12:35 .. Center 2
12:35-12:50 .. First part of Center 3
Recess
1:05-1:20 .... Completion of Center 3
1:20-2:30 .... Total group activities
```

In schedules III and IV, some of the centers are interrupted by a recess. Teachers often feel that this would be disastrous. However, if children have had sufficient time to get really involved in the work at a center and are interrupted by a recess, they come back from it and immediately become immersed in their work again. It is almost as if their minds never really left! On the other hand, when students return from recess and it is time for them to begin a new center, it is sometimes much more difficult for them to settle down.

In actuality, it is an advantage to have a recess fall during a center, rather than at the conclusion of a center.

CHAPTER III

Getting Started

Using Sociograms to Group Students

Once the number of centers you will operate daily is determined, the students are ready to be grouped. This can be done effectively by using a sociometric study. Dr. Mary E. Collins (1) pioneered in this field by developing a procedure for classroom teachers to administer an informal sociometric study in the classroom, and then to use the data as a basis for grouping children. This chapter applies many of these procedures.

One of the main advantages of grouping children sociometrically is that the students are assigned to groups which they helped choose, so they are anxious to cooperate. This type of organization is particularly effective if you establish with your students the golden rule on choices: "There will be lots of choices, as long as the choices don't disturb others and you can complete your own work. If your choices result in others

not being able to do their work, or you not being able to complete your work, then the choice will be mine—and you may not like my choice!" If this rule is firmly established, then problems with students who are breaking the basic rule can easily be resolved. You can privately confer with the students and explain that you know how much they want to be together, but you also know it is difficult for them to get their work done when they are together. Therefore, you are hesitant about putting them in the same group. If they can find a way to be in the same group and still get their work done and not bother others, then they may stay together. If they cannot work it out, the choice must be yours which, regrettably, will be to separate them.

The responsibility is now theirs. To help them shoulder the responsibility, suggest that they sit and work together at centers designed for talking and cooperation (manipulative math, science, Independent), and sit apart at centers which demand concentration (writing and math). Or you might suggest that if they sit together at all of the centers, they might put a reminder sign between them that says, "don't talk!"

Tell them it doesn't make any difference to you how they work it out. However, you are not responsible for reminding them, or enforcing the rule. It is up to them. In ninety percent of the cases the students find a solution, since it is important to them.

The development of cliques is a problem which sometimes surfaces with upper-grade students. The last thing you want to do is further their exclusiveness by grouping them together at centers. The most effective way to handle this is to discuss cliques in general with the entire class. Tell the class that you will be forming (or re-forming) groups, and that you feel it is important for them to get to know students other than just their close friends. Therefore, when you make up the groups, you will not place any students with the same people with whom they already spend most of their time on the playground, at lunch, etc. So—they should begin thinking about whom else they would like to be with in a group in the room.

When you administer the sociometric study, if a student names three people in a clique as choices for inclusion in a group, you can bring up the discussion and then ask for a list of different choices. Explain that otherwise you will have to make the choices, as you determine the groups.

On the day you plan to administer the sociometric study, the activities and assignments should be planned so that students can work independently. Explain that you will be talking to each student individually, and that you do not want to be interrupted unless it is

an emergency. If you have a teacher aide, it is an advantage to administer the sociometric study when this person is in the room so that any problems can be delegated. If not, students should hold their questions for the time being or quietly ask a neighbor.

You will need a pencil and thirty or more pieces of paper approximately 1½ by 3 inches. If you have a class picture, have it available on the table or desk. You should sit in a section of the room where you will have privacy while you are talking with each student. A screen or study booth is ideal. Or you can sit in a corner of the room with your back facing the students.

Call a student and write his or her name at the top of one of the little slips of paper. Explain that you are going to place students into three or four groups, or that you are going to change existing groups. Ask the child, "If you could have anyone in the class in your group, whom would you choose?" Some children will immediately answer. Others will stop and ponder. Still others will get up and look at the various students in the classroom. This is common in kindergarten or at the beginning of first grade. They really don't know yet who their friends are. But if an older student needs to look around the room to determine whom to have in the group, this is a valuable clue in terms of the child's feelings of peer identity. If a student is uncertain about whom to choose, you can help by displaying the class picture.

When the student decides upon a top choice for joining the group, write a "1" on the slip of paper and the name of the chosen student. Say to the child, "I'll try hard to get you with _____ , but in case I can't work it out for you, who would your second choice be?"

Write a "2" and the name of the second

choice. Tell the student that you will probably be able to arrange the groups to include either the first or second choice, but just in case it doesn't work out, who would a third choice be?

Nancy
1. Sally
2. Susan
3. Mary

Recording student choices

Be certain that the child understands that not all three friends will turn up in the group, but that almost certainly at least one of them will be a member of it.

Another question you might want to ask when you administer a sociometric study is, "Is there anyone whom you would not want to have in your group?" I am always hesitant about asking this as it seems to go against many of my principles. Yet interesting pieces of information emerge which I would have had no way of knowing otherwise. Once a boy answered the question, "Yes! I wouldn't want _____ (a girl) in my group. I hate the way she laughs!" I thought this particular girl was delightful. How would I ever have known that her laugh drove him up the wall!

Actually few students bother to name a person they would not want in their group. But those who do take the time to specify this information have strong feelings, and I suspect it is good for the teacher to be aware of these feelings. (Interestingly, few of the

so-called "trouble makers" are named. Perhaps the students figure they are kind of fun to include in their group!)

While the student is still at the table, take the piece of paper with the listed names and turn it face down or slip it into an envelope. Tell the child that, as far as you are concerned, those choices are a secret and under no circumstances will you tell anyone. Students are often put on the spot by friends wanting to know whom they chose. Suggest that the child reply, "That's a secret between the teacher and me, and I can't tell." This avoids potential hurt feelings.

Continue until you have talked with each of the students in the classroom. When the process is completed, put the papers in a secure place where there is no possibility of the students accidentally finding and going through them.

To eliminate or reduce the "I'll choose you if you choose me" syndrome, administer the sociometric test during a time when recess or lunch will not intervene.

If you have told the children that you are going to change groups, then it is important to follow through and actually alter the groups, preferably the next school day. It is often convenient to give the sociogram on a Friday so you have the weekend to plot the results.

Now the fun begins! First make a master list by writing all of the students' names alphabetically. Plot the information from each of the slips of paper. If Nancy's first choice was Sally, place a "1" beside Sally's name on the master list. If Nancy's second choice was Susan, place a "2" beside Susan's name on the master list. Do likewise for Nancy's third choice. Continue until you have recorded all the students' choices on the master list. This list then indicates how many times each student was chosen and whether as first, second or third choice.

Betty ①②①①②③①
Bill ②
Bob ③②①③
Cindy
Carl ①①②①②③②①①
Darleen ②③②
Don ①②②③②①①①
Ev ②③②②
Freddy ②③①
George
Hank ①②③
Linda ①②②①①③①①

Tabulating student choices

Generally, from four to six children are chosen by many of the students, (in the above list, Betty, Carl, Don and Linda). Put a star by these names as they will form the nucleus of each group. It is interesting to discover that often several of these are not the students whom you think of as leaders. They may be quiet students or not especially talented academically. But obviously they have the ability to make friends and are liked.

The easiest way to formulate your groups is to use the slips of paper on which you wrote the student's name and their choices. Using the previous illustration, for four groups you would place the most popular choices (Betty, Carl, Don and Linda's slips of paper) in four separate places on the floor or on a large table. If there were other students who were also selected by a large number of students, you should disperse them among the four groups.

The next students to be placed are the loners, those who were not selected at all, or were only chosen by one other student. (In the above list, the loners are Bill, Cindy and George.) Look at their slips and put them with their first choices, unless you feel that the combination would be a disaster. In that case, put them with their second choice. The loner had definite reasons for specifying a first choice. Whatever the reasons, give him or her the advantage of that first choice, if at all possible. In addition, keep an eye out for classroom situations where you can help the loner to become more accepted by others.

Many factors need to be considered in the grouping of students, particularly balance. In each group there should be approximately the same number of strong academic students, and approximately the same number of students who require extra teacher time.

The students who require extra time from the teacher are especially important. In this category fall the discipline problems, as well as students who are absolute jewels, but who need extra help in order to grasp new concepts. If you group too many of these students together, none will get the help and guidance needed.

One way to balance the number of "extra teacher time" students is to draw a nice bright red star on the slips of paper of these students. It will be obvious as you arrange the slips of paper whether you are maintaining a balance in this area.

By using the slips of paper to arrange the groups, it is easy to shift students from one group to another. The slips also indicate everyone's choices, so you can check on the development of inter-relationships. In some cases everything falls into place beautifully. Other times you will sit for hours arranging and rearranging.

When in the final stage of the grouping process, your emotional reaction to each of the groups should be about the same. (There should never be an "Oh, no! Here they come!" group.)

Invariably one student ends up being placed in a group that lacks all three of the chosen friends. Almost always this is a person who was chosen by a large number of students. In turn, this child's choices were other popular students who formed the nucleus of other groups. If this happens, place someone in the child's group whom you feel is a potential friend. You should talk to the student before school and explain that you know the personal preferences were _____ , _____ and _____ , and that you diligently tried to arrange the group so one of these choices could have been included but it just didn't work out. Say that instead you put _____ in the group because you thought they got along well, and ask if the student thinks that will work out all right. Every time I have had to do this, the student has said, "Oh, sure that'll be fine." I suspect it is because this child is the kind of student who gets along beautifully with everyone, so all the students in the group will be friends in no time anyway!

The last step is to make up charts of the groups. On four pieces of paper in neat bold letters, using a black felt pen, write each group's number, color or name. Under this write all of the students' names in that group.

These should be posted in a prominent place in the classroom the next morning.

When the students arrive, plan on five or ten minutes of bedlam as they read the lists and rejoice! Then you can start centers for the day.

If you start the school year with centers, you can make up the groups in one of two ways: random selection, or on the basis of student records. Many teachers do not like to look at a student's record prior to getting to know the student. In this case, determine groups by random selection. Otherwise, use the records and balance the groups as much as possible, mentally trying not to link student information and specific student names. It is easier than it sounds, as you are dealing with thirty completely unfamiliar names and records.

After approximately six weeks, the students should know each other well enough that you can administer a sociometric study and have *them* determine the groups.

New sociometric tests need to be administered periodically during the year. The interval between sociometric tests varies considerably.

Groups which have been functioning beautifully suddenly begin to bicker. Tensions are rising. Students will ask, "When are we going to change groups again?" Or, you will hear, "Oh, don't do that! That makes me so mad when you do that!" It may have been a month or six weeks since the last sociometric study, or it may have been four months. But believe me, you will know when the time has arrived!

Rotating Groups

If you have decided to rotate groups, obviously you must have a method to indicate to the students the scheduled rotation from one center to the next. Your goal should be for the students to become sufficiently independent so that it becomes unnecessary for them to rely on you for this information.

Grouping children and rotating them through the centers builds a sense of organization and structure. And structure is essential to the successful operation of an individualized program. The rotation lends both you and the students a sense of stability and confidence so that all of you know what is happening and what will happen next in the classroom.

The easiest way to have students rotate independently from center to center is to use color-coded signs at each center. These are successful with both readers and "non-readers."

The signs are constructed in the following manner from 9″ × 12″ construction paper.

fold

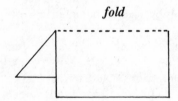

Fold the paper in half.

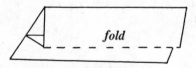

fold

Fold the top in half to form a triangle.

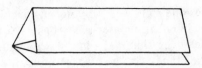

Fold the bottom in half and overlap either the top or bottom.

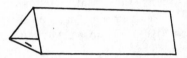

Staple or paper clip at either end.

A sign is placed at each of the centers. The rectangle in the bottom right-hand corner is color-coded to indicate the center to which the group should rotate.

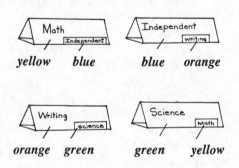

Math [Independent]	Independent [writing]
yellow blue	blue orange

Writing [science]	Science [Math]
orange green	green yellow

Color-coded signs indicate center rotation

To introduce students to the process of "reading" signs, begin at the first center and hold up the sign. For example, tell the students that the yellow sign will be used for the

Math Center. Point to the blue rectangle on the yellow sign and tell them it indicates the center that they go to next. Ask them what color is in the corner and then ask if anyone can see a center which has a sign that color. Walk to that center and hold up the blue sign.

Continue walking to each of the centers, holding up the sign, explaining the center, and pointing out the rectangle in the corner which indicates the next center. To help insure that the children understand, hold up the green sign and say, "Let's pretend that today you started here at the Science Center. Who can tell me which center you would go to next?" After the reply, walk to the next center and hold up that sign, and repeat this process at all the centers.

As a final orientation step, start a student at one of the centers and have her or him hold up the sign. Ask all the children to think about where they would walk if they were going to the next center. Have the student then walk to the next center and hold up the sign. Ask how many would have gone to that center.

It is important that you explain the rotation process several times, so that the students feel extremely confident before they actually begin. I have used the above system with kindergarteners and only had two children out of 32 "get lost," so I will vouch for its effectiveness. It also works well with upper-grade students.

You should *not* tell a confused student where to go. Although this is a faster method of solving the problem, it results in you doing the thinking for the student, building a dependence on you. Instead, take the time to ask the child where the last center was. Walk together to that center, and ask if there is anything that shows where the next center is.

If the student is still uncertain, point to the sign and ask about the little colored rectangle in the corner. Almost all children will say, "Oh, that's right. I remember . . ." If the child does not respond, explain the rectangle and ask whether there is a center with the same color sign. Then walk together to that center. Ask the child to look at the sign there and try to determine where to go next. By repeating this procedure a few times with the students who need assistance, you will very quickly have all of them rotating through the centers independently.

Generally, the child who needs extra help and reassurance is the type who is convinced that there is no way to understand what you are going to say. This student panics and "tunes out" before you even start your explanation. Have patience. The child needs your help and assurance. It is a giant step when this student feels sufficiently confident to begin rotating through the centers alone without coming to you for reinforcement.

If you use this system of color-coded signs, each group of students should be assigned a name or a number (Group 1, Group 2, etc.).

A reverse way to indicate rotation is to color-code the groups and number the centers. If the students are young, they can be helped to remember their color group by pinning on a colored luggage tag which corresponds to their group color. The metal border on the outside rim makes this type of tag much sturdier and more durable. Therefore it lasts much longer than standard name tags. At the end of the day, the children hang tags of the same color on a hook, tags of a different color on a separate hook, etc. These can then be easily retrieved by the students on the following day.

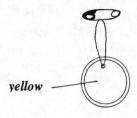

yellow

**Individual student
color-coded tags**

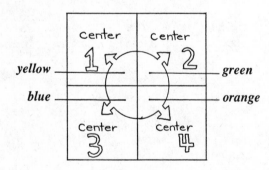

Creative Writing your choice
↓
Spelling-practice your words
↓
Math - stapled booklets
↓
Art- stitchery

**Diagram on chalkboard
indicating centers rotation**

A chart labeled Center 1, Center 2, Center 3 and Center 4 is placed on the wall. A brad is used to attach a separate "wheel" to the center of the chart. The wheel is divided into four colored sections to correspond with the color-coded groups. At the end of each center, the teacher or student turns the wheel to indicate where each group goes next.

yellow — Center 1 — *green*

blue — Center 2 / Center 3 / Center 4 — *orange*

Centers rotation chart

Another system for indicating the rotation of groups is to draw a simple diagram on the chalkboard of the centers and list the assignments. This also serves as a visual reminder of what was discussed with the students at the beginning of the day.

The first time you initiate learning centers, students should rotate at approximately the same time. To avoid the feeling of regimentation, go to the center which you think will need the longest time to clean up and ask the children to get ready to move to the next center. If someone needs a few more minutes to finish an assignment, that person should continue working. The others should put their materials away and move to the next center. As the first center begins cleaning up, go on quietly to the next center and have them begin the clean-up process. This way the rotation is slightly staggered. The noise level is lessened since everyone does not clean up and rotate simultaneously and a relaxed feeling prevails.

Gradually, more flexibility can be built in. But in the beginning, it is wise to establish a definite routine to help both you and the students know who belongs where.

Determining Daily Centers (Sample Schedules)

When you determine the specific centers for each day, you should make an effort to alternate centers which are primarily paper-and-pencil tasks with centers which demand a different type of involvement.

Creative Writing, a paper-and-pencil center, can be followed by Individualized Spelling where the students have a wide variety of ways to practice their spelling words. This can be followed by Computational Math which demands much concentration. In turn this is followed by Art, and so back to Creative Writing. This creates diversity, and results in greater student concentration at the more demanding centers.

Another example:

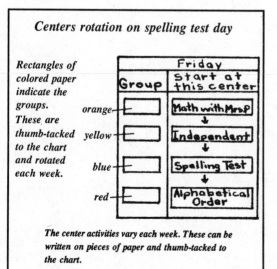

Centers rotation on spelling test day

Rectangles of colored paper indicate the groups. These are thumb-tacked to the chart and rotated each week.

	Group	Friday Start at this center
orange	⬜	Math with Mrs.P
yellow	⬜	Independent
blue	⬜	Spelling Test
red	⬜	Alphabetical Order

The center activities vary each week. These can be written on pieces of paper and thumb-tacked to the chart.

A different type of scheduling is required on the day individualized spelling tests are given (see Chapter VIII). The tests take approximately 18 minutes, while normally the length of the centers is 30 minutes or so. You can solve the test-day problem by planning four 18-minute centers. There are many assignments and activities which are ideal for a shortened center: art projects, instructional groups, directed games, etc.

If you have an aide who can give the individualized spelling tests, you are then free to work at another center. This is an ideal time to re-group students, according to ability levels, for instruction on skills such as telling time, money, fractions, etc. Re-groupings of this type allow you considerable flexibility in meeting the needs of individual students. In order to schedule these instructional groups, make lists of four ability groups for a specific skill. Post these lists and explain to the students that they will be re-grouped for one day only. They will return to their regular groups the following day. As the ability groups rotate to the center you are supervising, you can then vary the instruction and activities according to their skill level.

A related scheduling problem concerns activities which you feel are important, but that take only 10 to 15 minutes. These can often be effectively included at the Independent Center. You can require an assignment of this type for the first portion of time. The remaining time can be spent as the student wishes. When using the Independent Center for a required activity, be certain to select assignments which all of the students can complete in approximately the same amount of time. Otherwise, the less capable students are penalized.

One of the time schedules outlined in the previous chapter involved only two centers in the morning because of combined classes and team teaching in the afternoon devoted to music, physical education, science, social studies, health, and art. In this type of schedule, the range of subjects covered in the afternoon demands that math, spelling and writing become the morning's activities.

Four centers should be set up. However, each student goes to only two centers (one language-oriented, one math-oriented) on any given day. The following chart indicates the daily centers. A clothespin, attached to each chart, indicates the first center for each group on each day.

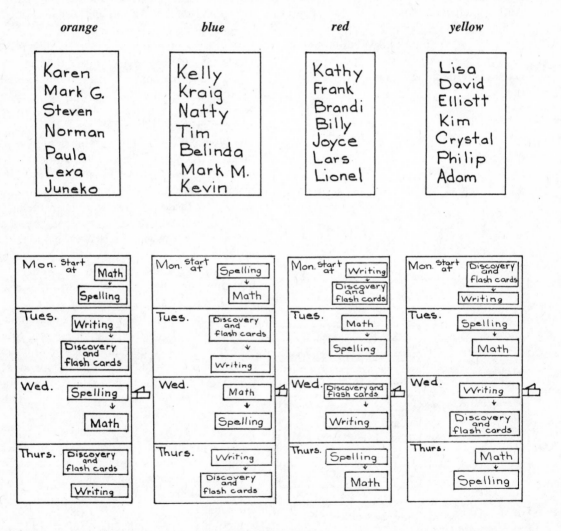

orange

Karen
Mark G.
Steven
Norman
Paula
Lexa
Juneko

blue

Kelly
Kraig
Natty
Tim
Belinda
Mark M.
Kevin

red

Kathy
Frank
Brandi
Billy
Joyce
Lars
Lionel

yellow

Lisa
David
Elliott
Kim
Crystal
Philip
Adam

Two daily centers

Because of the need to spend the entire centers' time on the basic skills, assignments at the Discovery Center should involve Manipulative Math experiences and practice with math flash cards. (See pages 218-219.)

One additional scheduling problem occasionally occurs when the alloted time for centers is shortened, perhaps on "library day," or when a speaker is scheduled. This necessitates reducing the number of groups and centers for that day.

Rather than making up completely new lists for groups, four groups can easily be converted to three groups in the following manner.

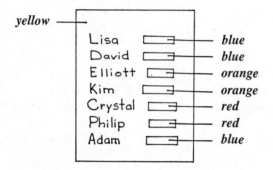

yellow

Lisa	*blue*
David	*blue*
Elliott	*orange*
Kim	*orange*
Crystal	*red*
Philip	*red*
Adam	*blue*

Four center groups become three

On the chart for the yellow group, for example, beside each child's name draw and color in a blue, red or orange rectangle. Explain at the beginning of the day that only three centers will be operating instead of the usual four. In the above chart, Lisa, David and Adam would go with the blue group. Elliott and Kim would go with the orange group, and Crystal and Philip would go with the red group.

The first few times you re-group the students in this manner you will need to explain the procedure to them. Thereafter, the "yel-

low group" needs only to be reminded to join the other groups as shown on the chart.

The group you choose to reassign should be composed primarily of students who have friends in other groups, as well as within their own group. This is an opportunity to enable them occasionally to be with their other friends. As a result, everyone is delighted when the groups are reshuffled.

Organizational Adaptations

As time goes by, you may find you want to build in more flexibility and allow the students to determine when and where they complete their assignments. Or you may wish to move into contracts. Adaptations of the basic learning-centers plan are accomplished easily once you and your students are secure with the organization and operation of the centers, and you have established your expectations. The degree of flexibility depends on what is comfortable for you and your particular group of students. With some classes it may seem advisable to stay with basic learning centers throughout the entire year. In other classes when the students' sense of responsibility becomes established and they are meeting or exceeding your expectations, it can be a pleasant change to try something different.

The Transition Plan

The students go to two centers a day. During a two-day period, three centers are assigned and students choose the fourth center. This can be an Independent Center where many choices are available, or a Structured Independent where you have specified or limited the choices.

The students go to the centers in any order, provided that there is room for them at the center. They must spend a minimum of 30 minutes at each center. (This results in the continuation of the previous center's time schedule.) Each student keeps a record sheet and hands it in daily for the teacher to check.

Sally		*May 24-29*
Monday 9:45–10:15	*Where I was.* math	*What I did:* stapled book pp. 3-6
10:25–11:00	*Spelling*	chose my words and made lists
Tuesday 9:45–10:15	*Choice*	worked on copying and illustrating my books
10:25–11:00	*Discovery*	task cards # 1, 3
Wednesday 9:45–10:15		
10:25–11:00		
Thursday 9:45–10:15		
10:25–11:00		

Individual student record
for "transition plan"

Another variation of the centers theme has been devised by one of my fellow teachers, Ethel Lagle (2). She selects a few students to work on contracts while the remainder of the class continues the normal rotation of centers. The "contract" students are not necessarily the most capable academically. Rather they are students whom she feels have the necessary self-discipline. She explains to them that contracts are simply a different way of scheduling their work at the centers. (The student must agree at the beginning of the week to complete all the work listed on the contract by the end of the week.) It is the child's responsibility to budget time so as to accomplish the tasks. Any "left-over" time can be used for special projects. One year, two students used their extra time to design and implement art centers for the rest of the class. Others undertook research projects in the library, etc.

When a student begins using contracts it is often necessary for them to have help in learning how to budget their time. To accomplish this, a "pacer" is assigned. This is a student who has used contracts for at least three or four weeks. This student will tell the other child, "You'd better get going, or you're not going to finish your contract by the end of the week. I think today you'd better start with your math. It looks to me like you're behind in this week's work . . ."

As might be expected, some students begin contracts and then request to return to the "regular" rotating centers. Other students request contracts and are given a trial period.

This seems to me an excellent way to meet individual student needs and learning styles. However, I would not recommend it until both you and the students feel secure with the organization and operation of the basic learning-centers environment.

Notes

1. Dr. Mary E. Collins, Extension Instructor, California State College, Sonoma, California.
2. Ethel Lagle, Teacher, Novato Unified School District, Novato, California.

CHAPTER IV

Mechanics of Operating Learning Centers

Building Independence and a Sense of Responsibility

Once you have determined the groups and introduced the students to the process of rotation, you are ready to explain the specific activities at each of the centers.

When you first begin students in learning centers it is wise to keep the activities simple and at a level enabling all to enjoy success. At this stage you are not at all concerned about individualizing. Instead your goal should be to get the students used to procedures of working in a learning-centers environment and to build their sense of responsibility and independence.

If you first establish what your expectations are, where the materials are located, where they are to put completed assignments, what they are to do when they finish the work at a specific center, etc., you will be free later to do what you wish most to do—

teach. In order to establish the students' independence in these matters, it is essential for the first several days that you are free to move about the room and handle any problems which surface. You want the students to know that you know whether or not work has been completed, whether it has been handed in, etc. This is crucial for the establishment of expectancies and a sense of structure and organization. If a child is disturbing other students, you should be free to move immediately to that center and handle the problem. If a student has not cleaned up work materials before leaving a center, you want to be able to say, "I believe you forgot to do something before you left the last center. Please take care of it."

Insisting on these basics at the beginning will mean that you will not need to worry about them later. They will be part of the students' routine. Then you will be free to diagnose individual student needs and plan programs to meet those needs.

For these reasons, the centers for the first several days, or even the first week, may be little more than busy work. The assignments need to be of the type that students can successfully complete with little help from you. This allows you to set the basic program in motion.

Math might consist of dittos which review skills previously mastered. Writing could consist of copying as neatly as possible a poem from the board, or an assignment reviewing capitalization and punctuation. An art project could be the third center. The fourth center could simply be a tape at the listening post and comprehension questions (upper grade), or listening to a story and following along in a book (primary grades). These are not exactly exciting centers, but neither will they tie you down.

If students are to learn to work independently, it is important for them to know exactly what to do when they get to each of the centers. You can help them build this independence by carefully explaining each center and then asking them questions and more questions. What are you going to do at the Writing Center? What are you to do if you finish the work at the center before it is time to rotate to the next center? Where are you going to put your paper when you are finished? . . .

During this period while the students are becoming acquainted with the new classroom environment and your expectancies, it is essential to remain very supportive. Most children will adjust easily to the new structure. But there are always those who need added reassurance and assistance.

When you sense that the new routine has become comfortable for all the students, you can begin to insist that they know the essentials about the system. When you explain the assignments for the day, remind them that this is the time to ask questions, while the class is together. If they get to a center and forget what the assignment is, or where the materials are, they should ask other students at that center. If no one can help them, only then should they come to you.

After this is firmly established, do not repeat basic instructions once the daily centers have begun, unless the student has already checked with others. Instead you can remind the child, "We talked about that at the beginning of the day. Have you checked to find out if anyone at your center remembers?"

A line of distinction needs to be drawn clearly between the request that a basic instruction be repeated and a need for help in working the assignment. The student must be assured that anytime help is needed with an assignment, it is all right to come to you. It not only is all right, it is what you want the child to do. But this is different from asking the teacher where the paper is!

The student's sense of independence should be encouraged at every center. Rather than relying on the teacher to pass out paste jars, get the scissors and paper, etc., these materials should be situated so the students can easily get them when needed. (See Chapter V, "Room Arrangement and Materials Storage.") Again, this frees you to *teach*. Students can also become responsible for notifying you when new supplies are needed.

I always keep a spindle in a prominent place in the room. As a student notices a supply getting low, he or she writes a brief note and sticks it on the spindle. I check it at the end of each day, and gather any of the needed materials. Frequently, along with the notes stating we need more yellow construction paper and pencils are running low, are reminders of things I may have promised to bring to students or to share with the class. Those are always my favorites!

The students should also be responsible for keeping track of their own work. Remind them the first several days that, when they leave a center, they must put their folders away so that they won't get mislaid. If a student comes to you to say that a math folder has been mislaid, say that you are very sorry, but that is why it is important to remember to gather up materials and put them away at the end of the center. The student may miss the entire center searching for that vital folder and have to make the work up as the day progresses, but it is a lesson well worth learning. Each person's materials are a strictly personal responsibility.

You may feel like an ogre demanding that students fulfill these responsibilities. Yet, if you do not insist on this in the beginning, you may well spend your entire year showing students where the paper is, repeating assignments, helping students search for their mislaid work, etc. Acquainting the students with the procedures of working in a learning-centers environment and building their sense of responsibility and independence at the start cannot be stressed enough.

Before students begin the centers the first day, the basic rule referred to in the last chapter should be discussed: "You will have lots of choices, as long as your choice doesn't bother other students. If your choice keeps you or others from being able to do their work, then the choice will have to be mine."

You can illustrate the rule by saying, "If everyone at the Art Center were busy at work and one student decided to mess up the entire center, do you think it would be fair for that to end the Art Center for everyone?" You will get violent protests that it would not be fair! Explain that this is exactly how you feel. If one student cannot follow the rules, it isn't right for everyone to get punished. Therefore, if a student has a difficult time making choices, *you* will make the choices for that person. You will not let one student destroy the situation for everyone else in the class.

It is important to discuss this with the students before any problems arise. Otherwise they will say, "I know who you're talking about," which is exactly what you don't want to happen.

If a student causes a problem, just say quietly, "Your choice is bothering other people and making it hard for them to get their work done. Do you want to make a new choice, or do you want me to make the choice for you?" The student almost always will answer that he or she will make the choice. It is important that you ask the child at this point, "What is your choice?" Perhaps the student replies, "I think I'll pick up my work and sit over there to do it." You can answer, "Fine. Then that is what I expect you to do. If I need to come back again, the choice will have to be mine."

A good motto is, "Warn once. Then stick to it." If you need to go back to the center, say, "I'm sorry, but it looks like I need to make the choice for you. My choice is _____." You can tell the child to work on a specific math or writing assignment and sit near the center where you are working, or move to a study booth to continue his or her assignment.

The main thing is to remove students from

situations they are unable to handle.

If you are not involved with other students at that time, you can discuss the problem with the child then by asking, "Do you know why it was necessary for you to leave your center? Can you think of some way you could handle the situation next time?"

At the end of the center, the child should be asked, "Do you feel you can rejoin your group and make a choice which will not bother others?" As teacher, you can then fol low through accordingly.

If you are busy supervising a center when a problem arises, it is best not to stop and discuss it with the student at that time. Instead, have the child move away from the assigned regular center and say, "I'll talk with you later."

If students are to become self-directed individuals, it is important that they feel the consequences of their actions, both positive and negative, and examine alternatives so they can learn to cope. Even very young children understand making choices. I recall one student in kindergarten who would see me coming from across the room and say, "I choose! I choose!" What's more, the child would then make a valid choice.

One of the main advantages of learning centers is that problems can be handled without commotion, or scarcely a break in the basic routine. Often, in a traditional classroom, there seem to be only two possible solutions to a problem: (1) stop and handle it with thirty students looking on; (2) ignore it, while inwardly you get more and more angry. In a learning centers environment, the students become so involved in what they are doing that there is little that one can do to disrupt the class. This may be discouraging to the student who has previously attracted attention through disruptive behavior. But for the overall operation of the classroom, it is a great asset!

The Independent Center (see page 5) is a marvelous place to begin building a sense of responsibility. You can describe the various choices and introduce it as a center you are going to *try* for one day. Explain that it is important for you to have the time to work with individual students at the Math or Writing Center. Therefore, if problems at Independent take you away from the task at hand, you will have to replace it with a different center. However, if the students can manage, the Independent Center will be scheduled again the following day. It is really up to them whether this center will continue.

The responsibility is now on their shoulders to make a success of Independent. This is one of the most important factors in a learning-centers environment. The students must become partners in assuring the smooth operation of the centers, since you cannot be everywhere at once. Be certain at the end of the day to discuss how things went at Independent and to follow through when planning centers for the next day.

Students almost always start off being very careful at Independent. As a result you will seldom have problems at the beginning with this center. As time goes by, however, they become more careless, and it may well be that you will need to withdraw the center for a period of time. Don't worry about it or feel guilty. Tell them you know they can handle the responsibility, and you will try the center again later. But for the present it will be necessary to replace it with another center.

A typical problem at Independent involves blocks. After several months the noise level grows louder and louder, and the blocks begin crashing. Stick with your old rule about choices. You can explain that you will warn individual groups once. But if you need to come back a second time, you will have to make the choice, and your choice will be for that group not to use the blocks for several weeks. Instead, they will need to find something else to do at Independent.

Then be certain to follow through. After several weeks, ask the restricted group if they think they can use the blocks now without bothering the other students. You will find they do a beautiful job and are marvelous about reminding each other to keep the noise level down. This is what you are after: building a sense of responsibility and a climate in which they support each other.

Potential Problems

Misuse of Equipment and/or Materials

Situations sometimes occur when students misuse equipment. If it is a matter of just one or two students who are causing the problem, it can easily be solved with the basic rule about choices. However, if many students are involved, it is a different matter. You should explain to the students that the equipment is expensive, or that you have spent considerable time constructing it. It is necessary once more to place the responsibility on their shoulders. Tell them that you cannot stand by and let them misuse materials. Therefore, they have a choice: either they assume the responsibility of taking care of it, or you will have to put it away. It is up to them.

You should follow this discussion by making an inventory of the needed material and equipment at the involved center(s). A list should then be placed at the center. The stu-dents are told that they are responsible for checking to be certain it is all there before their group leaves the center. When they have accounted for all of it, they should call you. In a few moments you can determine whether or not all of the material is there and whether any has been misused.

If a group cannot handle the responsibility, they are given alternate assignments at the centers. They quickly realize that it is much more interesting to use a microscope, than to read and answer questions about one Or that it is more fun to build something, than to read about building it!

Eventually you can ask them if they are ready to assume the responsibility for using materials properly; then gradually have them resume involvement with the regular center assignments.

Problems of this type are so minimal, but when they do surface, the teacher must face them head on. Otherwise, chaos will reign. At the same time it is extremely important to let the students know how you feel about problems of this nature. Be honest and say: "Look, it really bothers me when . . ." "I don't think it's fair when . . ." Help them realize that feelings, responsibilities, expectations and consequences are all interrelated.

Noise Levels

Another potential problem concerns noise levels. Learning centers do not by their very nature engender a silent classroom, but they should not create havoc either. What should be heard is an underlying buzz of students who are involved in their work.

Teachers are familiar with "quality noise," which is the sound of excited, involved students. However, even good noise needs to be held at a level which does not disturb others. Furthermore, an acceptable noise level for one person might be too loud for another, and the same person will tolerate different noise levels on different days.

When I was team-teaching, I can remember on some days saying to my teammate, "It is really noisy in here today." She would reply that she hadn't even noticed it. On other days the situation would be reversed.

I suspect that the same situation is true for students. Therefore, if a student comments about it being noisy, try to get the child settled in a section of the room which is more isolated, or suggest work in a study booth. Or have the student go outside to work. (When students work outside the room, ask them to check with you at the end of each center time, so you can be certain that they complete a reasonable amount of work.)

As far as noise is concerned, the important thing is to determine a level which is comfortable for you. You can often head off a potentially noisy situation by moving to a group of students when you first hear the noise level starting to build.

Problems usually develop when you become so involved with students that you are not aware of the growing noise level. By the time you realize it, the whole room is awash with sound. It is then necessary to stop and get everyone settled down.

One teacher I know, who has sensitive ears, simply taps her ring on the table when the noise level begins building and that is the signal for the students to quiet down. In that classroom the noise level never rises above that of the tapping ring!

Some teachers flick the lights on and off as a quiet signal. Others have the students take two deep breaths and let them out slowly. My favorite procedure is to have the students put their heads down for a minute.

This is not because I am angry with them, but because I want them to hear silence. When everything has been still for a few minutes, I quietly say, "All right. Those at the Math Center—put your heads up and go back to work. (pause . . .) O. K. Now the Writing Center . . ."

If students have difficulty settling down after recess, try stopping them before they enter the classroom. Ask them to think about which centers they are going to and what they will do when they get there. Then have them come in the room a few at a time. Or, as students come through the door, you can ask them to indicate quietly the centers they will be attending. What you want to accomplish is to help students readjust from the playground activity to the classroom environment.

If it is "one of those days," when the students seem exceptionally restless and noisy, (students seem to experience those days periodically, regardless of the classroom environment!), it is often effective to stop everything and call them together. Talk about the noise level, and ask them to help keep it to a minimum. Have them figure ways that they can indicate to a student to be more quiet, without making any noise themselves! You want to get them working with you, not against you! Once you accomplish this, they can assume a great deal of the responsibility by reminding each other about noise. One of my favorite classroom quotes is, "Silence is contagious!"

Giving Students Choices

Another potential problem concerns choices. Although choices are often included in a learning-centers environment, many students are overwhelmed by having too many decisions thrust upon them at one time. They simply do not know how to cope with them. Therefore, it is wise to introduce choices slowly and build in consequences— positive and negative. For instance, instead of giving them ten different ways to practice their spelling words, suggest two or three different ways. Tell them that, if they handle these choices well, one or two additional ways will be added the following week. Gradually the changes are made, additional choices are added, and student responsibility grows. They should understand that, if they can't handle the choices and responsibilities, it will be necessary for the choices to be eliminated. Again it is up to them. Don't take the responsibility on your shoulders.

For each of the centers, think about the potential problems and discuss these, plus the consequences with the students. They need to know that you are well aware of what could happen. Finger-painting is a great example of a potential problem area! Be sure you and the students are on the same wavelength about what could happen and what will certainly happen if problems erupt.

Eventually you will have helped them develop sufficient responsibility so that they will be able to have choices at the Writing Center, Spelling Center, Math Center and Independent. But these will have been gradually built into the program.

Rushing to Complete Work

Students who rush to complete their work so they can have free time can create another trouble spot. If this is allowed, the student discovers that what is important is not how well the work is done, or the amount of effort put forth, but rather the act of quick completion. Then we wonder why the quality of the student's work is unsatisfactory, and why study habits are poor!

To counteract this, tell the students you want them to stay at each center until the center time is completed. If, as yet, the work at the centers is not "on-going," explain what they are to do if they finish the assignment early: Math Center, practice with flash cards; Writing Center, illustrate what they wrote; Spelling Center, practice their words a different way, etc.

Once the work at the centers is individualized and continuous, a student should have no problems in beginning another project after finishing an assignment. At an "on-going" center, short, cut-and-dried assignments, with definite beginning and ending points which encourage rushing, do not exist. Instead, work is continuous. What is stressed is doing your best work. Sometimes this may involve speed (mastering basic math facts). Other times, it means working slowly and carefully. (Three lines written very neatly are much better than eight lines sloppily written!)

Unsatisfactory work should be reassigned. Gradually the students will begin to realize they are going to be at the center for the entire time, so they should work slowly and well the first time around, rather than rushing through only to have to repeat their work. This concept, "take it slow and do it well," requires much discussion and reinforcement. But what joy when students begin to take pride in their work and become involved in what they are doing!

Unfinished Assignments

When you first introduce students to learning centers, most of the assignments will be of short, one-day duration. In order to be certain that students complete and submit these assignments, specific places should be designated where work is to be handed in. Cardboard boxes cut to about three-inch depth, covered with construction paper or contact paper, serve as handy containers. One is placed at each of the centers as a "hand-in" box. At the end of the centers' daily time-block, while the students are cleaning up, the number of papers in each box can be counted. If any are missing, call the students together and say, "Before we go outside for P.E., I need to have all the assignments handed in. I hate to have your P.E. time wasted, but there are two writing assignments missing . . ." Sometimes, a student will immediately realize that he or she is the "culprit." At other times, it is necessary to have everyone stand and call off each of the names on the papers which have been handed in. As a name is called, the student sits down. Those left standing are the ones who need to find their papers. This is done for each assignment which has missing student papers. The point is made that this process is taking the time reserved for P.E. and would not have been necessary had all the papers been turned in.

You can acquire the same information by checking each of the students' papers against the roster. But I think it is important that the students are aware that assignments not handed in result in wasted time. Surely, it is better for them to feel their time wasted, rather than hear me talk about my time being mis-spent! In addition, a little peer pressure can create wonders. . . .

After several days of this slow procedure, amazingly all the papers are handed in! I immediately reinforce this with, "Good news! All the papers are in. Let's hurry up and get outside. We'll be able to have a nice long P.E. time today!"

Besides becoming aware of the fact that

misplaced papers cause wasted time, the students also begin to realize that the teacher knows whether assignments are handed in. This is important!

As time goes by and the nature of work becomes on-going, the only check lists needed are for those centers with a specific assignment for that day. The following type of check list is most helpful.

orange group	blue group
☐ Karen	☐ Kelly
☐ Mark G.	☐ Kraig
☐ Steven	☐ Natty
☐ Norman	☐ Tim
☐ Paula	☐ Belinda
☐ Lexa	☐ Mark M.
☐ Juneko	☐ Kevin
☐ Elliott	☐ Lisa
☐ Kim	☐ David
	☐ Adam

red group	yellow group
☐ Spencer	☐ Lisa
☐ Kathy	☐ David
☐ Frank	☐ Adam
☐ Brandi	☐ Elliott
☐ Billy	☐ Kim
☐ Kevin	☐ Crystal
☐ Lars	☐ Philip
☐ Crystal	
☐ Philip	

*Check list
for specific assignments*

The students' names are listed according to their regular groups. The names listed below the dotted line in each group indicate the students from the yellow group who will join the other groups on days when there are only three centers instead of four. (See page 23.)

Have students bring their papers to you when completed. Do not actually correct each paper at that time, but scan it to determine if it appears to have been completed correctly. Put your initials in the corner, a check by the student's name on the check list, and then ask the student to put the paper in the "hand-in" box.

At the end of a center, instead of having to scan an entire class list, you need only check the list of eight students who just completed that center. If there is no check by one of those names, call the student and ask to see the assignment. The child now discovers that you do not even need to wait till the end of the day to find out if an assignment has been turned in. You know immediately at the end of each center time!

While stressing the importance of completing assignments, you can use the Independent Center as an incentive by explaining that it is a center to which everyone is entitled, provided that assigned work has been completed. If you see a student wasting time at the Math Center, for example, you can point out that the privilege of the Independent Center can be retracted: "You know you are entitled to one Independent Center today. Right now you are using this center as an Independent Center, doing just what you want to do. That's all right, because you have one Independent Center coming. However, when your group goes to the Independent Center, I want you to come back to this center and get your work completed. You know you are to have one Math Center today, too!" Most students will say, "Oh! I didn't know that's how it worked." You can reply, "Yes, that's how it works. You have one Independent Center, but you must have one of each of the other centers, too."

Most students will immediately go to work after a discussion like this. Occasionally a student may elect to continue daydreaming, or otherwise wasting time and then return to the center during Independent time. The child quite possibly knows what is best. You have no idea what happened before the student left home that morning, what the family or personal problems may be, etc.

I recall such an instance of a student who was not able to settle down. After talking with the child for a few minutes, the problem spilled out. Though she knew she was forbidden to touch her sister's diary, she had gotten into it and accidentally broken the lock. Her problem was that not only had she disobeyed, but her disobedience was going to be discovered! I asked her if she thought it might help if she sat down and wrote a letter to her sister, explaining how she felt. Under these circumstances, insisting on her doing her regular school work would have had little effect on her inability to concentrate and accomplish the task at hand. Instead, she spent most of the morning working on the letter and took it home at lunch time to put with her sister's diary. In the afternoon she was back to her normal self.

I mention this because of the importance of remembering that students, like adults, have problems and need time to think about and solve them. It may be a better use of their time to do this at an academic center and complete an assignment when they normally would have been at the Independent Center.

Establishing Expectations

Once basic classroom structure is set, you are ready to start individualizing the instruction. Diagnosis is the first step and should be done initially at only one center. Based upon the diagnosis, students are assigned materials appropriate for them. At the same time, individual expectations for each student are established.

Requirements will vary according to each individual child's abilities and the concepts on which he or she is currently working. For instance, at a Math Center, it would be extremely unfair to tell a student who is just beginning "borrowing," to complete the same number of pages as a student who is working on building speed and proficiency in basic addition facts.

Daily expectations can easily be set during the first few minutes of the center by briefly discussing with each student how much work you think should be completed that day and marking that point by an "X."

> "This is really getting easy for you. I think you could probably do three pages today. Here, let me put a little crisscross on this page. See if you can get at least that far."
> or,
> "This is something completely new for you, so it will be slow going for a few days. Don't worry about it. Soon you'll be sailing along again. Why don't you see if you can get two lines done today?"

What you are doing is pointing out to each student that what you expect is determined by individual factors, and these factors will vary from time to time. In addition, you are illustrating the thinking entailed in setting realistic goals.

Once the students are familiar with the process of determining daily expectations, have *them* make the decision and place the

"X" at the anticipated ending-point. They also should indicate their starting-points by writing the date beside the first problem they work. Discuss with each student whether the daily expectation seems realistic. This only takes a few minutes and you may be surprised at how good they are in projecting what they can accomplish.

When you first begin this procedure, explain to the students that you are making a guess about how much they can accomplish. (Your expectations should be such that success is almost assured.) Once you know the capabilities of each student, you can begin to hold them responsible for getting at least to the "X," and going further if possible. It then becomes the equivalent of a minimum assignment which has been established for that specific person.

As the center becomes individualized, each student should have a definite feeling of success, since the material being worked is at an appropriate level. One of the interesting situations which always arises involves one of the more academically gifted students moaning because they are only going to get a few lines done that day. Then, one of the much slower students will offer sympathy by saying, "Don't worry. That always happens to me, too, when I start on something new. Just wait. In a few more days you'll be able to do as much work as I'm doing!" Now that's success!

On days when you do not work at the Math Center, take a few minutes at the beginning of the center to check the placement of each child's "X." At the end of the center, return to check whether they have each fulfilled their minimum requirements.

Eventually you will find almost all of the students are accomplishing much more than you would ever have asked of them. Only a few students will continue to need a daily check to determine if they have completed the required work. Ask those students to bring their booklet to you when the center is over, so that you can check on their progress.

In order to provide encouragement and support for these students, you might quietly say part way through the center, "Don't forget you need to be at least this far before you leave the center." This can be a friendly reminder which may help spur the student's concentration. The child is reminded that you do have a minimum daily expectation for each person. But, by the same token, you are rooting for the student to live up to that expectation.

At the end of the center, the child shows you that the minimum requirement has at least been met. Otherwise, the student stays over at the center until reaching the "X," unless some unforeseen circumstance arose which made the attainment of the minimum daily requirement impossible.

It is important to tell students that sometimes what appears to be a realistic expectation turns out otherwise. Assure them that if they have really been working during the entire center time, but do not make it to their mark, you will not hold them over at the center. However, if they have been talking or wasting time, that's different!

The same basic system can be used at the Writing Center. Generally all that is required at this center however, is a request that they do their best work. Nonetheless, there will be those few students who need the crisscross periodically to indicate a specified amount of work which they are to complete. I wish this were not necessary. But some students need more direction than others. If this is the case, my personal feeling is that the teacher must provide it, while attempting to capture their attention with work which is interesting and for which they see a purpose—easier said than done, I know!

If it is necessary for a student to stay at a center to complete work, it should not be to the detriment of other tasks. With a little foresight, centers can be planned to facilitate a period for catch-up work. If Math is followed by Independent, the student may need to go to Independent a few minutes late but will not be behind when the group rotates to the following center. Having Writing rotate to Art or Spelling accomplishes the same thing. This should be taken into consideration when planning the rotation of the centers.

Perhaps a student has not completed the minimum requirement. But you still want the child to rotate with the group to the next center. Then, you can instruct this student to finish the assignment during Independent Center or at recess. Be certain, however, that the child does complete the work.

During this time, while you are working on establishing basic expectancies, it is crucial to explain to students that you will never ask them to do something unless you think they can actually accomplish it. By the same token, you expect them to do their best on assignments because they are geared to the students' needs—not too hard, not too easy. This is sometimes hard for a student to understand who has had years of failure. The child has continually been asked to do tasks which could not be accomplished. Therefore, the student expects to fail. Much work is required in order to rebuild the child's ego. This student must believe you when you say, "You can do it. I know you can."

Stress that anytime you give a student an assignment too hard to figure out, you are the one who "goofed." You may have thought you talked with the child about it before, or perhaps you handed out the wrong material.

Every year, some student comes up to me and grins, "You goofed, Mrs. Petreshene. We've never talked about this." How delightful it is for a student to feel so secure that it just has to be the teacher's fault if an assignment cannot be handled!

It takes time and much reassurance to convince students that you want them to come to you if they need help. In order to establish this trust, the students must know that they will not be "put down," directly or indirectly, or made to feel guilty because they are having a problem. That is what you are there for, to help them learn.

Discussions should be held periodically, so you can be aware of how students feel about the work they are doing, and about the environment in general. This can also be accomplished by using one of the following two forms.

Name ____ Date ____ How do you feel about...	😌	😐	😟
Math			
Spelling			
Reading			
"copy work"			
writing stories			
Discovery			
Music			
P.E.			
Art			
your classmates			
My favorite subject is _____			

> Name_____ Date _____
> In the classroom I like
> _____
> _____
> But the one thing I like best is
> _____ because _____
> _____
> I don't like to_____
> because _____
> _____
> If I could change some things
> in the room, I wish we would
> _____
> _____

*Student evaluation and
attitudinal forms*

Students Who Have Problems Coping

Some students enter the classroom convinced that they will be unable to do the assignments. They have learned through bitter experience that to attempt a task and not be able to complete it results in failure. Therefore, they adopt the do-nothing strategy. Then they give the excuse that the work wasn't interesting. Or they didn't feel like doing it, etc. None of these may be the truth. But the student has learned to handle what may be an untenable situation (risking additional failure) in this manner.

Both you and the student have a problem with this attitude toward assignments. Much of the problem can be solved once the child becomes convinced that you will not hand an assignment to a student who cannot handle it. However, until this point is reached, it is often difficult to get the child involved in an activity. Positive statements can often help motivate the student if for no other reason than to receive recognition, or to gain a sense of having pleased the teacher.

In time, pleasing oneself will provide the motivation. It is the ultimate goal. Meanwhile, your displaying an interest in what the child is doing and making sincere positive comments may help.

"Have you done that much already?"

"This is the best work I have ever seen you do. Can you do this well again next time? Please let me see it."

"You have a good story started. I'm curious to find out what happens." (Children will follow you around the room saying, "I knew you'd want to know how this turned out.")

Other students need help in identifying the cause of their problems.

"Do you think you would be able to concentrate better if you moved away from the center? Sometimes sitting in a study booth makes it much easier to get your work done."

It is important not to make the students feel guilty if it is necessary to move them away from others, so that the work can be completed.

I always think of the child who spent the first month of school being distracted by anything that happened nearby. The tousled little head continuously popped up to see what was going on. One day I suggested that this student try working in a study booth, explaining that it might help concentration. The child came to me at the end of the center beaming. Three times more work had been completed than had ever been accomplished before. From that time, until the end of the year, this student always headed to a study booth during the Math Center. All you could see was the top of a little head busily bent over the work. If this student learned nothing else that year, at least the all-important discovery remained: that, in order to concentrate and do well, isolation produced results!

If you suggest working in a study booth to a child, but the idea is rejected, you might say, "All right. That's your choice. But then I expect you to settle down and get to work." (There is a difference between suggesting a possible solution and telling the student that it is necessary for you to make the choice.)

If a negative comment is required, as sometimes is the case, try to follow it with a positive statement.

"I know you can do better work than this. Let me see what you have accomplished in ten minutes."

By having the child check with you in ten minutes, you have indicated that now is the time to get to work! Provided that the student accomplishes some quality work, you can reinforce this effective behavior with, "Great! I knew you could do it!"

Although the work in an individualized environment almost guarantees success for each child, it does not eliminate all drudgery. Some skills require drill to master. If a task is important, it should not be eliminated from the curriculum just because it is "no fun." This is one of the factors which resulted in problems in many of the "open schools" of the 1960's. If a student says, "Do I have to do this?" try to be honest but firm.

> "I know this isn't exactly fun and you don't like to do it, but it is important because _____ . So I'm sorry, but yes, you do need to do it."

If it is not handled in this way, you are leaving yourself open for a verbal battle every time a student "doesn't feel" like doing an assignment! But, by the same token, it is important to look at the activity and see if you can think of a more interesting way to accomplish the same thing. (Often you can find an alternative way when you stop to think about it. We're all creatures of habit!)

Almost all students thrive in a learning centers environment. It is a joy to watch a child's self-confidence and sense of responsibility grow. Occasionally, however, there is a student who has great difficulty adjusting to this environment. Since it is of utmost importance that such a child not be allowed to destroy the smooth operation of centers for everyone else, some action needs to be taken.

It is helpful to try first the various strategies which previously have been outlined. If the child is still unable to cope, you might try the following. Talk with this student privately before or after school, and discuss honestly what you perceive as the problem(s). Explain that together you must find a solution. Or *you* will have to make all the choices. Since you really do not want to do this, you need to seek another way to solve the problem.

Say to the child, "I'm going to give you three choices. I want you to choose one of them for today. Choose the one which you think will help you get your work done without bothering others. (1) You can go to each of the centers and check with me at the end of each center to show me what you have been able to accomplish. Then, tell me how you feel things went. (2) You may go to each of the centers and select a friend at the center to be your buddy, one who will help remind you to get your work done. Both of you will then report to me at the end of each center. (3) You may get the materials from each of the centers and bring them to a place near the center where I will be working, and I'll try to help you concentrate on your work."

I have only needed to use this system one time. There was a long pause while the student thought, then said, "I think I'd better sit near you." I was disappointed because I had really hoped the child would choose one of the other options. However, he was right. For the first time, he had a successful day. I was able to give him sincere praise and positive reinforcement.

At the beginning of each day, I quietly talked with him for a few minutes and asked what his choice was for that day. He continued to want to sit near me. After approximately two weeks of this, I asked him to choose a center—one which he would enjoy and at the same time be able to handle. He chose Independent. There were no problems.

For several more days he went to one center, and spent the rest of the time working near me. Then it was increased to two centers, then three, and finally all four centers. For awhile he checked with me at the end of each center. Eventually he was "on his own." I'm not certain which of us was more elated! Some of my fondest memories are of this student, who caused so many problems at the beginning of the year, but eventually became a delight to have in the classroom.

When Everything Goes Wrong

Regardless of how well learning centers have been functioning, periodically it becomes necessary to "pull back" and tighten the structure. Teachers often feel guilty about this. They assume they must be doing something wrong. But in any environment there are times when everything seems to run beautifully, and other times when problems surface. At these times it is especially important to discuss your feelings with the students. Let them become aware of the factors which are bothering you.

By the same token, the students should have the opportunity to express their feelings. Sometimes problems can be solved then and there. Other times, it becomes necessary to take "two giant steps backward." Some or all of the choices may need to be withdrawn, and Independent Center replaced with another center. The resulting environment may be close to what it was at the beginning of the year. It may even be necessary to go to total group assignments, raising hands, remaining in their chairs, etc. You can say to the students, "If this is the only way we can get things done, then that is how it will have to be."

If centers are to be successful, they cannot just be "your thing." The students must want them and be willing to work to make them run smoothly.

Though it may seem discouraging at the time, before long you can slowly introduce choices again and work on building a sense of responsibility and independence. Along with the key word, "slowly," once more you will need to stress the inter-relationship between responsibility and consequences.

You should not become overly concerned about having had to "tighten up." It happens in all classrooms. The eventual environment and sense of cooperation may be stronger because of it.

When I first used learning centers, I felt terribly discouraged after about a month. Philosophically I agreed with learning centers and individualization. But it didn't seem to be working for me. I moved all of the desks into neat rows with the intent of going back to a "traditional classroom." When the students arrived the following morning, their faces fell a mile when they saw the room. A long discussion ensued. I told them the problems as I perceived them. They talked about the things they liked and the things they didn't like about learning centers. Together, we worked out solutions for their problems and mine. Together, we changed the room back into learning centers. That has been my classroom environment ever since.

At the time I was convinced I was the only person who had ever had these feelings of "just not being able to do it." I did not have access to anyone who had gone through the same thing and could assure me that it was typical. All I needed to do was discuss the problems with the students, and tighten up the structure. I accidentally discovered it for myself, and since then have found that it is almost universal. Everyone seems to go through it at one time or another. But how I wish I had known then what I know now!

CHAPTER V

Room Arrangement and Materials Storage

Determining the Basic Floor Plan

Before moving furniture, it is wise to make a sketch of the room and note the location of permanent fixtures. Include in your sketch:

1. Electric outlets
2. Windows
3. Sink
4. Student coat closets
5. Counters, shelves and storage
6. Chalkboards
7. Bulletin boards

Diagram the room on a ditto master. Duplicate several copies, and you are ready to determine your basic floor plan.

At this stage don't worry about the specific items needed at each center. The placement of the centers and storage areas should be your main concern.

The following factors should be considered.

1. Desks, tables, flip-top desks, flip-top desks with attached chairs. Any of these can be used for centers. Tables are the most convenient, but teachers are not always given choices about furniture! Desks are excellent at the writing center, as they clearly define each person's space. Tables often crowd students for writing. If the desks have a slant top, the lids can generally be propped up so they are level by inserting a kindergarten block, or a piece of wood inside the desk and letting the lid rest on the wood.

Consider various groupings of desks.

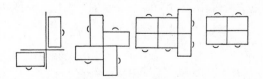

Desk groupings

2. Noisy areas/quiet areas. The actual placement of centers is extremely important. What seems logical on paper may be impossible, once centers are in action. Evaluate each center in terms of the probability for noise. The more active the center, (Independent, Art, Science, Manipulative Math), the noisier. These should not be located near a center requiring concentration.

It might seem logical to place Manipulative Math and Computational Math next to each other. However, in terms of noise level and movement, these centers are not compatible.

Quiet centers should be near each other. But the more active centers need to be placed in different sections of the room. If it becomes necessary to place an active and a quiet center near each other, separate them with some type of barrier. (See pages 45-47.)

3. Paths of movement. Watch out for temptations! If a student needs to go from one side of the room to another, in order to get supplies, or to rotate to the next center, there are many temptations along the way. Consider how close the possible paths of movement take the students past others who are trying to concentrate on their work.

Long narrow paths invite sliding. These can be broken by storage units or physical barriers.

4. Student coat closets. Furniture should be grouped so as not to interfere with access to these areas.

5. Doors. Furniture will need to be arranged so that closet doors can easily be opened. Or the doors can be taken off their hinges.

6. Bulletin boards. Bulletin-board space can be used to display charts related to specific centers: Ways to Practice Your Spelling Words, Beginnings for Stories, etc.

7. Art and Science area. These two activities should be planned close to the sink and will need access to storage.

8. Writing Center. Try to plan this so that the chalkboard will be visible from each of the seats. Instead of eight to ten desks together, consider two or more smaller groupings. Considerable storage area nearby will be needed.

9. Math Center. Tables or desks, or a combination of these, will work well for this center. Nearby storage should also be planned.

10. Reading (instruction) area. A round table is particularly convenient for reading instruction. A chalkboard and storage for books are also desirable.

If you plan a separate block of time for reading instruction, this area can be used during centers time for spelling and listening post activities. If you intend to use it as a listening post center, be certain there is an electric outlet nearby.

11. Independent reading area. This section of the room can generally serve several functions. It can be used as the Independent Center for leisure reading during the reading time-block, and as a place for the total group to meet at the beginning and end of the day, as well as for music and movies.

If you intend to use it for total group activities, it will need to be large enough to accommodate all the students. Shelves, for leisure and reference books and storage for activities for the Independent Center, are necessary. A couple of chairs, or a couch and a rug, make nice additions.

Because the area will be used for reading, the lighting should be good.

The size of this area will be determined by whether you plan to use it for total group activities, or only for small groups.

12. Extra tables and desks. For students who elect to do additional work at a center, or who are required to remain to complete their assignments, extra desks and chairs must be available at each of the centers. Or a central area for "overflow" should be provided. Several small tables or desks, placed in the middle of the room, can eliminate the need for extra chairs at each center.

To make the overflow area (two small tables will do) even more flexible, have a large piece of masonite available. When needed, the two tables can be pushed together and the masonite laid on top, which results in a large table. This is also ideal for many Discovery Center activities.

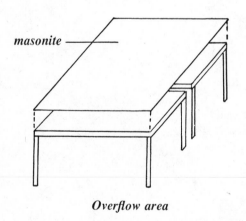

Overflow area

13. Storage for materials at each center. If there is not sufficient storage space in your classroom (there never is!) you can easily make additional shelves with 12-inch square cement blocks and unpainted shelving. These come approximately 11½ inches by 6 feet, 8 feet. . . . up to 16 feet in length. They can be painted or covered with paper. Shelves between 4 and 6 feet long seem to work well with cement blocks. If you want to

have the shelves extend beyond 6 feet, insert additional cement blocks at the mid-point.

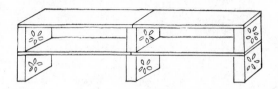

Storage areas 1

The shelves can also be used to define a corner and provide storage space.

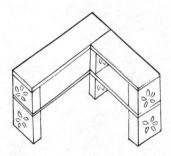

Storage area 2

Desks with bars mid-point in the legs can be used for storage. Push the desks together and lay shelving across the bars, to provide two tiers of storage at minimal cost.

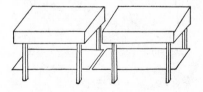

Storage area 3

14. Storage of student possessions and materials. Many of the student's materials will be kept at each specific center. However, they still need a place to keep books they are reading, papers which are to be taken home, etc. Therefore you need to consider whether these things will be kept in individual desks, or in some type of storage unit.

Individual cubby-holes can easily be made from five-gallon ice cream cartons, painted in a variety of bright colors with tempera paint. Thirty cartons can be arranged in the following manner.

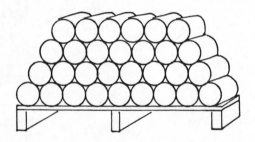

Cubby holes

The trick to assemble them is to secure the bottom row before building upwards. (Otherwise the pressure on the bottom cartons will cause them to spread apart).

For easy access, the bottom row should be elevated. A 7-foot shelf, approximately 11½ inches wide, should be attached to sturdy legs. (An old railroad tie sawed into 11½ inch sections makes wonderfully sturdy legs, as the shelf and legs can be nailed together.)

Fasten the bottom row of ice cream cartons together, using brads, acco fasteners, or yarn. Place this row of cartons on the shelving and nail each carton into the board. This will give you a good sturdy base on which to build. Continue building each successive row, attaching adjacent cartons with brads, acco fasteners, etc.

Use a permanent felt pen to write each student's name on a piece of 1″ masking tape. Attach near the top of the cubby hole.

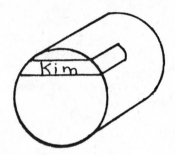

Close-up of individual cubby hole

To facilitate passing out papers, the names can be placed on the cubby holes in alphabetical order, reading from left to right. Or you can number the cubby holes in consecutive order. (Write the number on the tape along with the child's name.)

If you use the numbering system, each student should write the number of his or her cubby hole on any papers handed in. This will help locate the child's cubby hole quickly when papers are being passed out.

15. Private spaces. It is particularly important in a learning-centers environment that a private area be established. Physical barriers (see below) can often simulate this feeling. Study carrels are also quite helpful. These can stay permanently at certain desks or tables. Or they may be folded flat, and stored in an accessible part of the room. These enable students to create a sense of privacy whenever they feel the need.

The study carrels can be made from cardboard, cut from boxes, or from heavy railroad board or chipboard. The three pieces are hinged together with masking tape. The exact size will be determined by the sizes of the desks or tables. The side pieces should be several inches away from the edge of the desk, to avoid having them slip off.

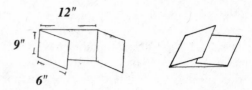

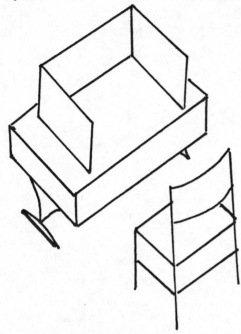

Sturdy carrel

A modified small scale study carrel can be made from two pieces of 9″×12″ tagboard. Although quite small, students enjoy using these to conceal their work.

STEPS IN CONSTRUCTING A SMALL SCALE MODIFIED STUDY CARREL

16. *Physical barriers.* Some teachers like to be able to survey the entire classroom at a glance and are therefore uncomfortable if barriers prevent them from doing this.

Other teachers are happier with barriers, as they believe that noise and student distraction is minimized. The final choice should be determined by what is comfortable for you.

Hanging physical barriers can be made by glueing dowels to the top and bottom of a piece of fabric. Wire or string is attached to the top dowel and the divider is hung from a light fixture, or from hooks screwed into the ceiling.

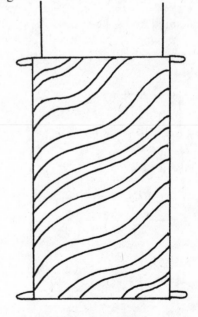

Hanging divider

Versatile dividers can be made from sturdy cardboard cartons in which freezers and refrigerators are shipped. They can be obtained free of charge from appliance stores. Rather than attempting to transport large boxes intact, take along a razor-blade knife. While you are at the store, cut along the seams of the cartons so that the pieces can be stacked. You can then easily put these into your car and take them to your school. The size you eventually cut them will depend on the specific function they are to serve in your classroom, the sizes of tables, desks, etc. It is usually wise to walk around your room and place the cardboard in various locations to get the feel of the room before actually cutting it to desired size.

Use the razor-blade knife to cut the cardboard to the exact size you need. Hinge the pieces together with masking tape. The cardboard can also be held together by cutting interlocking slits in the two pieces. An alternate method for keeping it in an upright position can be effected by placing it between two desks, or between desks and shelves.

The card-board can be made attractive by: (1) papering with compatible wallpaper patterns from a sample wallpaper book (attractive and free), (2) painting with latex, (not enamel), (3) attaching colorful commercial pictures, or (4) covering with student murals.

Both the cardboard and cloth dividers can be used for displays.

DIVIDERS

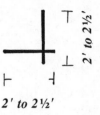

2' to 2½'

2' to 2½'

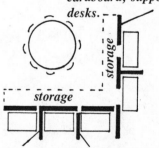

Free-standing pieces of cardboard, supported by desks.

storage

storage

Free-standing pieces of cardboard, supported on both sides by desks and storage shelves.

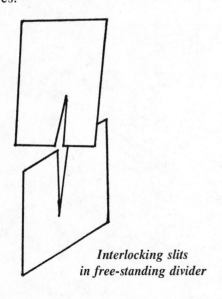

Interlocking slits
in free-standing divider

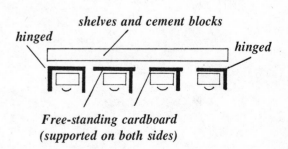

shelves and cement blocks

hinged

hinged

Free-standing cardboard
(supported on both sides)

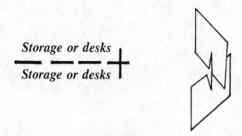

Storage or desks

Storage or desks

also be used for the Independent Center and/or leisure reading).
2. Writing Center.
3. Math Center.
4. Spelling/Listening Post/Discovery Centers.
5. Art/Cooking/Science/and/or other Centers.
6. Overflow area.

After consideration of all these factors, draw several floor plans on the room diagram. Be certain to provide the following major areas:

1. Total group meeting area (which can

The activities at the last three centers will vary considerably from day to day and should be considered as you experiment with various floor plans.

A sample floor plan follows:

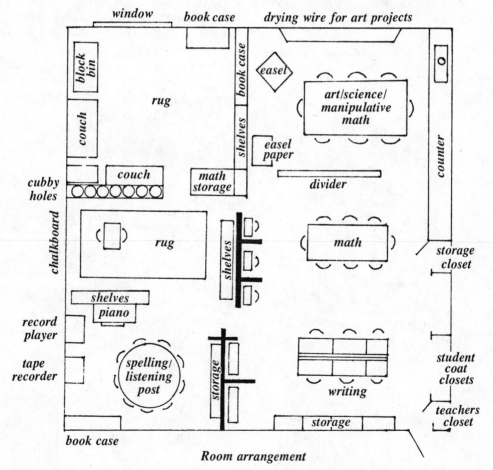

Room arrangement

Planning for Each Center: Materials and Storage

Once you have determined your basic floor plan, and the materials needed at each specific center, the storage of same must be considered.

Independent Reading/Total Group/and Independent Center

If possible, try to procure a rug for this area. In addition, some throw pillows and a couch or chairs make it most inviting. If bookcases are not available, books can be stored in cardboard boxes. It may be necessary to cut down the boxes so they will not be too deep. Cover them with attractive self-adhesive paper. This also makes them more durable.

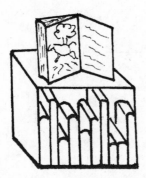

*Cardboard box for
book storage and display*

Display some of the more interesting books on top of the box so students will be attracted to them. (Students often will not be drawn to a book area if only book bindings are showing.)

Arrange the Independent Center activities on the shelves. (These activities should be frequently changed in order to maintain interest.) This is also a good location for blocks and animals (fish, mice, rats, lizards, snakes, guinea pigs, etc.). The area should also provide maximum visibility if it is to serve as the movie center.

A most useful addition to this center are six to eight cut-outs from formica counter tops. This is the part which is cut out and thrown away when a sink is installed in a counter top. Often cutouts can be obtained from cabinet-makers free of charge. When a student elects to work at the rug area, during the Independent Center, a "cut-out" provides a smooth surface on which to write.

In the primary grades, if there is room at the Independent Center, you might include a large refrigerator box. This can be used as a puppet theater, store, bank, etc. It can also be used to display student work.

Computational Mathematics Center

The materials needed for the Computational Mathematics Center include:
—Boxes to hold the students' math file folders. Two shallow boxes usually work better than one deep box. Only half the students' folders are stored in

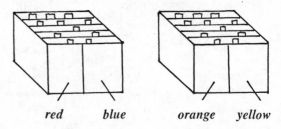

red   blue   orange   yellow

Storage for student math file folders

each box, so they do not have to look through as many folders in order to find their own. It is helpful to color-code the front of the boxes, to indicate which groups' folders are in each box.

—Large number ladder or number line attached to the wall.
—Miscellaneous math materials: counters, individual ladders or number lines, Number Blox, etc.
—"Hand in box." This can be made by cutting a cardboard box so that it is approximately 3 inches deep and covering the box with attractive paper. The box should be approximately 1½ to 2 inches larger than the papers which will be handed in.

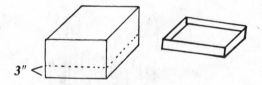

Constructing a "hand-in box"

—Pencils, erasers. Pencils can be kept at the center in frozen-juice cans which have been covered with self-adhesive paper, or in egg cartons which have been taped closed and painted. Holes are punched in each of the "cups." Pencils can then be inserted in each of the holes.

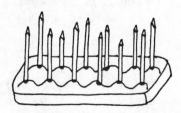

Pencil holder made from egg carton

Pencil holder made from frozen-juice can

Writing Center

The materials needed for the Writing Center include:

—Color-coded boxes to hold student dictionaries, or these can be kept in cubby holes if they are nearby. (The students should keep their individual creative-writing folder and record sheet inside their personal dictionary, as well as the creative-writing material on which they are currently working.) Storage boxes for each group can be made from large detergent boxes.

Space-saving storage box

Folders face forward in this box

—Student copy work-books. If the copy work books are large (primary size writing paper) they can be kept in four color-coded 5-gallon ice cream cartons, one for each color group. Otherwise, they may be stored in the student cubby holes, or placed on nearby shelving. In order to keep the various groups' copy work books separate, pieces of colored paper, which correspond to the color groups, can be taped to the shelves; and the copy work books arranged accordingly.

—Pencils, erasers.

—Stapler.

—Commercial dictionaries.

—Story starter chart, placed so that it will be visible from all seats at the Writing Center.

—Lettering chart, placed so that it will be easily seen.

—Various-size papers. These can either be put on a nearby storage shelf, or in a cardboard carton with partitions. Sturdy boxes of this type can be obtained from liquor stores.

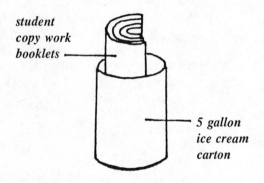

student copy work booklets —

5 gallon ice cream carton

Storage for writing paper

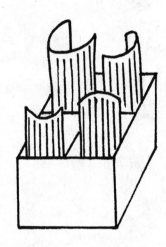

Partitioned cardboard box stores writing paper

—Box or vegetable bin containing mounted pictures, manila envelopes containing story-started dittos, and stands to hold pictures.

—Box or vegetable bin containing teacher's master copies of the copy work books.

—Creative writing task cards.

—Hand-in box.

—Two or three-pound coffee cans covered with self-adhesive paper to hold current story starter dittos, or specific assignments.

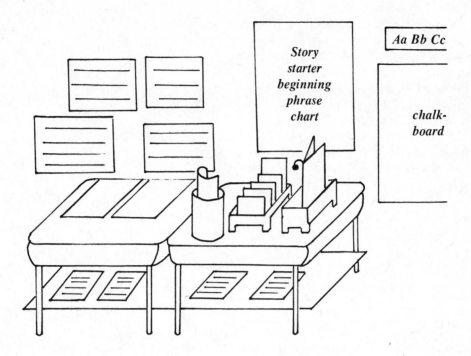

Chart labels: *Story starter beginning phrase chart*, *Aa Bb Cc*, *chalk-board*

Writing Center storage area

Individualized Spelling/ Listening Post/ Reading Instruction

The materials needed for the Spelling Center include:
— Boxes to hold students' books with lists of words, or these may be kept in their cubby holes if they are nearby.
— Yellow and blue books: (one in which they write their weekly list, and the other which is used for their spelling test). These may be stored at this center, or kept in their cubby holes.
— Pencils, erasers.

The equipment needed for the Listening Post Center includes:
— Earphones and listening post.
— Tape recorder.
— Record player.
— Film strip projector (optional).
— Movie projector (optional).
— Screen (optional).

A movie projector can be plugged into the listening post. This enables a small group of students to listen to and watch a film without disturbing the other students. The jack from the listening post is too large for the opening in the movie projector. You will therefore need an adapter.

A full-size screen is not necessary at the listening post, since only a small group of students will be viewing the film strip or movie. A piece of 12″ by 18″ white construction paper can be pinned to the wall and used quite effectively as a screen, provided that direct light does not fall on it. A box painted black, both inside and outside will also serve nicely. A piece of white paper is attached to the back of the inside wall of the carton for a "screen."

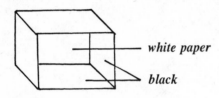

white paper

black

"Screen" for film or film strips

"Fourth Center" Activities (Science, Manipulative Math, Art . . .)

Since this center often changes in character from day to day and serves many functions, a range of materials needs to be in proximity. If storage space is limited, the materials may be stored in boxes and displayed for specific units of study.

Some of the materials which should be readily available for this center include:
—Hand-in box.
—Pencils, erasers.
—Coffee cans for dittos (assignment for that day).
—Individual folders (see illustrations below) to hold current work, stored in a box at the center or in the students' cubby holes.

INDIVIDUAL FOLDERS

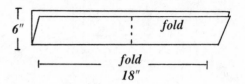

Fold one piece of 12″×18″ construction paper.

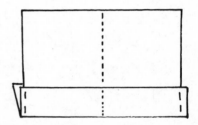

Insert a second piece of 12″×18″ construction paper which has first been creased in the middle. Staple the edges.

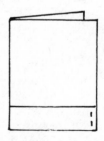

This results in a four-pocket storage folder.

—Boxes to hold task cards. (These can be made from detergent boxes.)

STORAGE BOX

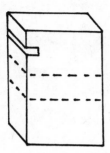

Tape closed the "spout" on the side of the empty box. Cut the box in half, making two storage boxes.

Cut the boxes so the back is higher than the front.

The storage boxes should be covered with self-adhesive decorative paper to strengthen them.

Art Center

Basic supplies which should be stored at this center include:

—Crayons
—Paints
—Colored chalk
—Paste
—Paste brushes
—Tempera
—Paint brushes
—Orange-juice cans
—Egg cartons
—Easel paper
—Colored construction paper
—Small bowls
—White art paper
—Watercolor sets
—Newspapers
—Scissors
—Smocks

Scissors can be stored in egg cartons, as previously diagramed for pencils. This makes a very handy container for twelve pairs of scissors. At a glance you can determine whether all of the scissors have been returned.

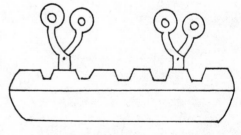

Storage for scissors

Paste can be stored in baby food jars. Eight of these jars can be kept in a small box. It can be moved to other centers when paste is required.

Smocks will often be needed at the art center. A pattern for a smock which young children can easily put on, and which requires no buttons or snaps, is illustrated in the Appendix.

Paint can be available at a center without fear of spillage. Use only the top of an egg carton. Discard the section which has the "cups". Trace three circles using a frozen-juice can on the inside of the lid of the egg carton.

Constructing a paint holder

Cut out the three circles. Turn the lid over and insert three juice cans containing tempera paint. Add brushes and place in the middle of the center. Several of these will make a nice painting center with no worry about spilled paint!

Paint holders

Easel. Free-standing easels can often get in the way. Wall easels are space-savers and serve the same purpose. Staple or thumb tack oil cloth to a wall area. Nail metal clips or wooden clothespins (to attach students' easel paper to the wall) near the top of the oilcloth. Nail a paint rack from an easel to the lower part of the oilcloth. Egg-carton lids, as illustrated above, should be put inside the paint rack so that paints will not spill.

Paintings and other art work can be dried by attaching two parallel pieces of wire to the wall, preferably near the art center, and clipping wooden clothespins to the wire.

Wall easel and drying area

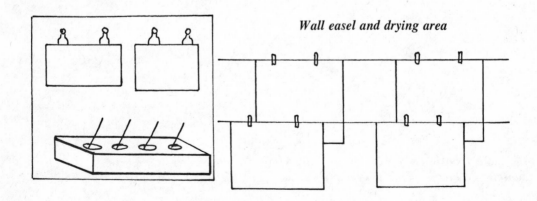

Other Materials

Dittos can be kept in file folders, and stored in a cardboard box. Or, if file folders are not available, the sets of dittos can be stacked on top of each other with a piece of 9″×12″ colored construction paper inserted between each set. The construction paper should extend approximately 1½″ beyond the front of the dittos. On this extended part, write the source of the ditto and the page number. This makes it easy to find the specific ditto you need, or to find the original source if extra copies need to be duplicated.

DITTO STORAGE

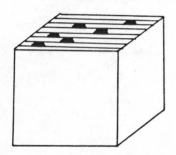

File folders

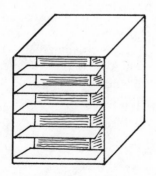

Colored paper dividers

Labels

Use one color of construction paper as dividers for dittos from each source.

Color coding is also useful for sorting dittos on specific skills. Be certain to note source and page number when dittos are stored in this manner.

A spindle can be made by pounding a nail through a piece of wood. This can serve for the students to leave notes, indicating which materials need to be replenished.

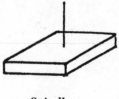

Spindle

A check-in board eliminates the tedious process of taking roll each day. Paint a 22″×40″ board and a paint rack from an easel. Screw thirty cup-hooks into the board, and attach this to the wall. The paint rack should then be attached below the cup hook board.

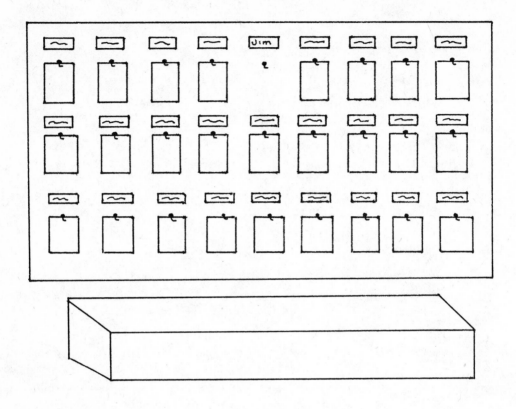

Check-in board

Pieces of sample formica (available from cabinet shops and building supply companies) are put in the paint rack. Each student's name is written on a piece of masking tape, and put above one of the cup hooks.

As they arrive in the morning, each student takes a piece of formica and hangs it on the cup hook under his or her name, enabling you to tell who is absent at a glance.

A class picture with the students' names adds a personal touch to the classroom and is greatly enjoyed by the children. In addition it can be helpful to substitute teachers, as well as teacher aides.

CHAPTER VI

Keeping the Lines
of Communication Open

Of utmost importance when you are contemplating a change in classroom organization is keeping the lines of communication open between you and your principal, and you and the parents.

Once you have fully thought out the reorganization of your classroom, the first step is to describe it to your principal. Any change should also be approached slowly. As previously noted, it is far better to begin individualization with one successful center, than to attempt to individualize four centers simultaneously. That could result in disaster!

Once your principal's approval has been obtained, hold an orientation meeting for parents. "Back to School Night" in the fall is not the appropriate time to discuss classroom reorganization with parents because of the limited time. You need their undivided attention.

At the orientation meeting, explain why you are making a change, what you hope to

accomplish, how this will be handled, and how it will affect their children. Professional experiences and personal descriptions are helpful to use in a meeting with parents. When I talk with parents, I try to communicate the range of abilities that exist, even at the kindergarten level, and that this range widens with each successive year. To illustrate this important point in favor of individualized instruction, I tell this story:

During the first week of kindergarten at a Discovery Center, an aide was working with one or two children at a time. They were putting a small amount of water in the bottom of a baby food jar, adding a few drops of one food coloring, followed by another few drops of a different color. One child came running up to me and with great excitement said, "Wook!" I asked her what had happened, but all she could say was, "Wook!" She was not yet at a level where she could express what she had seen happen.

Not two minutes later another kindergartener walked up and said, "Look, Mrs. Petreshene. I put a little water in the jar. Then I put in three drops of yellow food coloring and two drops of red food coloring. Look what happened! It turned orange!"

These two children were obviously miles apart, not only in experience, but particularly in their ability to communicate. To expect the same level of achievement from them would be ridiculous.

Similar differences are apparent in all curriculum areas. Frequently, one or two children enter kindergarten already reading quite well. Other children enter, not knowing any of the letters of the alphabet or corresponding sounds. More important, they have not reached a stage where they are even interested in letters or words.

I explain to the parents that, if this kind of gap exists in kindergarten, they can imagine what the spread is by third, fourth, or fifth grade. At these stages some children are still operating at the first or second-grade level. Others have acquired junior high or even high-school skills. Once again, to expect the same achievement from each of these students and to give them the same assignment is unrealistic. Also, I discuss some of the problems encountered when I had a "traditional" classroom. (See Chapter I.)

When you have your orientation meeting, be certain to explain to parents *what* you hope to accomplish. In my case it is the establishment of an environment in which the children feel successful, where they learn a sense of responsibility and develop independence, where they have opportunities to learn about getting along with others, and at the same time grow academically in accordance with their abilities.

Describe your classroom organization (the *how*): keeping track of individual student progress, determining the strengths and skill deficits of each student, providing for improvement and growth, how and what materials will be used, determing if students are using their time effectively, etc.

It is important that parents understand the underlying structure and organization of your program and how you will be able to determine and provide for the needs of the students. Many parents have experienced, or have heard about environments wrongly called individualized. Many associate this type of organization, however erroneously in this case, with the "swinging-from-the-chandelier" type of classroom. You must convince the parents that their children are going to profit from being in your classroom.

If your school policy allows parents to volunteer in their own child's classroom, the meeting is an excellent time to recruit volunteer teacher aides. Parents are often so excited and curious about the type of environment you are describing that they will volunteer time on the spot. When requesting volunteers, stress that by yourself you can accomplish a certain amount of individualization. But, if there were two adults in the classroom, more one-to-one interaction and instruction could take place, thus benefiting *their* child.

Discuss the variety of classroom activities in which they can become involved: academic centers (helping children write stories, math, reading, science, spelling), or enrichment centers (arts and crafts, cooking, music, drama). Assure them that you will acquaint them with the materials, how to use them, and familiarize them with any concepts they need to know before they are asked to "run" a center. Stress that they will not be asked to do anything that may be uncomfortable for them. Also mention the need for home volunteers and special project volunteers as well. Ask them to leave their names if they think they could volunteer in the classroom in any of these capacities, and tell them you will contact them individually.

The parents should also be invited to visit the classroom. Ask them to clear this through the office first. Try to arrange for them to arrive at a time when you can talk with them for a short while before the centers begin, perhaps before school or during a recess. You can show them some of their children's work and discuss what they will be doing at each of the centers that day.

All of the information discussed in the orientation meeting could of course be communicated in a letter. But I personally prefer an "in-person" orientation meeting. Regardless of how you decide to accomplish it, the important thing is to keep the lines of communication open.

CHAPTER VII

Recruiting and Training Teacher Aides

Introduction

Teachers who have never used aides in their classroom are often uneasy about having another adult in the room. Much of the uneasiness stems from the uncomfortable feeling that someone will be watching every move they make.

In a learning centers environment, the teacher no longer is the "center of attention," standing at the front of the class with all eyes riveted in that direction. Instead, the teacher is quietly involved with a small group of students in one area of the room. The teacher aide is equally busy with other students in a different part of the room, while the remaining children are absorbed in their own work. Since there is only a soft buzz of activity, a feeling of privacy results. Discussions do not carry beyond the immediate group. The sense of being in the spotlight then disappears.

With volunteers, it is a marvelous opportunity to acquaint them with the actual organization and operation of your program. Week in and week out, they see individual growth, and the excitement and involvement of students. This feeling of excitement, and the awareness that the needs of individual students are being met, are communicated to your aides. As a result, the volunteers become supporters of your program. Since neighbors do talk over the backyard fence, why not have some goodwill ambassadors who understand what you are doing, since they have actually been involved?

In addition, if the volunteer aides are parents of students in your class, they learn more about their own child's strengths and weaknesses. In reporting to these parents when there is a problem, there usually is no need to convince them that it exists. Once the problem has been perceived the immediate concern of both the teacher and the parent is what can be done to solve it.

Other parents may place inordinate pressures on their child. They are relieved to discover, through aiding, that their child is doing quite well; and extreme pressures are not necessary. This results in a much healthier home atmosphere for the student.

With few exceptions, using parent aides results in benefits to the class as a whole, and to the individual child, parent and teacher. Situations do occasionally arise which indicate it would be best for the parent not to continue working in the class. It is important that this possibility is discussed with volunteers before they actually begin their classroom stint. It must be stressed that the well-being of the child is of utmost importance. Therefore, if either the parent or you feel the student's behavior or work is adversely affected by the parental presence in the classroom, an alternate solution needs to be found. Perhaps the parent can assist by doing work at home for you, or by assisting in another classroom. The deciding factor must be what is best for the individual child.

Sometimes, administrators do not wish parents to volunteer in their child's classroom. In this case, work out a "trade agreement" with another teacher on recruiting aides. You or the administrator can explain the school policy to parents. Assure them that they will be able indirectly to help their child by aiding in a different class, since in return this means someone will help in their child's classroom.

If the administrator is uncertain about the use of volunteer aides, it is important that you take the time to communicate your feelings about having these helpers in your classroom. As the year progresses, be certain to tell your principal about instances where the class has benefited, or a specific child has been helped. Talk about the positive aspects of having teacher aides in your class. So much of an administrator's time is spent being bombarded with problems that it is essential for teachers to take the time to communicate successes. Your principal must have this type of information in order to be able to make valid policy decisions. If you can present a convincing case to show that volunteer aides have been an asset to your program and have facilitated student growth, the administrator will be much more receptive to the idea of parents volunteering in their own student's classroom.

Recruiting Teacher Aides

Teachers often wonder when they should begin recruiting and incorporating teacher aides into their classroom program. There is no clear-cut answer. Some teachers prefer to get the entire program underway before starting to use teacher aides. Others prefer to start with aides as part of the environment from the beginning of the year. One of the advantages of starting the year with teacher aides in the classroom is that they are not faced with a completely individualized program. Instead, they are introduced more slowly to the process of individualization, as you gradually make changes in the program.

The most effective means of recruiting parent aides is through a parent-orientation meeting as described in Chapter VI. Several weeks after the orientation meeting, it is helpful to send a letter home with each student, briefly explaining again the need for volunteers and how classroom teacher aides result in benefits to their children. Mention the number of volunteers you currently have, how many more are needed, and why. Explain the type of activities for which volunteers are needed. Assure parents that they will not be asked to undertake an activity until they are thoroughly familiar with it. You also might mention how much it seems to mean to students to have parents actually involved in the classroom. A letter of this type will almost always result in several additional volunteers.

There are parents who would like to aid in the classroom, but for one reason or another are hesitant. Contacting them directly is generally the best procedure. You might hear a student frequently talking about being involved in art projects with family members, or mention some person's interest in macrame, sewing, etc. This relative would be an ideal person to contact for help at the art center or on special projects. Keep attuned to student's comments about their parents' interests, parents who do not work, etc., as this will provide clues as to whom you might contact directly.

In addition, check with your local secondary schools and community colleges. Many offer credit for students who serve as teacher aides.

Another often overlooked resource are senior citizens. They generally have the time to volunteer, are reliable, and add a "special ingredient" to the classroom.

At the primary level, upper-grade students are also helpful. Many upper-grade teachers are receptive to the idea, provided it does not result in students neglecting their own studies. Problems sometimes occur because cross-age tutors take advantage of the situation by staying away from their own classrooms for longer and longer periods of time. To avoid this, a schedule should be posted which indicates the names of volunteering students and their scheduled arrival and departure times. Explain to the students that they will have to assume the responsibility of leaving on time. Tell them it is important to you that they not stay beyond their scheduled time, since this will result in them not being allowed to aid. By reminding them of this again and by remaining adamant that they leave on time, they will quickly assume the responsibility. (Students are more inclined to take advantage of the situation if they feel that you will back them up. This then places the upper-grade teacher in the position of being the tyrant who is unfair.)

Frequently the students considered for aiding are those who are bright and finish their work ahead of everyone else. However, academic success does not necessarily insure that a student will work effectively with younger students. In fact, the more gifted students are often quite impatient and intolerant of students who need help. Often, they cannot understand why concepts are not grasped immediately. Therefore, it is wise to observe the interaction of cross-age tutors and the younger children.

Upper-grade students who are experiencing limited success academically should not be overlooked as potential classroom aides. An aiding experience often helps them gain a sense of accomplishment and importance. They can become some of your most dedicated and valued aides.

Fourth, fifth, and sixth-grade students rarely can supervise a center which requires them to maintain the attention of seven or eight younger children. They are most effective used when working with two or three students on a one-to-one basis, or at a high-interest center (art, cooking, science). They can also keep things running smoothly at a center by handing out materials, checking in-coming work, etc.

Scheduling Aides and Compatible Tasks

When recruiting aides, it is wise to get some general information which can be used to determine their initial classroom assignment. Find out the length of time a person has lived in the community, previous experience working with children, the types of classroom activities enjoyed, activities which might be uncomfortable, and the days and hours available for aide work. With this information you should be able to place an aide in a situation which will assure success.

Keep in mind that, as time goes by, some aides may want to change centers. Others prefer to become thoroughly acquainted with one subject area and then continue to work at that center.

The interests and abilities of volunteer teacher aides vary tremendously but should be used in ways that are beneficial and rewarding to all. Certain talents or abilities remain hidden. Some of your aides or volunteers may be shy about revealing any talents they may have. Through observation and discussion, you can learn about these abilities and make the kind of placement which maximizes a person's ability or effectiveness.

Don't overlook those who don't want to teach, yet are willing to correct papers. Math booklets or spelling workbooks can be sent to such persons. You can also try to convince them to spend one day each week helping the students make the corrections. Or you may have a corrections center one day.

The following day, the correction aide can supervise the center, checking student corrections, tearing out completed pages, and sending work home.

You may discover an adult or upper-grade student who has special talent in drama, music, poetry, science, movement, etc. If this person cannot come during centers, perhaps a lunch-time visit, one or more days each week for a month or so is possible. Many students will be thrilled to spend their lunch time working in a small group with someone who has a special talent which interests them.

You will be amazed at the variety of ways volunteers can assist you and your students.

Taking time to get to know your aides and their strengths, and then planning assignments accordingly, is an important aspect of running a program in which teacher aides are successfully incorporated as an integral part of the classroom.

Encouraging Reliability

Many potentially good aides stop working in the classroom because of three factors: (1) They are uncomfortable doing the tasks asked of them. (2) They are given insufficient information and direction and are left with the feeling of not knowing what to do. (3) They do not feel needed.

Teachers often convey the feeling of non-importance with comments such as, "I'm sorry. We're scheduled to _____ today, so I won't need you after all," or "Oh, is today your day to aide?" Non-importance is also conveyed by wasting the aide's time while the children are involved with the teacher in total group activities and the aide sits by, idly watching.

To avoid problems of this type, it is essential that you keep a list of the day and time each aide is expected. You should plan in advance exactly what you want the aide to do, gather needed materials and write directions, if necessary. If this has been taken care of prior to the aide's arrival, you indirectly indicate that you value the time of this volunteer. It also conveys that you are counting on the aide being present. This not only improves the aide's feelings of being appreciated and needed, but as a consequence cuts down on "absenteeism."

To cut down further on potential absenteeism, you should stress before an aide even begins working in the classroom that you will be setting up specific activities which need supervision, or which the children would be unable to do without adult assistance. Explain that if, for any reason the aide cannot come on the scheduled day, it is essential for you to know ahead of time. Otherwise you will end up trying to supervise two activities in different parts of the room, both of which require adult assistance, and everyone will suffer. If you are notified ahead of time, you can substitute an activity which the students can manage on their own.

To stress further the importance of prior notification, give the aide your home phone number and the time you generally leave in the morning. Then, if something comes up at the last moment, the aide can call you early, giving you the time needed to plan an alternate activity.

If an aide does not show up when scheduled, call that evening and briefly mention the problems which occurred, or say, "I may have mentioned to you how hard it is . . ." or "I may have forgotten to give you my phone number . . ."

If aides do not show up and you say nothing, or if they frequently cancel without being told that you are sorry because you had hoped to schedule a certain activity on that day, they may well feel that it doesn't make any difference.

In addition, it is wise to mention periodically how helpful it is to have their assistance, as well as the experiences provided the children that could not have been obtained otherwise. You should also emphasize that you would not have been able to work nearly as closely with the students, had you been trying to cover all of the centers at once.

A few minutes spent each day, explaining a particular activity or aspect of the classroom about which you are excited, is good public relations. It is also an enjoyable experience of sharing with someone who becomes involved in your enthusiasm. This is particularly important for the weekly volunteers. A few minutes of personal conversation bridges the gap and helps the aides feel they belong and are important, which they are! Adults, as well as children, need to have these feelings communicated.

Communicating Observations

The aide needs an established procedure for passing on observations to you. Imagine the frustration of working with a child and noticing something which you feel is important, but not knowing whether or how to communicate this information to the teacher.

The aide needs to know what type of observations are important to you: problems the child had; techniques or materials which worked or were not particularly successful; and the interest or disinterest of students.

The individual record-keeping systems described in the subject chapters include a section titled "comments." The teacher aides should be encouraged to jot down comments which they feel may interest you. This ensures that their observations are in writing and that you will be aware of them.

A few moments spent with aides before they leave can be most profitable. All that needs to be said is, "Thanks again for helping today. Were there any problems or anything I need to know about?" This opens the door for any comments about the children which the aide feels are important. In addition, it gives the aide the opportunity to indicate areas in need of additional instruction. Then try to remember the next time the aide is in the classroom to make a brief comment about having followed up on the observation(s).

Building a Consistent Environment

If aides are to be an integral and effective part of the classroom, it is essential that they know your expectations, the process by which you set up requirements, how you want problems handled, etc. Once teacher aides understand your style, a consistent environment is established. And students know what to expect from day to day. If, each day, different aides set different expectations for students, an unstable environment results.

As the aides become familiar with individual students, they will learn what are realistic expectations, who needs a great deal of help, and who works well independently. However, when an aide first begins helping in the classroom, all of this can seem overwhelming. It is wise to acquaint the aide

gradually with your expectations and the procedures for setting the varying requirements. In addition, be certain to indicate the overall expectations that you have stressed with students.

Second, you will need to assist the aide in knowing what to expect of individual students. Of great assistance in this respect is a folder with samples of each child's very best work, or a list of the students' characteristics in terms of proficiency, level of independence, study habits, etc. Explaining the list and applying it to possible situations will relieve many uncertainties on the aide's part. Lists of this type should be kept at each of the centers. Instructions and procedures for the centers can also be written. This immediately enables the aide to feel comfortable in the classroom and know what is expected. As the aides become familiar with the students and the operation of the centers, they will need the lists less and will rely on their own judgment.

While the aides are becoming acquainted with the classroom, you should be available to handle problems and provide support. Check the center several times. At the end of the center, before the students rotate, ask in a voice just loud enough for the group to hear, "Is there anyone whom you feel hasn't used the time well and needs to stay over at the center and get some work completed?" This immediately indicates to the students that the aide is not just a "glorified baby sitter." You have shown that you respect the aide's opinion. It also builds the aide's authority with the students.

If the aide indicates that Johnny had spent most of his time talking and, as a result, has not completed much work, you should quietly go to Johnny and mark a reasonable amount of work for him to complete at the center while the others rotate to their next center. He then checks not with you but with the aide before he leaves the center, to show the completed work.

This reinforces the environment and procedures that you have set for the students. The aides will be able to set the basic expectancies once they are familiar with the routine. Be sure to explain to the students that, when a teacher aide is at a center, it is just the same as if you were there. If an aide feels a student is not using the time well, the child may have to stay over at the center just as if you were there. Then be certain to back the aide's decision when one is made.

The aide's authority must be built, or the situation will be uncomfortable. This in turn will affect the smooth operation of the classroom.

Students will often test aides, just as at the beginning of the year they test the teacher. Often they are really asking to have the limits defined, and trying to discover if the same rules apply, even though a different person is involved. Once they discover that the rules remain the same and the environment consistent, the testing disappears.

There are always one or two "supreme testers." Aides generally are tempted to react to these students in one of two ways: capitulate and back down, or get into a verbal debate with them. Neither method produces a satisfactory solution.

Your professional expertise needs to be shared with the aide. If the expectation is reasonable, the aide should be instructed to restate this expectation and then leave the student. There is no way that a student can be forced to pick up a pencil and get to work. Therefore, arguing with the child accomplishes nothing other than elevating blood-pressure levels! The student needs to be told

the expectations, the consequences, and then must make a decision.

A common example of the "supreme tester" is the student who is told what is expected at the center and promptly says, "I'm not going to do it!" The aide will naturally be shaken by this and usually will relate the incident to the teacher. The teacher must then speak to the student and reiterate the requirement. The consequences should also be explained, (such as staying in at recess, lunch or after school, until the work is completed). If it becomes necessary to enforce the consequence(s), it is unfortunate. However, when situations are handled in this way, the student rarely repeats the episode. Fortunately, "show-downs" of this type are few. But in these cases the students desperately need to know your limits. Once this is made clear, they are almost always willing to conform.

Students who have special problems should be mentioned to your aide at the beginning. The most effective manner of handling these students should also be explained.

If you are following the suggestions in Chapter IV you should discuss these with your aide. You also might ask the aide to read that section of the book to help create a consistent and supportive environment.

Techniques for Communicating Directions to Teacher Aides

As previously mentioned, one reason teacher aides stop working in the classroom is because they have been given insufficient information and directions. Therefore, they feel insecure and uncertain. A method needs to be provided for clearly communicating directions so that the aide understands exactly what to do and has the opportunity to ask questions.

In some cases this can be handled in a few minutes during recess, prior to the start of centers. In other cases time will need to be set aside for instructing the aide. At the academic centers the aide will need experience working with the material and training sessions before attempting to teach concepts and processes. This can most effectively be handled after school when neither you nor the aide is rushed.

Other centers which involve short-term activities need only written directions which can be kept from year to year. This saves you considerable preparation time in the future.

The aide can read the directions and become acquainted with the materials during the recess prior to the start of centers, and while the students are all together for their class meeting. When the students go to their first center, you should ask the aide if there are any questions and perhaps briefly demonstrate the use of the materials. This can be done while students get out their materials

---

LICENSE-PLATE GAME
(VISUAL MEMORY)

Needed:
Sets of cards
Small chalkboard for each student and eraser or rag
Chalk

Directions:
There are three sets of cards inside the envelope: 3 digits (yellow), 4 digits (blue), and 5 digits (green). Distribute a pile of 3-digit cards to each student. Tell the students: "There has just been a robbery and you see the get-away car driving off. Pretend the card in front of you is the license plate of the get-away car. You are to see if you can remember the license plate and write it down."

The cards should be placed face down on the table. When you say "up," each student is to turn up the top card and try to memorize it. When you say "down," the child must place it face down again. Then the student writes the number and checks to see if it is correct.

Adjust the length of time they look at the numbers, longer if they are having trouble, shorter if it is easy for them.

As you see some students doing this easily, give them a set of 4-digit cards and remove their 3-digit cards; later, 5-digit cards.

(You may simultaneously have some students using three-digit cards, other four-digit, and still others with five or six digits.)

Direction Sheet For Aides

and settle down to work.

If you ask your aides to arrive just prior to centers, they have the opportunity to become familiar with the materials and directions for that day. They also are able to hear your specific instructions to the students about the center they will supervise. This further helps with their understanding of the activity.

If you decide to use written directions for short-term activities, they can be placed on pieces of 9″×12″ construction paper. These direction sheets can be kept in a folder which is labeled "Teacher Aide Directions— Please return direction sheets to the folder when you are finished with them."

The sheet should indicate the needed materials, purpose of the activity, and step-by-step directions. In some cases a sample of the finished product should be included.

Envelopes constructed from pieces of 12″×18″ tagboard can also be used. Fold a piece of the tagboard in half, and staple along both sides to form a pocket. Place the appropriate materials inside, and write directions on the outside. These envelopes are then stored, upright, in a box or vegetable bin.

The following check-list may help you determine whether you have covered verbally or in writing the essential instructions with an aide.

1. Location of materials
2. Purpose of the activity
3. Directions on how the materials should be presented; (demonstrate) or, if it is an on-going center, the basic procedures
4. Directions that are to be followed to the letter and those in which the aide can use personal initiative
5. Questions the aide might ask the students to further their understanding (particularly important in science and manipulative-math experiences)
6. What to watch for
7. Record-keeping procedures and communicating observations
8. Grouping of children (ability-grouped, sociometrically grouped . . .)
9. Special characteristics of individual children
10. Tricks and ways of helping children with problems
11. Setting basic expectancies and completion of minimum requirements
12. Procedures for children who remain at the center
13. Storage and clean-up (placement of papers, folders, materials)
14. The importance of keeping privileged information confidential

The following check-list should be used for providing additional information for specific centers.

WRITING (PRINTING/CURSIVE) MECHANICS

---

1. Proper formation of letters—(Is a reference available?)
2. Is the sequence of strokes important to you?
3. Children with good small-muscle control, and those with poor small-muscle control . . .
4. Ways of helping children with problems. Any tricks?
5. Proper way to hold pencil and what to do about children who hold their pencil a different way . . .

MATH

1. Children who generally find math easy, and those who may need special help . . .
2. Ways of helping children with problems . . .
3. Reversals (ς instead of 5) Should the aide ignore the reversal or correct the child? If so, how . . .
4. Is it all right for a child to count on his or her fingers?

CREATIVE WRITING

1. How to help the child who is stuck . . .
2. Ways to get children started on a story . . .
3. What to do about the child who enumerates the objects in a picture rather than writing a story about it . . .
4. How to handle: proofreading
   capitalization and punctuation
   misspelled words
5. What to do if a child wants to know how to spell a word . . .
6. Children who generally find creative writing easy, and those who may need special help . . .

READING

1. How to handle: the child who doesn't know a word
   the child who can't answer comprehension question
   the child who interrupts

other children
2. Children who may need special help and encouragement . . .

ART

1. Mixing paint . . .
2. Paste (procedure)
3. Clean-up procedure
4. What to do if the child doesn't know how to draw a _____
5. Purpose: creativity, or to duplicate the sample as nearly as possible . . .
6. Is it all right for the child to copy?
7. Coloring pictures: Is it important for the child to stay inside the lines?
8. How much mess is acceptable?

Helping Students Versus Thinking for Them

When a student comes to an aide for help, the aide may often wonder whether the child actually needs help or is trying to take the easy way out. If the aides are to help develop a student's thought-processes and sense of independence, it is essential that the child be encouraged to think independently and to become proficient at reading directions, etc. By asking questions, the aide can discover whether the student actually needs help, or is attempting to avoid independent thinking. If assistance is needed, the aide's questions can help guide the child's thinking.

If a student says, "I don't know what to do on this page," the following set of questions could be asked by the aide:

1. *"Have you read the directions?"* If the student says, "No," the aide should ask the child first to do so, and then to come back

if help is still needed. If the student returns, the aide can say,

2. *"What do you think they want you to do?"* Often the student needs only to have thoughts confirmed by an adult. This question eliminates lengthy (and often unnecessary) explanations if the child just needs reassurance. If the student does not understand the directions, the aide can say,

3. *"Instead of reading the entire set of directions, it is often helpful to read a sentence at a time and figure out the meaning. Read the first sentence. What does that mean?"*

4. *"O.K., now read the next sentence. What does that mean?"* When the student has read the entire set of directions, the aide should ask,

5. *"So what is it they want you to do?"*

By using this method, the aide has forced the student to think, and at the same time has guided and supported the child.

Several sessions like this may help clarify the process for the student. However, if looking for an easy way out was the idea, the child will soon discover it is quicker just to read the directions for oneself!

It is important to train aides to ask questions in a manner which results in *the student discovering the answer.* If the student does the thinking, this will almost always result in a satisfying discovery of the answer. However, if the aide tells the child what to do, step by step, this is the adult doing the thinking, while the student merely plays secretary! Suggest that, when the aide is in doubt, the question to ask oneself is, "Who is doing the thinking?"

Each aspect of preparing aides to work effectively in the classroom takes time. But the time spent more than pays for itself.

When you have competent aides who understand your program and are able to contribute successfully to the classroom, everyone benefits!

Problems With Aides: How To Handle Them

Should problems arise with aides, such as unreliability or incompatibility with you or your classroom, they should not be ignored. It is essential that they be handled in as delicate and diplomatic a manner as possible.

If an aide is unreliable, despite your efforts requesting prior notification of absence, the best solution is not to count on this person. Instead, set aside some tasks that you would like accomplished but which are not essential for that day. This might consist of student corrections which need to be handled on a one-to-one basis, assisting a student in making changes in content or format in a story, checking individual students on reading vocabulary words, etc. If the aide appears, it is a bonus, and these non-crucial tasks are taken care of. If not, the program will run smoothly without the aide.

Occasionally (fortunately, very seldom), an aide does not work out in the classroom. It could be a case of an overly protective parent who interferes with your instructions to the child. Or the aide continually contradicts what you have said. Perhaps the aide responds negatively toward students, making derogatory remarks about the quality of their work, effort put forth, and/or intelligence.

Obviously, these situations cannot be allowed to continue. Unfortunately, there is no "easy way out." The first step is to try assigning the aide to work with individual students. Sometimes if the pressure of supervising an entire center is removed, the aide relaxes and works successfully with students on a one-to-one basis. (In the case of the overly concerned parent, direct contact with the child is removed.) If the aide has been working at an academic center, another possible solution is a new assignment, to art, cooking or reinforcement games. Also make constructive suggestions to the aide and discuss ways you would like situations handled.

If none of these positive actions result in improvement, discuss the problem with your principal, and elicit suggestions. Talk with the parent and, as diplomatically as possible, present the problem as you perceive it. Explain that sometimes, despite the best intentions on both your parts, aiding in the classroom may not be feasible. Tell the aide you appreciate the effort made. Then, mention that you would be delighted to have the person volunteer in a different capacity, such as correcting student work, making materials for the classroom, duplicating and/or collating materials, etc. Indicate that assistance in these areas is valuable. It allows you to spend more time developing programs and materials which benefit the children. In this way the aide can continue indirectly to help in the classroom.

I have not as yet experienced this problem in my own classroom, but I have gone through it with other teachers. It is not a pleasant experience. But it must be dealt with for the sake of the students and the smooth operation of the classroom.

One unique way to avoid potential problems of this nature was devised by Bob Vasser (1). He asks parents for help on a special project for a four-week period. If, during this time, the volunteers become a real asset to the classroom, he tells them he finds their help invaluable. He urges them to continue aiding throughout the year. Almost all of the parents are so delighted with his obvious endorsement of their work, they continue helping in the classroom. If, in rare instances, a parent has not worked out successfully at the end of the four-week project, he thanks the person for the time and effort. That concludes the classroom stint, with no feelings hurt.

Notes

1. Bob Vasser, Teacher, San Rafael School District, San Rafael, California.

CHAPTER VIII

Individualized Spelling

Introduction

The program described in this chapter should enable you to (1) diagnose the skills a child possesses, as well as those skills needing further development, (2) provide for those deficits.

The program does not send the child off to the corner to work alone. Instead, it provides opportunities for the child to interact with peers. The routine weekly assignment, "Write your words five times each" is replaced with a variety of interesting ways to practice spelling words. Of great importance is the fact that, while the children are increasing their spelling skills, they are encouraged to make choices. In addition, they develop responsibility and a sense of independence. This program was adopted and expanded from a system for individualized spelling developed by Dr. Mary E. Collins (1) which combined individual spelling books and high-frequency-word lists.

The program described in this chapter is adaptable. It can be used in a traditional environment, allowing the teacher to experiment with individualization in one area of the curriculum while the remainder stays unchanged. It works equally well for children on contracts, or in a learning-centers environment.

At the outset the teacher needs to spend time making the necessary materials and organizing the program. But, once this initial work is completed, the program is self-sustaining for the remainder of the year with almost no additional time required. As a result, you will find that implementing the individualized spelling program is one of the easiest ways to start individualizing in the classroom.

The spelling program begins with a non-threatening diagnostic test to determine which skills each child has mastered against the skills in which further work is needed. On the basis of this information, the teacher prepares a booklet of words appropriate for the skills in which each child needs additional practice. Naturally, the booklets are different. They vary in length according to the skills to be practiced. (See word lists on pages 80-87.) One child's booklet may have short vowel words. Another child concentrates on spelling demons. Still another child is working on digraphs and blends.

On a specified day each week, each child selects words, from his or her booklet, to study for that week.

A test on the words selected is administered weekly. Any word missed is automatically carried over to the next week's list, so that the student has additional days to work on it. If the word is missed again, it is carried over once more to the following week's list. The focus is on the importance of learning to spell the word correctly. Sometimes this can be done in one week. Other times it takes several weeks.

As spelling skills increase, the word list in the child's individual booklet is changed so that new and different skills present their challenges. Thus, the words in each child's booklet always reflect skills which currently need practice. Review of previous words is also built into the program. In addition, words which the student misspells during Creative Writing are incorporated as part of the weekly individualized spelling list. (See pages 203-204.)

Diagnosis, Placement, and Word Lists

It is extremely important that the informal diagnostic test is administered in a non-pressured atmosphere. Each child should leave the testing situation with a feeling of having done well.

Tell the children that you are going to give them a few words to write so that you can find out which words they already know how to spell and with which words they need help. Do not use the word "test," since it carries negative connotations for many children. Also, be certain to stress that you are interested in finding out how you can help them become better spellers.

On pages 75-77 you will find a list of words to be used for the diagnostic spelling test. The list consists of short-vowel words; long-vowel words, blends and digraphs; three-letter and four-letter, and more difficult sight words; frequently misspelled words; and spelling demons.

Test a small group of seven or eight children around a table. (The remainder of the class should be occupied with a different activity.) Walk behind the children in the group, giving each child a different word to spell. Begin with the short-vowel list. Eventually each child should spell one word from the short "a" column, one word from the short "i" column, one word from the short "u" column, etc.

If you begin by giving all the children words from the same list, invariably one child will recognize what you are doing. This student will cue the others with, "Oh, I know what you're doing. You're giving us short "a" words to spell." You can avoid this by rotating the lists among the students (short "a" word to the first child, short "u" to the second child, short "o" word to the third child, etc.).

The rotation of the words will allow you to ascertain quickly those children who can spell short-vowel words, enabling you to move into more difficult words with them.

After the children have spelled one word from each of the short-vowel lists, use the same procedure for words from the long-vowel lists. If a child has difficulty with both the first and second long-vowel words, from then on give short-vowel words that can be spelled easily. Once you determine where the child is having difficulty, you have the information you need in terms of that list of words you will want to put in the child's Individualized Spelling Book to study. There is no need to frustrate the child by giving harder and harder words in the test.

Diagnostic Spelling Test

(To determine which word list is appropriate for each child, see pages 78-80.)

SHORT-VOWEL WORDS (LIST I)

man	*fed*	*fit*	*hot*	*nut*
sad	*wet*	*his*	*not*	*bug*
ran	*bed*	*big*	*lot*	*fun*
cap	*get*	*hit*	*dog*	*cup*
mad	*ten*	*did*	*box*	*rug*
fan	*bet*	*sit*	*not*	*gun*
lap	*men*	*hid*	*job*	*hug*
gas	*met*	*lip*	*mop*	*rub*

LONG-VOWEL WORDS (LIST II)

came	*hide*	*bone*	*paid*	*team*	*load*
bake	*kite*	*note*	*say*	*beat*	*boat*
same	*side*	*home*	*wait*	*seem*	*soap*
gave	*bite*	*hole*	*way*	*need*	*toad*
cake	*five*	*cone*	*nail*	*read*	*coat*
late	*ride*	*hope*	*rain*	*seat*	*road*
game	*dive*	*nose*	*tail*	*real*	*goat*
made	*mine*	*pole*	*pain*	*heat*	*loaf*

BLENDS (LIST II)

best	ask	ship
hunt	bent	chop
gift	skip	then
lift	plan	shop
held	kept	chin
just	glad	that
rest	drop	chip
flip	mask	shut

DIGRAPHS (LIST II)

with
much
wish
bath
such
dish
rich
rush

2-3 LETTER SIGHT WORDS
(LIST III)

are	our	sure
the	few	they
you	any	from
saw	put	here
for	of	have
was	who	give
do	one	some
all	new	want

4 LETTER SIGHT WORDS
(LIST III)

been
long
many
very
what
your
year
were

MORE DIFFICULT SIGHT WORDS
(LIST III)

because	please	large
around	another	thought
where	every	mother
pretty	great	through
brother	guess	friend
would	summer	heard
should	teacher	morning
school	people	country

WORDS MOST OFTEN MISSPELLED
BY CHILDREN IN THE ELEMENTARY GRADES
(LIST IV)

animals	received	February
happened	you're	different
threw	money	clothes
babies	course	believe
interesting	beautiful	decided
dropped	frightened	they're
woman	surprise	cousin
children	caught	bought

SPELLING DEMONS
(LIST V)

studying	ache	height
whether	answer	separate
trouble	among	cough
loose	women	Tuesday
lose	passed	forty
meant	sugar	fourth
truly	Wednesday	straight
built	minute	hoarse

200 IMPORTANT SPELLING WORDS
FOR UPPER GRADE STUDENTS
(LIST VI)

young	service	information
possible	enough	American
world	group	receipt
enclosed	president	social
though	advise	company
government	system	toward
attention	account	amount
business	office	general

In order to create a success-oriented atmosphere while diagnosing the children's abilities, it is essential to revert back to easier words as soon as you discover an area where a child is unsure. As a result, as the test continues, one child will remain on short-vowel words, whereas another may be on long-vowel words. Still another child is continuing on to more difficult words.

This is all done as subtly as possible. The children should be unaware of the fact that you are adjusting the difficulty of the words to match what you have found out about each child. As the children leave the test, you want each child to feel successful in having spelled almost every word you asked.

The key to administering the diagnostic test is observation. Each time you give a child a new word, you should glance at his or her paper to discover whether the spelling is still successful or beginning to encounter problems. Later, when you carefully examine the test papers, it will be apparent where each child experienced difficulty. Therefore, it is not necessary to keep a written record as you give the test. However, if you make an observation which it is crucial to remember, you may want to write it on the child's paper afterwards, when you are alone.

When you have finished working with the first group of eight children, compliment them on their good work and proceed with your next group. It takes approximately 15 minutes to test each group.

HOW TO ANALYZE THE DIAGNOSTIC SPELLING TEST

Unsure of all short vowels. Place in List I and have student take only short "a" words. (See page 108.)

Needs to review short vowels and work on long vowels. Place in List II.

Unsure of short vowels. Place in List I.

```
John        hunt
not         left
lap         chinn  chin
cup         that
hit         wuz  was
bet         do
hide        frum  from
same        hoo  who
home
```

Has almost mastered short and long vowels, blends, and digraphs. List III will review these concepts and begin providing practice on sight words.

When you have finished testing all the students, you are ready to determine which list of words is appropriate for each student.

List I.   Short vowel words (page 80)

List II.   Short vowel, long vowel, blends, digraphs (page 81)

List III.   A Basic Spelling Vocabulary (high-frequency-word list) (pages 81–83)

List IV.   One Hundred Words Most Often Misspelled by Children in the Elementary Grades (page 83)

List V.   127 Spelling Demons (page 84)

List VI.   200 Important Spelling Words for Upper-Grade Students (selected more difficult high-frequency words) (pages 84-85)

List VII.   Words to be used for practice on specific phonetic elements, (ar, er-ir-ur, or, oi-oy, ou-ow, silent letters, etc.) (pages 86-87)

The words on List I and List II provide practice on beginning phonetic principles and the concept of "sounding out" words. List I should be used for children who had difficulty spelling short-vowel words during the diagnostic test; whereas List II should be used for children who need to work on spelling long-vowel words, blends, and/or digraphs.

List Three, "A Basic Spelling Vocabulary," should be used with children who have essentially mastered the spelling of phonetic words but who need work on basic sight words. I developed this spelling vocabulary by cross-indexing three widely used high frequency word lists: Madden-Carlson (2), Rinsland (3), and Dolch (4). Words which were found on at least two of the three high-frequency lists were compiled to form "A Basic Spelling Vocabulary."

List IV, "One Hundred Words Most Often Misspelled by Children in the Elementary Grades," can be used successfully with students who have mastered the "Basic Vocabulary." Johnson (5) compiled this list by analyzing the creative writings of 14,643 students from throughout the United States (grades three to eight). After the original diagnostic test, students who are placed in List IV should be given an additional test at a later date on all of the words on the previous list ("Basic Vocabulary") to make certain that they can spell each of these words. Any words missed should be added to their individualized spelling book. The test can be administered by grouping these students while the remainder of the class has a different assignment.

List V, "125 Spelling Demons," is a good review list for almost all students. Despite the fact that 100 of these demons were selected by Jones (6) many years ago, they continue to be "demons" today! Twenty-five words have been added to Jones' original list. Many of the added words "complete a confusing pair." For instance, Jones lists hoarse, whole, there/their, choose. Words frequently confused with each of these (horse, hole, they're, and chose) as well as other frequently misspelled words complete the list.

List VI, "200 Important Spelling Words For Upper Grade Students," was developed by using the findings from two monumental studies: the Kucera-Francis (7) ranking of words most frequently used in newspapers, magazines, and books; and Horn's (8) study of words most commonly written by adults. The 236 words of highest frequency from each of these lists were cross-indexed. I omitted the easier words from this compilation (all, am, an, etc.). The remaining words comprise List VI, "200 Important Spelling Words For Upper-Grade Students."

For the more capable spelling students who pass the diagnostic tests for each of the previous lists, see pages 108-109.

List VII, "Words to be Used to Work on Specific Phonetic Elements," is explained in detail on page 88.

Individualized Spelling Lists

LIST I
SHORT VOWEL WORDS

am	box	had	led	on	run
an	bug	ham	leg	pad	sad
and	bun	hat	let	pan	sat
as	did	hen	lid	pat	set
at	dig	hid	lit	pen	sit
ax	dip	him	lip	pet	sip
bad	dog	his	log	pig	six
bag	fan	hit	lot	pin	sun
bat	fat	hot	mad	pop	tag
bed	fed	hum	man	pot	tan
bus	fit	hug	map	pup	tap
but	fix	if	men	rag	ten
cab	fog	in	met	ragbag	tip
cap	for	into	mix	ran	top
can	fox	is	mom	rat	tub
cannot	fun	it	mop	red	tug
cup	gas	job	mud	rid	
cut	get	jam	nap	rip	
dad	got	jet	net	rob	
beg	gum	kit	not	rub	
bet	gun	lap	nut	rag	

80

LIST II
SHORT VOWELS AND LONG VOWELS
BLENDS AND DIGRAPHS

and	go	made	rain	tell
as	get	may	road	ten
ask	got	make	ride	that
ate	game	me	say	them
best	gift	much	see	this
big	glad	must	sing	then
boat	had	mine	sit	time
bath	has	much	six	thing
bite	help	no	so	those
bake	him	not	stop	up
cut	hot	name	she	use
coat	his	need	seen	we
came	hole	note	seem	wish
did	hand	no	stay	with
day	hunt	play	swim	well
drive	held	pick	stove	went
drop	if	plan	sent	will
drove	into	red	stone	wait
each	jump	ran	save	way
eat	just	ride	smoke	when
fast	keep	run	same	
five	kept	reach	shape	
feel	let	read	smile	
fine	late	real	take	

LIST III
A BASIC SPELLING VOCABULARY

*a	*am	asked	been	boys
about	*an	*at	before	bring
after	*and	away	best	brother
again	another		better	*but
all	any	back	*big	by
along	are	*be	black	
also	around	because	book	called
always	*as	*bed	boy	*came

81

*can	give	little	over	there
car	*go	live		these
children	going	long	people	they
Christmas	good	look	place	thing
cold	*got	looked	play	things
come	great		please	think
coming		*made	pretty	*this
could	*had	*make	put	thought
country	happy	*man		three
	*has	many	*ran	through
day	have	may	read	*time
days	*he	*me	*red	to
dear	heard	*men	right	today
*did	help	more	room	told
didn't	her	morning	*run	too
do	here	*most		took
*dog	*him	mother	said	town
don't	*his	*much	saw	tree
door	*home	*must	say	two
down	*hope	my	school	until
	house		*see	*up
*each	how	*name	*she	*us
*eat		never	should	used
every	*I	new	small	
	*if	next	snow	very
father	*in	nice	*so	
few	*into	night	some	want
find	*is	*no	something	wanted
first	*it	*not	soon	was
*five	*its	now	started	water
for			summer	way
found	*just	of	sure	*we
four		off		*week
friend	*keep	old	*take	*well
from	kind	*on	teacher	*went
*fun	know	once	*tell	were
		one	*than	what
*gave	large	only	*that	when
*get	*last	or	the	where
getting	*let	other	their	which
girl	letter	our	*them	while
girls	*like	out	*then	white

82

who	*with	write	years	
*will	work		you	
*wish	would	year	your	

*Easier phonetic spelling words (See pages 88-89.)

LIST IV
ONE HUNDRED WORDS MOST OFTEN MIS-SPELLED BY CHILDREN IN ELEMENTARY GRADES (9)

again	didn't	jumped	running	tried
all right	different			two
always	dropped	knew	said	
an		know	school	until
and	every		some	
animals		let's	something	very
another	February	like	sometimes	
around	first	little	started	wanted
asked	for	looked	stopped	went
	friend		surprise	were
babies	friends	many	swimming	when
beautiful	frightened	money		where
because	from	morning	than	with
before		mother	that's	woman
believe	getting		their	would
bought	going	name	then	
		named	there	you're
came	happened		they	
caught	hear	off	they're	
children	heard	once	things	
clothes	here	our	thought	
coming	him		threw	
course		people	through	
cousin	interesting	pretty	to	
	it's		together	
decided	its	received	too	

83

LIST V
127 SPELLING DEMONS

ache	country	hoarse	once	tear	very
again		hole		than	
all right	dear	horse	passed	their	wear
always	doctor	hour	past	then	Wednesday
among	does		piece	there	week
answer	done	instead		they	where
any	don't	its	quiet	they're	whether
		it's	quite	though	which
been	early			through	whole
before	easy	just	raise	tired	whose
beginning	enough		read	to	women
believe	every	knew	ready	tonight	won't
blue		know	really	too	would
break	February		receive	tries	write
built	forty	laid		trouble	written
business	fourth	loose	said	truly	writing
busy	friend	lose	says	Tuesday	wrote
buy			seems	two	
	grammar	making	separate		you're
can't	guess	many	shoes	used	your
carrying		meant	since	using	
choose	half	minute	some		
chose	having	much	straight		
color	hear		studying		
coming	heard	none	sugar		
cough	height		sure		
could	here	often			

LIST VI
200 IMPORTANT SPELLING WORDS FOR UPPER GRADE STUDENTS

about	against	American	asked	been
account	ago	amount	attention	before
advise	almost	another	away	being
after	also	any		believe
again	always	around	because	best

better	government	night	service	very
between	great	note	shall	
business	group	nothing	shipment	want
		number	should	war
called	have		since	was
cannot	having	of	sir	water
check	head	office	small	way
city	hear	once	social	week
company	here	one	some	went
copy	herewith	only	something	were
could	high	or	soon	what
course	himself	order	state	when
credit	house	other	still	where
	however	our	sure	which
		over	system	while
days		own		who
dear	information			why
didn't	interest	part	thank	without
does		people	their	work
don't	kind	place	there	world
during	kindly	please	these	would
	knew	point	they	write
enclosed	know	possible	think	
enough		present	those	year
even	later	president	though	years
ever	letter	price	thought	young
every	little	program	three	your
eyes	long	public	through	yours
	love	put	to	
fact			today	
feel	many	receipt	told	
few	matter	receive	too	
find	might	received	toward	
first	more	return	try	
found	morning	right	two	
from	most	room		
	mother			
general	Mr.	said	under	
give	Mrs.	school	United States	
given		send	until	
glad	never	sending	upon	
going	new	sent	use	
good	next		used	

WORDS TO BE USED TO WORK ON SPECIFIC PHONETIC ELEMENTS: R-CONTROLLED VOWELS, VOWEL DIGRAPHS, SILENT LETTERS, 'TION, HARD AND SOFT "C" AND "G."

er, ir, ur	bark	fort	fare	coil	boundary
bird	barn	horn	hair	coin	bow
birthday	car	north	hare	enjoy	brown
burn	card	shore	pair	hoist	cloud
chirp	cart	short	pare	join	clown
church	chart	sore	share	joy	couch
curl	dark	sort	square	loyal	count
curve	far	sport	stair	moist	crouch
dirt	farm	storm	stare	noise	crowd
fern	farmer	tore		point	crown
fir	farther	torn	**au, aw**	poison	drown
firm	hard	wore	August	soil	flower
first	harm		automobile	spoil	found
fur	harp	**eer, ear**	automatic	voice	fountain
germ	jar	appear	awful		ground
girl	march	beard	because	**ow, ō**	growl
hammer	mark	cheer	claw	blow	hound
hunter	market	clear	crawl	bow	howl
hurt	park	dear	draw	bowl	loud
perfect	part	deer	drawn	crow	mountain
perhaps	scarf	ear	fault	fellow	mouth
person	sharp	fear	haul	grow	our
purple	smart	hear	hawk	low	plow
serve	star	near	jaw	mow	pound
shirt	start	queer	law	row	powder
sir	war	tear	lawn	shadow	proud
skirt	warm	year	paw	show	round
stir	warn		shawl	slow	scout
third	yard	**air, are**	straw	snow	scowl
thirsty	yarn	air	yawn	throw	shout
turn		care		window	shower
ar	**or, ore**	chair	**oi, oy**	yellow	sound
apart	before	dairy	annoy		south
arm	born	dare	boil	**ou, ow**	towel
art	corn	fair	broil	blouse	tower
bar	fork	fairy	choice	bounce	town

oo, ew	ŏŏ	knew	tion	decide	twice
blew	book	knife	action	difference	vegetable
bloom	foot	knock	attention	distance	village
boom	look	know	correction	face	voyage
boot	shook	known	direction	fancy	wage
broom	stood	calf	education	general	
chew	took	chalk	nation	gentle	'c, g'
cool	wood	half	station	giant	(mixed)
crew	wool	salmon	transportation	ginger	baggage
drew		stalk	vacation	huge	bicycle
flew		talk		ice	carriage
food	silent letters	walk	'c, g'	juice	cigar
grew	bought	yolk	(soft)	lace	circus
igloo	bright	whole	ace	large	college
loop	brought	whose	advice	magic	garage
moon	caught	wrap	age	mice	
new	daughter	wren	announce	nice	
noon	eight	write	balance	orange	
room	fight	written	bounce	ounce	
rooster	fought	wrote	cage	package	
scoop	frighten	climb	ceiling	palace	
shoot	height	comb	celery	pencil	
smooth	high	crumb	cent	place	
soon	light	lamb	center	police	
spool	might	limb	certain	price	
spoon	neighbor	thumb	chance	race	
stew	night	castle	change	rice	
stool	right	fasten	citizen	sentence	
threw	straight	listen	city	since	
tool	taught	often	dance	slice	
tooth	tight	soften	danger	space	
zoo	weigh	whistle	December	strange	

LIST VII

List VII, pages 86-87, is intended to be used in a different way than the previous lists. It provides a means of practice on various phonetic elements which the child has not mastered. After the student has learned to sound out basic phonetic words and has learned many of the basic high-frequency words, it is useful once again to administer an informal diagnostic test. In this evaluation, check seven or eight children at a time for the phonetic elements found on List VII ("r" affected vowels, oi-oy, ou-ow, silent letters, etc.).

As soon as you have found one phonetic element on which the child needs additional practice, you can insert in the student's Individualized Spelling Book the "special" list of words which provides practice on that concept. (The lists should be typed so there is only one concept on any given page: the "er, ir, ur" words on one page; the "ar" words on a separate page, etc.)

Tell the child to take three or four words from the personal "special" list each week, and to include them on the list of words to be written in his or her blue book (My Spelling Words, see page 89). The student should continue taking three or four words from the "special list" each week until all of them have been studied, or as many as you deem necessary. This insures that the child will study words utilizing that concept for a period of several weeks. When the student has mastered that particular concept, you may again insert in the child's Individualized Spelling Book a list of new words on a different phonetic concept.

This allows the child to concentrate on learning one phonetic principle at a time. Meanwhile, the student continues learning high-frequency words from the Individualized Spelling List.

Materials

Once you have administered the Diagnostic Test, you will be able to determine which of the word lists need to be reproduced for your students. You may purchase the supplement to this book, which contains the seven word lists in a reproducible, black, large print format. Or you may type the needed word lists on ditto masters, using a primary typewriter. If you decide to type the word lists, use the supplement format, as shown on pages 90 and 91. Page 90 is the first page of the short-vowel list as it would appear in the child's Individualized Spelling Book. Use this same basic format as you type each list of words. (The only exception is List VII, see preceding column.) Alongside each word are two small squares. When a child selects a word to place on the weekly spelling list, he or she writes the date in the square next to the word: ☐ ☐ . If, at a later time, you feel it would be advantageous for the student to study the words a second time (see pages 104-105), the second square is dated, when the word is selected.

Page 91 is the first page of the Basic Vocabulary List as it should appear in the child's Individualized Spelling Book. The dot in the square by some of the words (e.g., ▣☐ bug) indicates that it is an easy word. (See asterisks on the Basic Vocabulary List, pages 81-83.) These easier words may be handled in one of two ways: 1) If the Diagnostic Spelling test indicates the child has already mastered these easier words, the student is told not to take any of the words marked with a dot. This assures that the student studies only the more difficult words on the list. 2) If the student needs a brief review of the easier words, he or she is told to practice these words only one time. When studying words a second time, the student skips any of those marked with a dot.

Before duplicating ditto masters, look at the original diagnostic-test results. Tally the number of children who need each list. Be certain to make extra copies of each list to accommodate children who move to your classroom during the year, or for children who master the skills on the preceding list and are ready to begin practicing a new skill.

Example:
List II
4 sets . . . for children who placed at this level on the diagnostic test
2 sets . . . for children who may move to this classroom during the year
5 sets . . . for children who are starting in List I, but will probably move into List II before the end of the year
Total needed: 11 sets of List II

Determining number of lists to duplicate

By planning ahead, you will be spared much work at a later date. Also, if the materials are available, you are able to move children into new skill areas as soon as they are ready. (There is a big difference between having the materials ready for the child, versus having to ditto one new set of materials for the child who is ready to change skill levels!)

In addition, you will need to duplicate three copies of "Words I Want To Learn" for each child. (See page 92.)

Now you are ready to assemble an Individualized Spelling Book for every child. Covers should be sturdy, such as tagboard or washable wallpaper. If you are interested in having the children make their own covers, using fabric and cardboard from boxes, see Appendix II for directions. Covers made this way are especially nice since they are both sturdy and personalized.

Put, inside the covers of each child's Individualized Spelling Book, the word list most appropriate, based on your evaluation of the informal diagnostic test. (See pages 74-80.) Insert three copies of "Words I Want To Learn" in the back of each child's book.

Each child will also need two smaller stapled booklets. "My Spelling Tests" is used by the child each week at spelling-test time. "My Spelling Words" is used at the beginning of each week to write the list of words which the student selects to study for that week. Different color covers help differentiate between the test and practice booklets.

STUDENT BOOKLETS

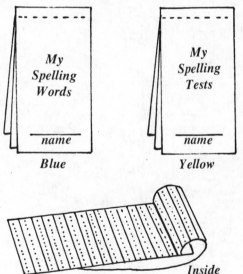

My Spelling Words

name

Blue

My Spelling Tests

name

Yellow

Inside

INDIVIDUALIZED SPELLING WORDS

☐	a	
☐	an	
☐	and	
☐	as	
☐	at	
☐	ax	
☐	bad	
☐	bag	
☐	bat	
☐	bed	
☐	beg	
☐	bet	
☐	box	
☐	bug	
☐	bun	
☐	bus	
☐	but	

☐	cab
☐	can
☐	cannot
☐	cap
☐	cup
☐	cut
☐	did
☐	dig
☐	dip
☐	dog
☐	fan
☐	fat
☐	fed
☐	fix
☐	fog
☐	for
☐	fox

INDIVIDUALIZED SPELLING WORDS

[•] a	[•] at
[ ] about	[ ] away
[ ] after	[ ] back
[ ] again	[•] be
[ ] all	[ ] because
[ ] along	[•] bed
[ ] also	[ ] been
[ ] always	[ ] before
[•] am	[ ] best
[•] an	[ ] better
[•] and	[•] big
[ ] another	[ ] black
[ ] any	[ ] book
[ ] are	[ ] boy
[ ] around	[ ] boys
[• •] as	[ ] bring
[ ] asked	[ ] brother

91

WORDS I WANT TO LEARN

_____	_____	_____
_____	_____	_____
_____	_____	_____
_____	_____	_____
_____	_____	_____
_____	_____	_____
_____	_____	_____
_____	_____	_____
_____	_____	_____
_____	_____	_____
_____	_____	_____
_____	_____	_____
_____	_____	_____
_____	_____	_____
_____	_____	_____

Use colored construction paper, approximately 4½"×12", for the front and back covers of these booklets. Inside of each booklet, place one sheet of lined handwriting paper (approximately 4½"×12") for each week in the school year. The type of lined paper which you use inside the stapled booklets will vary according to the ages (and small-muscle control) of the children. In general, for primary children, use larger lined paper, and for upper-grade children, smaller lined paper

---

Individualized Spelling

These are the words I want to work on this week.

Name_____
Date_____
_____
_____
_____
_____
_____
_____
_____
_____
_____

Students' "Take Home" List
(Approximately 4½"×11")

Each week, the child selects words to study from the Individualized Spelling Book, and makes two lists. One list is written on a copy of the ditto shown above. (You will need a large supply of these.) The student takes this list home to study the words. But first, the student makes a duplicate list in the blue stapled booklet. (See page 89.) This booklet *always* stays at school, so that the child's current word list, as well as a list of all the words studied during the year, are always available.

Weekly Plan for Individualized Spelling

The Individualized Spelling Plan may be used in different ways. Most teachers have the children choose ten to twenty words from their Individualized Spelling Books on Monday. (Remember these are words which provide practice in a specific skill area which the child needs to study.) It is best to start children with ten words. As their confidence grows, you can suggest to some who are finding spelling easy that they attempt fifteen words. Later, some may be able to build up to twenty words. The result is a wide spread in the number of words each child takes each week. It is important that you help each child determine the number of words appropriate for the time being, and set expectations accordingly.

If you are testing on Friday, it is well to have the children practice their spelling words on Thursday. (See "Ways to Practice Spelling Words," pages 95-102.)

What happens on Tuesday and Wednesday really depends on what you feel is important. If you want the children to alphabetize the words every week, then you can schedule that on Tuesday or Wednesday. Or if you want the children to write their spelling words in sentences, you would schedule that one day of the week.

Instead of having all students take the test on a specific day, some teachers prefer a box in the room in which the children place their blue book whenever they feel they are ready to take a spelling test. The teacher then has a volunteer aide, or an older student give the child the test. After it is corrected, the student is ready to select new spelling words. This is a less formal method, whereas the "Friday test" provides more structure. You should decide on the method most comfortable for you.

Introducing the Individualized Spelling Program to Your Students

When you have assembled all the necessary materials for each of the children, you are ready to introduce the individualized spelling program to your class. Show them an Individualized Spelling Book, and explain that there is one for each student. Point out that there are words listed on each page inside. Explain the squares beside each of the words and the procedure of dating the square when the word is selected.

Let them know that they will select their words from their own Individualized Spelling Book. Each person's weekly list will be different! Show them the blue stapled booklet, "My Spelling Words." Explain that each child will have one, for writing the words chosen from the Individualized Spelling Book. Stress that no more than two words should be selected from any one column. (Otherwise the child's list ends up with all very similar words: a, an, and, any, etc.) As the student selects words, each in turn is copied on the first page of the blue book. The child should choose a total of ten words.

Point out that there are some easy words in the Individualized Spelling Book and some harder words. The children should try to balance their lists so that approximately half of their words can be easily learned. The other half of the words they select should be ones that they will really have to study. Explain that if they take all the easy words first, then they will be stuck with nothing but hard words later. By the same token, if they take all the hard words first, they will have to work hard at first, then later be bored because only easy words remain. You will be surprised at how efficient children can become at balancing their lists, and verbalizing exactly what they are doing. This is one more step towards independence and responsibility.

Each child may also select two "special" words which do not appear in the Individual Spelling Book. The student may want to choose names of pets, members of the family, dinosaur names, or words which give particular problems in writing stories, reports, etc. The child should list the two words selected on the page in the back of the book entitled, "Words I Want To Learn." (See page 92.) The two words should then be written in the blue booklet, "My Spelling Words."

It is important that you emphasize that the list in the blue book is to stay at school. Consequently, they need to copy the list of words from their blue book onto the sheet entitled "Individualized Spelling . . . Words I Want to Study This Week." (See page 93.) This ditto sheet they may take home.

When they have made their two copies of the list of spelling words they are going to study for the week, they should bring the two lists to you (or to an aide), so that you can be certain that they have spelled the words correctly and not transposed any letters. Put your initials on the sheet they take home, and write the date on the list in the blue book. This will make it easier for you on test day. You will be able to see at a glance that you actually have the current week's list of words.

Be certain to indicate what you want the children to do after they have completed the assignment of making the two lists and having them checked. Otherwise you may have seven or eight children who have finished their spelling assignment and are bothering others (directly or indirectly). You could have them study their words. Or perhaps you may want to prepare an alternate activity for them. But it is important for them to know from the first whether they are to stay at the spelling center, and if so, what they are supposed to do. Or, if they do not have to stay at the center, what other acceptable alternatives are available. By giving these directions to all students at the beginning of the day, you will save yourself much repetition during centers time.

Later in the week, you can introduce the procedure of practicing their words and taking the spelling test.

Ways to Practice Spelling Words

It is a good idea to have a variety of ways available for children to practice their spelling words. Encourage the children to find out how they best learn to spell words. Some children find it easier to learn the words by feeling the letters. Others learn words better if they can see the letters. Still others need to hear the letters of the words spoken. Many children learn best if they use a combination of approaches: tactile, aural, and visual.

When you introduce the children to different ways of practicing their spelling words, be sure that the choices you present are ones which will cause little commotion. For instance you might start with just two choices: writing words three times, or crayon trace. (See page 96.) You would not want them to start by writing their words in damp sand!

Explain to the children that, if they handle the first two choices well, the following week, another choice will be added to the ways they can practice their words. Be certain to compliment them at the end of the day about a choice wisely made and a job well done. Remind them that because they did well, they will get to make a choice again the next week.

At this point your primary concern is to lead the children to make choices and to be responsible for their decisions. As their independence and sense of responsibility grow, you can successfully introduce more choices. If too many choices are thrust upon children before they have had time to learn to deal with decisions, the net result will be chaos! So take your time introducing choices. Be certain they understand that continuing to have choices depends on how well they handle themselves.

As you introduce ways to practice spelling words, put the needed materials in a box, and include a sign which gives brief instructions. (See pages 99-100.)

Continue to introduce one or two new ways to practice spelling words each week. After a while you may want to put a chart up in the room, listing the various ways you have shown them, as well as suggestions they have made. (See page 98.)

Each week the number of boxes with ways to practice spelling words increases. At the same time there is growth in the children's sense of independence, since they can read the directions, and the necessary materials are readily available. If a child asks, "Where is the paper to practice my words?" you can respond with, "Where should it be?" The child will remember, "Oh yes, that's right. It's supposed to be over with all the other spelling things."

It is amazing how many different ways there are to practice spelling words. Here are some possibilities:

1. | Crayon Trace | . . . The child writes one of the spelling words with a color crayon. Next, a differently colored crayon is used to trace over the word. The student continues doing this until five different colors have been used. As the child traces the word, the names of the letters are softly said out loud. Later you can make available a "wash" made of thin yellow paint. The child brushes this over the crayon-traced words, resulting in an even more colorful paper.

2. | Decorate or illustrate words | . . . The child illustrates the meaning of the word. For instance, if one of the words was "ring," the student might draw a picture of a telephone and write the word "ring" above it. Or the child could use the configuration of the word to suggest its meaning.

3. | Have friends give each other a spelling test |

4. | Write spelling words three times |

5. | Board Erase | . . . The child writes one of the spelling words on the classroom chalkboard, or on a small chalkboard. Each of the letters is then traced, the student softly saying them aloud. The child continues tracing the word until it disappears!

6. | Magnetic letters | . . . Two children work together. One child spells one of the words of the week, using magnetic letters. The other child then removes one or more of the letters, and the first child must say what is missing, and replace the letters in the correct positions. They continue this way, taking turns.

7. | Snakes of Clay | . . . The child forms coils of clay, and then uses these coils to spell out words.

8. | Graph Paper Cut-Up | . . . Using one-inch squared graph paper, the child writes one letter of a word in each of the squares. The student then cuts the squares apart, mixes them up, and rearranges them in correct sequence. Next the word is reassembled, pasting the letters on a piece of paper in correct order. The child continues practicing each spelling word this way.

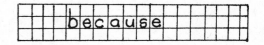

9. | Sand | ... Put sand, which has been dampened with water, in a dishpan. Children practice their words by writing them in the damp sand.

10. | Printing Set | ... Buy an inexpensive rubber stamp set which has each of the letters of the alphabet. (These are usually available in dime stores, variety stores, and toy stores.) The child practices words by using an ink pad, and stamping each spelling word. If the set comes with only thin rubber letters, it is easy to provide a "handle" for the children by glueing each letter to a wooden bead or small piece of wood.

11. | Magic Slate | ... Buy an inexpensive magic slate. (The top sheet is clear plastic and the surface underneath is black.) The child writes spelling words on the top clear plastic sheet, and then lifts the sheet to erase the words.

12. | Alphabet Macaroni | ...The child writes words with alphabet macaroni and then glues them on a piece of dark construction paper. When the glue dries, the child takes a crayon (yellow is a good color) and rubs across the top of the letters to make them stand out more. Or, the macaroni can be dyed, before the children use it. Pour about half an inch of rubbing alcohol and some food coloring in a jar. Add the macaroni, put on the lid, and shake well. The macaroni should absorb almost all the liquid. If there is much liquid remaining, add some additional macaroni and shake again. Spread the colored macaroni on newspaper to dry. This will take 5 or 10 minutes.

13. | Concentration | ... The child selects eight of the hardest words. Each of the eight words is written on two slips of paper. Then the student and a friend can play concentration with these spelling words. When a word is turned over, the child must say and spell the word.

14. | From Here to There | ... The child looks at one of the spelling words, and then walks to the chalk-board and writes it. The student then walks back, sits down, and checks to see if the word is spelled correctly. The child continues this way through the remaining words on the spelling list.

15. | Crossword Puzzle | ... The child connects the words to form a crossword puzzle.

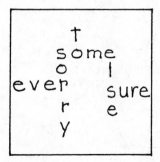

The following chart, which lists fifteen ways to practice spelling words, is helpful as a reminder for the children.

WAYS TO PRACTICE SPELLING

1. *Crayon Trace . . . 5 times* fun
2. *Decorate or illustrate your words* fly
3. *Have a friend give you a spelling test*
4. *Write your spelling words 3 times*
5. *Board Erase . . . trace with your finger*
6. *Magnetic Letters . . . "What's missing?"*
7. *Snakes of Clay . . .* sun
8. *Graph Paper Cut Up . . .* l o o k
9. *Sand . . . Write your words in damp sand*
10. *Printing Set . . . stamp your words*
11. *Magic Slate*
12. *Alphabet Macaroni*
13. *Concentration . . . 8 words (pairs)*
14. *From Here to There . . . Look at a spelling word. Walk to the board and write it*
15. *Crossword Puzzle . . . use your words*

Boxes with the needed materials and simple directions for practicing spelling words should be readily available.

Have a friend
give you a
spelling test

A shoe box works well. Inside, put lined paper.

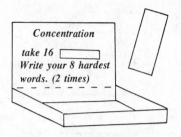

Concentration

take 16 ▭
Write your 8 hardest
words. (2 times)

This can be a rather small box (5″×5″ approximately). Inside put lots of 4″×1″ rectangles cut out of manila or white construction paper.

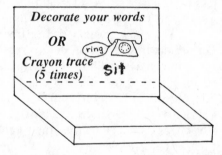

Decorate your words

OR

Crayon trace
(5 times)

A ditto master box is a perfect size. Inside put plain white ditto paper, or white construction paper.

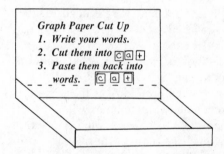

Graph Paper Cut Up
1. Write your words.
2. Cut them into
3. Paste them back into
   words.

Use a ditto master box. Inside, put plain white ditto paper. (The child will glue his graph paper squares onto this paper.) Also put 1″ square graph paper cut to 4½″×6″, paste jars, and scissors in the box.

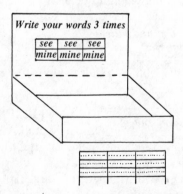

Write your words 3 times

see	see	see
mine	mine	mine

This needs to be a box which is large enough to accommodate the children's regular writing paper. Before putting the paper in the box, fold it in thirds.

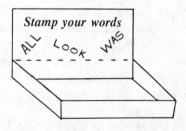

Stamp your words

ALL LOOK WAS

You will need a box which will accommodate plain white ditto paper cut to 6″×4½″. Also put in the box the set of rubber stamping letters and an ink pad.

Alphabet Macaroni

A shoe box works well for this. Inside, put a jar which has the alphabet macaroni in it, a glue bottle, and black construction paper cut 4"×4½".

The other materials needed for the fifteen ways listed on the chart are: a magic slate, plasticene clay, chalk and a small chalkboard, magnetic letters and a metal board, and a dishpan with sand in it. Generally the children look at these materials and immediately remember what to do with them. However, you could also set up a box for each of them, with a direction card attached to each box.

All the materials can fit into one larger box for storage, or the individual boxes of materials can be kept on a shelf.

More Ways to Practice Spelling

To add variety, you might want to have some additional direction cards which you periodically pin up next to the chart. On the days you pin up any of the extra cards for ways to practice spelling words, be sure to put out the additional materials.

16. | *White crayon on manila paper/black paint* | Using a white crayon, the children write their words on a piece of manila construction paper. They paint over the paper with a wash of thin black paint, and their spelling words "appear."

17. | *Tape Recorder say and spell words listen and check* | The child looks at one of the spelling words, says it into the tape recorder, and then spells it from memory, continuing in this way through the entire list. The student then replays the tape, and checks the spoken words against the spelling list.

18. | *Scrambled words* | The child takes pieces of construction paper, cut to 4"×1", and on one side, writes a spelling word correctly.

| *ftrea* | *after* |
back of card

On the other side the student mixes up the letters. After doing this with each spelling word, the child looks at the scrambled words and tries to write them correctly on a separate piece of paper. To check independently, the student turns each card over.

19. | *Glue and beans* | The child writes the most difficult words by using glue and beans.

20. | *Yarn and glue* | The child writes the most difficult words using yarn and glue. (This works especially well for children who are writing in cursive.)

21. | *Sand and glue* | The child writes the most difficult words using sand and glue. (Write the word with glue and then sprinkle sand over the glue. Wait for it to dry and tap off the excess sand.)

22. | *Ghost Writing with Q-tips* | The child dips a Q-tip in a small amount of bleach, then uses the Q-tip to write each word on black con-

100

struction paper. As the bleach dries, words appear like magic!

23.
> | l
> | lo
> | loo
> | look

On the first line of the paper, the child writes the first letter of the word. On the second line the student writes the first and the second letter of the word, continuing in this way until the entire word is written. This is especially beneficial for a child who has difficulty with the sequence of letters within a word.

24.
> **Special ditto—write your words**

Make a fun ditto or seasonal ditto for the children. Have them write their spelling words on it (10).

Balance your words on Elmer's trunk.

25.
> **Special ditto—write your words in ABC order**

Make a fun ditto or seasonal ditto for the children. Have them write their spelling words in alphabetical order (11).

Line your words up alphabetically on the field.

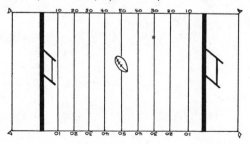

26.
> **Jigsaw Puzzle**
> **write all your words**
> **cut into puzzle**

The child writes all of the spelling words on a piece of paper, then turns it over and draws curved lines on it to make it look like a jigsaw puzzle. Next the student cuts it apart and tries to reassemble it, by using the letters of the words as clues.

27.
> **Alpha Bits**

Each child "writes" one of the words, using Alpha Bits (sugar-coated breakfast cereal); then spells the word, without looking, to a friend. The word spelled correctly can be eaten! (Anyone who catches someone else eating a word without having spelled it to a partner, may claim the other person's word and eat it!)

28.
> **Scratch Words**
> 1. **color a card**
> 2. **cover with black**
> 3. **scratch a word**

The child colors on a piece of construction paper cut to 4½"×6", with different colors of crayons, completely covering the paper. Next, the student colors on top of the colors, using a black crayon, then takes a paper clip, which has been opened, and scratches the same words on the paper.

29.
> **Typewriter**

The child types out the spelling words.

30.
> **Alphabet Ruler**

The student uses a ruler which has letters of the alphabet cut out of the center part. By placing a pencil in the appropriate "cut-out" spaces and tracing the letters, the child writes out each spelling word.

There are undoubtedly other things that you already have in your classroom which would make interesting ways for children to practice their spelling words. You might consider such things as:

Felt letters	use with a felt board
Spill and Spell letters	(commercial game)
Try Kit letters	(commercial perceptual kit)
Link Letters	(commercial letters which snap together)
Letter templates	(can be purchased commercially)
Scrabble letters	(commercial game)

Spelling Test Procedure

It may be overwhelming to think of trying to test thirty or more children, each with a completely different list of spelling words. But actually it is a simple procedure.

If your classroom is basically traditional, call seven or eight children to a table, while the other students go on with their assigned work. If your class is working in a learning-centers environment, give the spelling test to each group of seven or eight students as they rotate to the spelling center.

The procedure is similar to the one used in the informal diagnostic test. The children should be seated at the table before you begin collecting their blue booklets, "My Spelling Words." They should have their booklet opened to the current week's list of words. Collect the books, stacking each under the other in sequence, so that the books are in the same order as the children are seated. The children open their yellow booklets, "My Spelling Tests," to the first page.

Walk up behind the first child and look at the first word on the top blue booklet. Say "Your first word is _____ ." As soon as the student begins to write the word, move behind the second child. Turn to the second blue booklet and quietly say, "Your first word is _____ ." Continue this way on

around the table. When you get back to the first student, he or she should be ready for the second word, and you should be back to the top blue booklet! It takes a few times before you get the timing figured out, but you should strive to get back to students at just about the same time as they finish writing their previous word. If they have to sit for a long time waiting, they will get restless. There is no need to watch a child writing out the word. So as soon as you are certain that the student heard the word, move on to the next person.

One of the advantages of a test of this nature is that cheating is eliminated. There is considerably less pressure on the children than is often the case in regular spelling tests. If you get back to a child and see that there is a problem in trying to figure out a word, you can quietly say, "That's all right. Go on and think about that word for a few more minutes and then I'll be back with you." You can continue around the table giving the other children their next words, while the child who needs additional time to think about a word, can figure it out. Remember that some children will have more words, so it does not make a student feel conspicuous to sit out a round or two. This child may still be the first one finished with the test. As the children write their last word, ask them to sit quietly while you finish giving the other students the rest of their spelling words..

As soon as everyone is finished with the test, start correcting the test pages, by comparing the blue and yellow books. If a child misses a word, put a line through the word. Then turn to the next page in the *blue* book, and, with a red pencil or pen, write the word missed on the top line. This insures that the student will automatically take that word again next week as it will be the first word on the new list.

You will find it takes approximately 20 minutes to give eight children their spelling tests and to correct them.

Other Spelling Activities

If you feel that the students in your classroom will not be frustrated by the word lists in commercial workbooks, you can assign workbook pages as part of center activities. Or they can be assigned during reading time. Explain and discuss the pages with all students prior to making the assignment. Although they may know how to spell some of the words, the intent of the workbook is to give them practice on those as well as to introduce words they may not know. A check will be made later to determine which of the words they actually need to learn. The following week the students can include only those words as part of their individualized spelling lists.

Later in the week, (Friday afternoon works particularly well), dictate to the group as a whole, spelling sentences which incorporate the words in the commercial workbook. Any words which are missed should be written in red, on the next page of the student's blue booklet, "My Spelling Words." This means that, on Monday, when

the child selects spelling words for the week, the list will contain: (1) words missed on Friday's individualized spelling test, (2) words missed in spelling dictation, (3) words which have given the student problems in creative writing (see pages 203-204), (4) additional words chosen from the student's Individualized Spelling Book.

This procedure works well, provided that the commercial workbooks are not too difficult for the students. Otherwise, use the workbooks as supplements, only for those students who will have success with them. They can be assigned as part of their written reading work, or as a center activity. (Other students at the center would have assignments appropriate for their current spelling skill level). In this case, if you wish to include spelling-sentence dictation as part of the weekly activities, you can re-group the students for centers one day each week, according to spelling level. Spelling dictation would then vary according to the level of each group. If the students' reading and spelling levels closely parallel, as is often the case, you may prefer to administer spelling dictation during reading time. (The students will already be grouped appropriately).

Another activity, often incorporated as part of weekly spelling assignments, is having students write each of their spelling words in a sentence. This type of exercise should be used only if the meaning of the words is unfamiliar to students, which generally does not occur until the upper grades. Most spelling words are part of the speaking vocabulary in the primary grade. Therefore the activity serves little or no purpose.

Alphabetizing spelling words is another frequent spelling assignment. Be aware that the word lists are already alphabetized. Since most students select their words sequentially from the list, this results in the weekly list being automatically alphabetized! Therefore, other more practical assignments should be used for drill on alphabetizing.

Record Keeping

It is helpful to have a record-keeping system stapled or taped inside each child's Individualized Spelling Book. This can easily be filled in during the week, as you work with the child, or as you review assignments. In a short time, some useful information about how the child is progressing in spelling will be compiled.

On page 106 there is a sample of one type of record-keeping system which is quite useful. This was developed by John Fitzpatrick (12) to correlate with this program. The child writes in the date that words were selected, and the number of words chosen. When the two lists are brought to the teacher (or aide) to be checked, initial the third column.

If you are using a commercial spelling workbook in conjunction with the individualized program, you could have a column to date and initial when you have finished checking the child's spelling workbook. A column for spelling sentences, if this is done on a weekly basis, can also be added. Later in the week, the child should write on the record a key word which indicates the way that the words were practiced. (See page 98.) (It helps to underline one or two key words for each way listed on the chart. For instance, "crayon" might be underlined as the key word for "Crayon Trace . . . five times;" "decorate" could be the key word for "Decorate and illustrate your words," etc.)

When you check the student's spelling test, fill in the record with a star if all the words were spelled correctly, or the number of words missed. A glance down that column will quickly tell you how the child is doing in spelling. The final column labeled "comments," provides a place for you to write a few words concerning your observations, discussions you have had with the child, etc.

It is also helpful to keep an alphabetical composite class record. This can be filled in as each group leaves the center. Write an "a" by the names of any students who are absent. A blank space should be used to indicate a perfect score on the test, and numbers to indicate the number of words misspelled. (This system makes the chart much easier to read.)

At a glance you can tell which students, if any, had considerable difficulty with their spelling test, and follow up accordingly the next week. (Remind the student that already there are words left over from the previous week which are difficult so that easier words should be chosen to complete the list. Also ask how the child practiced these words— was it a different way? If so, perhaps it is not an effective method for this particular child.)

In addition, if possible, give the student a practice test on the day(s) the others practice their spelling words. Provide assistance as needed to insure that each child is confident about taking the spelling test.

Determining When a Child's List of Words Should Be Changed

It is important for you to be aware when a child has mastered the spelling skill under study. It is no longer necessary for the student to continue studying that particular word list!

Usually it will be many months before you need to change the list of words in the child's Individualized Spelling Book. Occasionally though, it becomes necessary to make a change even though the student has had the list for only a short time. This usually indicates that either the child has had a sudden growth in spelling skills, or that the results of your original diagnostic spelling test were misleading. The student may have been tired, ill, or tense.

Generally, those children placed in the high-frequency lists (Basic Vocabulary, Frequently Misspelled Words, Spelling Demons, or Important Words for Upper Grade Students), will need to study all the words on their list. This is necessary because many, if not all, of the words are sight words. When a student completes one of these lists, there are two options: (1) repeat the words a second time; (2) repeat only those words that were spelled incorrectly on tests.

Having the student repeat the entire list is appropriate for anyone who has not mastered the words. Or, if the next list might be too difficult for the student to handle successfully, the old list can be repeated.

A quick review of a student's yellow, "My Spelling Tests" booklet, listing all the words written in red (words which were originally missed on spelling tests), is sufficient review for the good speller. Such children should draw a small square by each of these words. (You may want to draw up the list of words for younger students.)

Once the review list is made, the student should take as many words each week, as the two of you feel are appropriate. As each of the words is taken, the child should date the adjacent square. When the entire review list

has been mastered, the student is ready to begin a new list.

Sometimes you will find that a child is learning spelling words with little effort. If this happens, have the student spell several words, from his or her Individualized Spelling Book, which were not previously practiced. If the child spells the words easily, give several words from the next more difficult list. Continue this way, until you find a list which is appropriate for the student's present level of skill development. Remove the current list from the Individualized Spelling Book, and insert the new appropriate list.

Children placed in List I (short vowel words), should be moved on to the next more difficult list once they show competence in the spelling skills which they have been studying. When a child can easily spell five or six of the words in the Individualized Spelling Book (words which were not previously studied), it is time to move on to the next more difficult list.

If you feel that a child would be frustrated if required to learn a harder list of words, it may be wise to concentrate on the same list for the entire year. It is better to have a child remain in the same list and feel successful, than to change the lists and see a student undergo frustration and failure.

Adapting the Spelling Lists

It is possible to adapt some of the lists according to the needs of particular students. For instance, if you place a child in the basic list, but you know many of the words will be too difficult, you can tell the student only to take the words which have a dot in the adjacent square. (See page 91.) This will in-

Date	Number of words	Spelling Workbook	Choice of Practice	Spelling Test (number missed)	Nancy
					(name) COMMENTS
9/15	10	9/17	Decorate #2	☆	9/10 Starting with long and short vowel list/blends digraph
9/22	10	9/25	Crayon #1	☆	
9/29	15	10/	Friend #3	1	9/27 Suggested she try 15 words next week
10/5	15	10/7	Friend #3	☆	10/3 Says she thinks spelling is fun — likes to work on spelling at home with her older sister

Student record

CLASS SPELLING RECORD

	9/15	9/23	9/30	10/7			
Anne			1				
Bill	1						
Bobby		1		4			
David			2				
Denise	a			1			
Eddie							
Frank	2	5	1				
Ginny				1			
Helen							
Jane	1		1	2			

Composite class record

sure the child is selecting the easier words. Or you might tell the student to select two words that do not have a dot by them (two harder words), but the remainder of the words chosen should have a dot in the square next to them.

When the student has studied all of the easier words on the Basic Vocabulary list, you can decide whether you want them studied a second time (write the date on either side of the "dot"), or whether you feel that the child is now ready to study the other more difficult words on the list.

The short vowel list (List I) can also be adapted by, for example, having a child choose only words with the short "a" sound. (Put a small check [✔] next to each short "a" word on the list. This will help the student find the words to take.) This means that, for the present time, all the child has to concentrate on is the first and last sound in the word. Later you might have the student take words which only have the short "i" sound, etc.

List II can be adapted similarly. Children only select words which have a certain blend or digraph. Or you might ask a child to choose words which end in "e."

What is important to remember is that the spelling program should be flexible. It must help you to work with each child in a manner which you feel is best for advancing individual achievement.

Providing for the More Capable Student

When students have mastered the phonetic lists and high frequency words, you may want to consider incorporating the commercial kit, *Continuous Progress in Spelling* (13). Rather than using this kit in the manner suggested by the publisher, it can be scheduled in exactly the same format as the spelling program described in this chapter.

This enables all the students in the class to be on the same basic schedule, while maintaining the individualized spelling program.

A colleague, Ethel Lagle (14), has combined this program and the *Continuous Progress in Spelling* program in the following manner. Students who are using the commercial kit (those who have mastered the phonetic, high frequency, and spelling-demon lists), are tested by the teacher and placed at an appropriate level in the kit's materials.

When designing the groups for the centers, the teacher makes certain that there are pairs of students in each group using the spelling kit. To insure honesty and fairness, and to minimize wasted time, the partners should not be good friends, as they must assume the responsibility for testing each other on spelling words.

On the day the other students in each group select their spelling words from their Individualized Spelling Books, the partners select their appropriate word lists from the *Continuous Progress in Spelling* kit. They then test each other until each has a list of ten words which were missed. These become their spelling list for that week. (The students check each other's tests, and then an aide or the teacher re-checks the corrected tests.) By the end of the center, if one of the students has not missed a total of ten words, the teacher has a back-up list of difficult words for them, which often relates to current social studies or science units of study.

For the remainder of the week, all the students follow the same spelling-center procedures of practicing their words in a variety of ways, taking their individualized spelling tests on Friday, and carrying over any misspelled words to the next week's list.

Notes

1. Mary E. Collins, extension instructor, California State College, Sonoma.
2. Richard Madden and Thorsten Carlson, *Word List for Success in Spelling*, World Book, Yonkers-on-Hudson, 1956.
3. Henry D. Rinsland, *A Basic Vocabulary of Elementary School Children*, Macmillan Company, New York, 1945.
4. Edward W. Dolch, *Teaching Primary Reading*, Garrard Press, 1960.
5. Leslie W. Johnson, "One Hundred Words Most Often Misspelled By Children In The Elementary Grades," *Journal of Educational Research*, 44: 154-155, October 1950.
6. W. Franklin Jones, *Concrete Investigations of the Materials of English Spelling*, University of South Dakota, Vermillion, South Dakota, 1913.
7. Henry Kucera and W. Nelson Francis, *Computational Analysis of Present-Day English*, Brown University Press, Providence, Rhode Island, 1967.
8. Ernest A. Horn, *A Basic Writing Vocabulary—10,000 Words Most Commonly Used in Writing*, University of Iowa Monographs in Education, First Series, No. 4, University of Iowa, Iowa City, Iowa, 1926.
9. Johnson, loc. cit.
10. Blair Gamble, Teacher, Novato Unified School District, Novato, California.
11. Ibid.
12. John Fitzpatrick, Teacher, Novato Unified School District, Novato, California.
13. Edwin A. Read, et. al., *Continuous Progress in Spelling*, Economy Company, Oklahoma City, 1972.
14. Ethel Lagle, Teacher, Novato Unified School District, Novato, California.

CHAPTER IX

Handwriting Center

Introduction

Individualizing the mechanics of printing and/or cursive requires a variety of materials. Once the necessary materials are made they can be used throughout the months of school, year after year. The time spent making up these materials seems less burdensome because of the long-term usage.

All of the materials do not need to be prepared at once. Staying just ahead of the fastest students has an advantage, as the handwriting samples require concentration and neatness. (You can write neatly for just so long, before your hand becomes overly tired, and mistakes begin to appear!)

Once the preliminary sets of material are made, the students can begin individual programs, rather than everyone practicing the same thing whether they need it or not! The variety of materials and some simple diagnostic tools at your disposal insures that stu-

dents work on specific skills appropriate for them.

When students have mastered the basic mechanics of letter formation (printing or cursive), you will want them to apply these skills, by copying written work. In the primary grades this is an excellent opportunity to reinforce the students' reading vocabulary. But it is next to impossible to accomplish if all students are given the same assignment, such as "copy the story from the board." In addition, this type of assignment usually is of little interest to the students. The quality of handwriting suffers as a result.

To help overcome these problems, this chapter deals with materials and methods appropriate for designing an individualized handwriting center. These include: readiness activities, diagnostic and record-keeping procedures, sequential materials for individualized practice on the mechanics of letter formation (printing and cursive), individualized copy-work material designed to reinforce the reading vocabulary of beginning readers, and high-interest material for students with more extensive reading vocabularies (riddles, jump rope jingles, poems, tongue-twisters, selections from the *Guinness Book of World Records*).

Geometric potato stamps

Readiness Writing Activities

At the readiness level, the main objective is to teach students the strokes necessary to form letters of the alphabet. At this stage, there is no need for the child either to write the letters "per se," or to identify letters. The development of small-muscle control, to be applied later, is what is important.

Young children are intrigued with patterns such as:

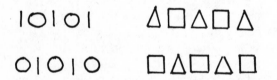

Therefore they are ideal for practicing strokes of the alphabet. Before the students draw the patterns, introduce and develop the concept. This can be done with potato prints. Cut a potato in half and then cut away the outer edge to expose a raised geometric shape. Use two shapes for potato "stamps," a circle and a square. (You may want several duplicate potato stamps, so that a number of children can work at the same time.)

To make prints, the children take 1 to 1½-inch brushes, paint tempera on one of the potato designs and then stamp the design on paper. Or stamp pads can be made by placing a piece of foam rubber, or several layers of paper towels in a shallow pan, and saturating with tempera.

Two different colors of paint, one for each of the geometric shapes should be used. Otherwise the colors will get mixed, and look muddy; therefore, one shape to one color!

Designs can also be made, using permanent stamps. These are easily constructed by cutting a shape from Dr. Scholl's Moleskin Adhesive Cushioning, and pressing this self-adhesive material onto a small piece of scrap wood. (These stamps can be re-used, year after year.)

When you are ready to set up a pattern-making center, fold large paper into 3″ to 4″ squares. (Colored newsprint works well.) There should be an odd number of squares across the paper. This results in the pattern automatically being repeated correctly on the next line.

Discuss patterns with the children. Demonstrate the process of making a pattern with the potato prints. Students can then stamp potato-print patterns under the supervision of an adult or upper grade student, who can guide and assist them as needed.

PATTERN MAKING

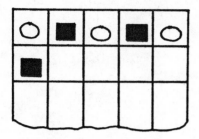

Right
The student will automatically place a square at the beginning of the second row, as it continues the pattern: circle, square, circle, square _____

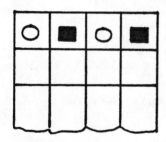

Wrong
The student will want to place a circle at the beginning of the second row: circle, square, circle, square, _____

Later, other geometric shapes and colors of paint can be added. The student selects any two, remembering the one shape to one color rule.

Either as an extension of this activity or as an introduction to patterns, the children can lay objects (Pattern Blocks are ideal), or shapes cut from construction paper, on a table to form a pattern. Another variation is the use of a duplicated ditto master with a drawn grid. Students follow the same procedure in forming a pattern, but now paste the construction-paper geometric shapes to the ditto.

Commercial stamps are available at most variety or toy stores for less than a dollar. These can be used with a commercial stamp pad to create pattern designs which delight children.

Once the concept of patterns is established, you are ready to set up a writing center which includes basic strokes of the alphabet as the elements of patterns.

On ditto masters, make two grids. One should have five squares across and four squares down.

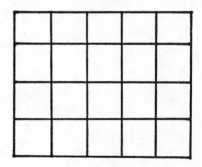

Grid for patterns

The other grid should have ten squares across and eight squares down. For your reference, make some sample patterns. (See page 114.) Add a supply of color crayons, and your center is ready for business.

While a student watches, start a simple pattern on one of the 2″ grids: red vertical line, blue vertical line, red vertical line. Ask the student what would come next. Then have the student draw the line. Continue this process until the student seems secure. With another student use a different pattern, perhaps horizontal lines instead of vertical, with alternating colors.

In the above patterns, the child concentrates on only one element—changing colors in each square. The shape and size stay the same.

If you use different-size patterns, keep the color and shape the same: tall red line, short red line, tall red line. . . . Likewise the shapes can be varied, but then keep the size and color constant: blue circle, blue line, blue circle . . .

Sample beginning patterns include:

Alternate colors ||||| _ _ _ _   OOOO xxxx *("x" may be difficult for some students to write.)*

Alternate sizes (same color) |ı|ı OₒOₒ XxXx

Alternate shapes (same color) |O|O |–|– O–O–
XOXO X–X– X|X|

Later you can introduce two variables.

Alternate colors and size |ı|ı|ı   *(red, blue, red, blue . . .)*

OₒOₒ   *(yellow, green, yellow, green . . .)*

Xx Xx Xx   *(purple, orange, purple . . .)*

Alternate colors and shape |O|O| *(purple, yellow, purple . . .)*

|–|–| *(blue, orange, blue . . .)*

–O–O– *(green, red, green . . .)*

X|X|X   *(brown, orange, brown . . .)*

X–X–X   *(purple, green, purple . . .)*

XO XOX *(black, yellow, black . . .)*

Alternate shape and size (same color) |o|o| |x|x ıXıX
OıOı OxOx ₒXₒX

Ask the child to identify the colors as you begin drawing a pattern. If the student is uncertain, indicate the colors. Then, have the child repeat them softly, while completing the pattern.

As soon as the student is able to draw vertical, horizontal, and slanted lines, and circles, introduce some of the following patterns on the 2″ grid paper. (Again, start the pattern for each child.)

Patterns using squares, circles and triangles

(alternate colors)

(same color at first—later, alternate colors)

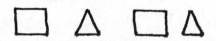

(alternate color)

(same color—later, alternate colors)

(same color—later, alternate colors)

If the student has difficulty drawing a square, suggest drawing two "walls,"

then add the "ceiling,"

and lastly the "floor."

If triangles are difficult, suggest that first the child draw a "teepee" or tent, using two downward strokes: "Down."

Then the pencil should be put back at the top of the stroke, and the second downward stroke drawn.

Lastly, the student should pick up the pencil and put it in the left-hand corner and draw across to form the "floor."

After this, you can introduce patterns involving size, shape, and color.

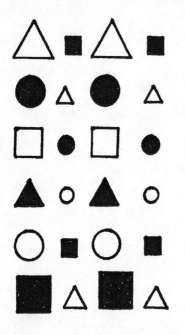

Alternating colors, size, and shape

Some students also enjoy using the 1″ grid paper, and coloring in the squares in alternate colors.

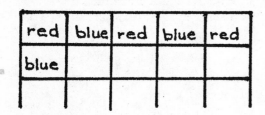

Colored pattern

Patterns can also be drawn on the 1″ grid paper.

A student should progress through these steps at a purely individual pace. Each stu-dent's patterns, the size of grid paper, and complexity of design, should be selected to match personal levels of ability.

Before interest wanes in patterns of this type, change to "seasonal patterns." These are also exercises in basic strokes, but the children perceive them as something completely different.

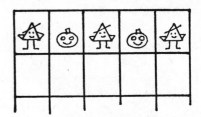

Seasonal pattern

Designs for seasonal patterns

Seasonal pattern, with varying sizes

116

Additional ideas for beginning stroke practice can be found in Louise Binder Scott and J.J. Thompson's book, *Phonics in Listening, in Speaking, in Reading, in Writing* (1). Although this book is currently out of print, most teacher-professional libraries or instructional-materials centers have copies. It contains amusing stories and poems which you can use for illustrating basic letter strokes. The child copies the strokes as the teacher makes them. Individual chalkboards are ideal for this. Students are delighted with the results, and enjoy going home and retelling the story with illustrations!

Louise Binder Scott also has a simple beginning-writing book called *My First Writing Book* (2). In this book, a line and a rectangle turn into a flag, a circle and a line turn into a lollipop, two circles become a snowman, etc. You may find that the size of the lines and shapes are larger than is comfortable for some children to draw. However, it should provide many useful ideas for your writing center.

At this stage most children are interested in learning to print their name correctly. Teachers are often tempted to write the child's name, and then have the student trace over the written letters. However, a child tracing letters without supervision, may form many poor habits. Strokes may be written in the wrong sequence, wrong direction, etc.

To avoid this, the teacher should start work with the student on a one-to-one basis. Have the child watch as you write the first letter of the surname, first name, or nickname, whichever is most meaningful to the young participant. The child should then write it, with you giving directions and/or illustrations as needed. Continue with this procedure for each letter of the name. This process should be repeated, perhaps for several days, until the student understands the procedure and the proper sequence of strokes. At this time it is fun to introduce an acetate pocket and name card. The acetate pocket can be made by taping a piece of clear, heavy acetate to a piece of heavyweight, dark-colored poster board. Four to eight of these are ideal for a writing center.

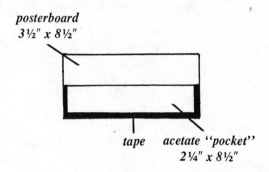

posterboard
3½" x 8½"

tape   acetate "pocket"
2¼" x 8½"

Acetate pocket

In addition to the acetate pocket, prepare a card for each of the students in your class by printing their names with felt pen on pieces of tagboard.

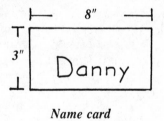

Name card

Make certain that the writing does not extend into the top 1" or the bottom ¼" of each card (shaded areas in the following diagram).

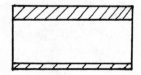

Placement of writing on name card

When the student is ready to use the acetate pocket to practice name writing, insert the name card into the pocket.

Name card inserted in acetate pocket

The child carefully traces over each of the letters in sequence, using a light-colored crayon. The student then removes the name card and the letters written with the crayon (the name!) are visible. The child can erase the name by using a piece of fabric or a paper towel.

You should supervise the tracing for students until they have mastered the proper sequence of strokes, after which they continue on their own.

Students may also enjoy using their index fingers to trace over the letters of their names, formed in fluffy flocking. Making a set of flocked name cards is fun for a center activity. (You could easily do it yourself, but the children are fascinated by the process.) Use pieces of tagboard, approximately 3″×8″. Write a child's name lightly with pencil on one of the cards. Then have the child gently squeeze a line of glue onto the outline of each letter. If this process is difficult for the student, you can do this step.

As soon as the glue is on all of the letters, have the child place the name card on a sheet of newspaper. Lightly sprinkle flocking over the letters. (Flocking is a fuzzy powder-like substance which can be purchased at hobby shops). The card should be allowed to dry for a short while. Then the child can hold the card upside down over the paper, and gently tap it, to knock off the excess flocking (which can be saved and re-used). The name card should dry until the following day. It can be used as a tactile card, for the child to trace with index finger. Once again, be certain to supervise initially the sequence of strokes.

Outlining name with glue

For those students who continue to have difficulty writing their names, use name cards with raised letters. By covering the raised letters with a sheet of paper, and rubbing with the side of a crayon, an imprint of the child's name can be made. The student can then use this as a model to trace: first with supervision, later alone.

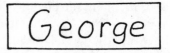

Name card with raised letters

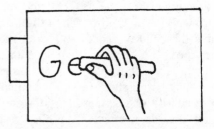

Child places paper on top of name card, and uses a crayon to make a rubbing of name

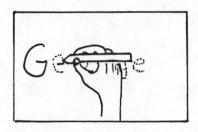

Student carefully traces name with a pencil or crayon

The name cards with raised letters can be made on tagboard cards, approximately 3″×8″. The child's name is written with a permanent felt pen, the letters outlined with glue, and dried. This provides a raised, somewhat bumpy surface. It is ideal for crayon rubbings.

For additional ways students can practice writing their names, see pages 95-102, "Ways to Practice Spelling Words."

At about the same time you are working with children on writing their names properly, begin working on the proper formation of numerals, a difficult task for some students. The same procedure should be followed, providing step-by-step guidance until the student seems secure. The student then can continue working alone using an acetate pocket, glue rubbing, etc.

Students who have difficulty with reversals of letters or numerals [7 , can often be helped by having them think about the direction of the stroke: toward the hand that is holding the paper, or away from the hand which holds the paper. For a right-handed child a "7" goes away from the hand holding the paper. The jingle, "Seven and three, away from me," is a cute way for the child to remember. Another memory jogger, "Six, nine, and eight, think my hand's great!" Explain that since the numbers think that hand is so great, they want to come toward it.

Obviously the "coming toward," or "going away from," process will be reversed for children who are left-handed!

Another appropriate activity at the writing-readiness stage is captions which the child dictates for paintings and other art work. Have the student watch you as you do the writing on the paper, as this will help to reinforce the left-to-right progression of the letters. Supervise as the child traces the letters to make certain the strokes go from top to bottom, etc., or, if you have upper-grade students helping in the classroom, they can be a great help supervising the tracing process, once you have given them instructions.

Another tracing experience can be combined with rhymes. Duplicate the illustrations on pages 120-123.

Set up a center with these pages, scissors, paste, paste brushes, and stapled booklets (one per child). The booklets should each contain nine pages of construction paper, 6″×9″, stapled at the top.

Rhyme book

After introducing rhymes, the center can be used for reinforcement.

At the rhyming center, a child is given one of the pages of rhyming pictures. The first task is to trace carefully each of the words,

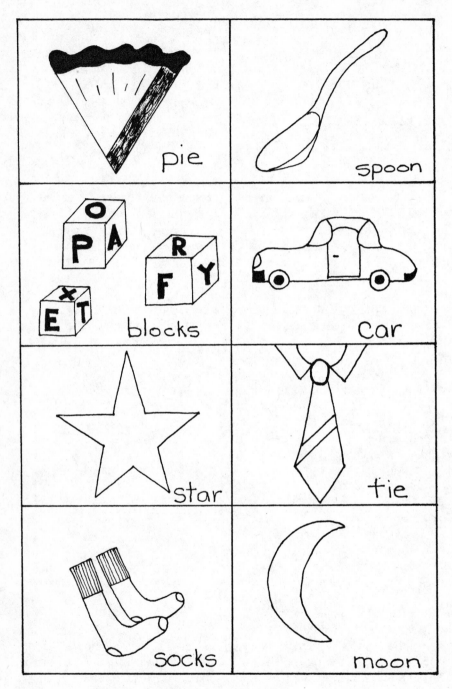

Pictures for rhyme book

120

lock

truck

house

Cake

duck

clock

rake

mouse

light

fan

hook

book

key

can

kite

three

and identify each of the pictures. The student then cuts out two of the pictures which rhyme, and pastes these on the inside of the cover. The next two rhyming pictures go on the next page. Both sides of each page should be used.

Inside pages of
rhyme book

on the dotted line or the top line. Draw the following illustration on a ditto master. Duplicate copies for all of the students in the class, plus extra "back-up" copies. Cut the ditto in half, so the child begins by working only the top half.

If any children leave the center before completing the page, they should tuck the remaining dittos inside their stapled booklets, so that nothing gets lost. All of their materials are then together when they return to the center.

Introduction to Printing
(Formation of Letters)

Students often have difficulty printing letters correctly, because they are uncertain about the placement of the letter, (where it belongs in relationship to the lines on the paper). So tell students that all letters, both upper case and lower case, (with the exception of lower case "t"), bump their heads on either the middle dotted line, or on the top line. Add that all letters stand on the bottom line, (although some have tails that hang below the line). Many of their potential problems will be eliminated as they grasp this.

The first step is to differentiate between tall and short letters. Once this is established, the student will be able to determine whether the letter is going to bump its head

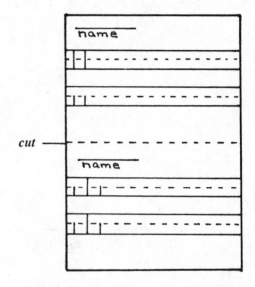

Tall lines and short lines practice page

The sample tall and short lines should be green, to distinguish them from the top, middle, and bottom lines. If you buy a single green ditto master (available at stationery stores), you can use it for parts of all the following pages.

When introducing this ditto, work with one child or a small group. Have the child compare the two green lines in the top row with the two green lines in the second row. Introduce the terminology "tall" and "short." The top lines are "tall." The lines in the second row are "short." Point out that the tall lines bump their heads on the top line and then stand on the bottom line. They

124

don't hang below the bottom line, nor do they stop before they get to the bottom line. They stand right on the line.

Have the student trace the two green "tall lines," being very careful to place the pencil right on the top line, and to stop as soon as it touches the bottom line. Watch as the child does this. Provide guidance as needed. Have the student complete the first row in this fashion. (Be certain to check the spacing between tall lines.) Some children will put them close together, while others spread them too far apart. Once underway, ask the child carefully to complete the top line and let you check it.

When you introduce the second line, point out that this is a "short line." It bumps its head on the dotted line. Repeat the previous procedure, making certain that the student understands this time that each short line is to begin on the dotted line.

This procedure will enable the child to understand where and how to place the letters.

When the student works on the second ditto (the bottom half of the illustration), review the terminology of tall lines and short lines. Make certain that the child understands the pattern of tall line, short line, tall line, etc.

Some children will need to complete several of these dittos. Stress that the child should do very neat work. What is important is not how quickly the student does the work, but how carefully. This needs to be repeated again and again. It is extremely important to get this concept across to students, especially at an early age.

For those students who need additional work at this level, duplicate the following illustration. The beginning letter in each row should be green.

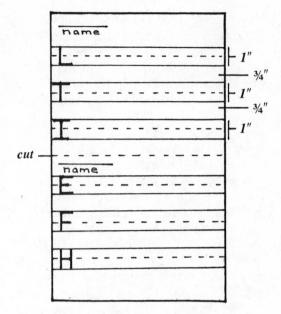

Practice page for "tall letters"

Repeat the discussion on the placement of letters. Continue with other supplemental writing-readiness experiences with any students who have difficulty with this step. The other children can begin work on the following material.

Printing and/or Cursive Mechanics

The following material, discussed as it applies to printed letters, is equally appropriate for cursive. The sequence begins with the easiest letters. Similarly formed letters are then grouped. For instance, once a child has learned to make a "c," the following letter is "a." The student is told, "Now that you know how to make a "c," just putting a short line next to the 'c,' makes an 'a.' ".

Lower case "l" and "i" are the first letters in the sequence, followed by the "c" group (a, d, q, g). The hump letters (n, m, h, and r), and the slant letters (v, y, w, x, and z) are next. The left-over letters, which are difficult for many students (f, s, u, and e) complete the sequence.

Ditto masters for each of the letters should be prepared. (See below.) By requiring only half a sheet to be completed for each letter, the quality of writing will often be higher. On each of these pages there are a series of guiding symbols. The letter is first written as it should be. A green dot indicates where the student is to start each letter. (Green is for go.) The direction of the stroke is indicated by a green arrow. The dotted letters for tracing, are on regular purple ditto master color. The students first practice tracing dotted letters. Gradually each of these guiding symbols disappear, and the students are on their own. (See illustration below.)

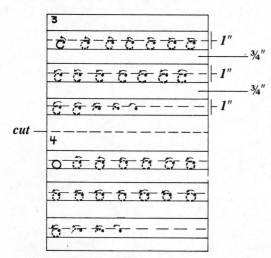

cut

Sample half-sheet ditto for lower case letters. The arrows and dots should be green.

Make dittos for each of the letters of the alphabet following this sequence: l, i, c, o, a, d, q, g, j, p, b, k, t, n, m, h, r, v, y, w, x, z, f, s, u, e. The "dotted line" can be made by running a tracing wheel over the ditto master. (Tracing wheels can be purchased at stores which carry sewing notions.) Store each set of duplicated dittos in a piece of 9″×12″ construction paper, folded in half.

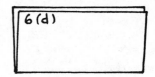

Storage folder for each set of printing dittos

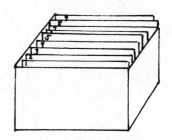

Box of storage folders

Make a student storage/record folder by duplicating the following illustration on 9″×12″ construction paper. (One for each child.) These can also be stored in a small box at the center.

As a student has completed a ditto and it has been checked by the person supervising the center, it should be placed in the individual's record folder. The corresponding box on the front of the folder can be checked off and initialed by the teacher or aide.

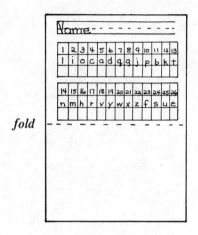

fold

Student storage/record folder

The student should progress at a self-set pace through this series of pages. It is better for the child to spend two days on one page and have it neatly completed, than to rush through it in one day. If the finished page is not of the quality which you feel is appropriate for that student, have the child complete another copy of the same page. However, first be certain to discuss what needs to be improved. The repeat work should begin under your supervision, so that you know that the child has understood the problem. The completed page should then be compared with the first page. Ask the child which is better, and why. Then ask if the student would like to keep both pages, or just the best page. Almost always the child will want to throw away the sloppy page.

Whenever a new page is begun, you should work with the student individually, correlating the new page to concepts developed in previous letters. Remind the child about placement. Watch the student write several letters, providing guidance as neces-

sary. When you feel that the child understands the proper sequence and directions of strokes for the new letter, the student can begin practicing alone, while you help others at the center.

When the student has finished all of the letters, the folder is brought to a corner of the room, away from windows and doors, and all the papers are spread out on the floor. They are then assembled in alphabetical order, and stapled inside the record folder. The child then has a booklet of "My Neatest Writing," which can be taken home.

To test the students, duplicate the illustration below. Have the student trace over each of the dotted letters while you watch. Make a note of any letters that the child writes in an unusual way, (for instance if the student wrote a "d" by first making the "tall line," and then the "c"). Do not correct the child, but record your observation.

Test for writing lower case letters

After the child has traced the dotted letters, the next task is to write the entire alphabet on the bottom part of the ditto. This test informs you (1) whether the student can look at a letter, and copy it in a different place, (2) the letters about which the child is uncertain, (3) the letters that are written incorrectly.

If the student cannot write a letter, say, "Just leave a space and continue with the next letter." Or you can offer to write it for the child. Record any difficulties, uncertainties, or incorrect sequence of strokes.

If a letter is causing the student a problem and you can explain this simply and sympathetically, you will be building willingness to listen and try to change. On the other hand, do not re-teach the proper sequence of strokes, if the child has a perfectly satisfactory way of writing the letter. The student will make a great effort to write it your way while the two of you are working side by side. But, as soon as you leave and the child is no longer concentrating on that letter, the old familiar way will reappear from force of habit.

If there are only a few letters on which further practice is needed, you can immediately administer the capital letter test. (Without much practice on the upper case letters, many of the students can write them quite satisfactorily.)

set of half-sheet dittos. Or you may wish to use commercial material for a change of pace.)

Additional review and copy-work materials, which can be used throughout the year, can be made from a sheet of student handwriting paper, cut in half.

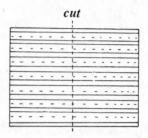

Handwriting paper for copy-work models

Write the letters by categories: slant letters, etc. Glue this to a piece of construction paper approximately 1″ larger, and cover it with clear contact paper or laminate. This becomes a model for the student, and can be used over and over.

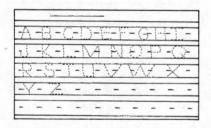

Test for writing upper case letters

The results of these diagnostic tests indicate where the student needs further practice. (If follow-up work is needed on upper case letters and/or numerals, you can make a

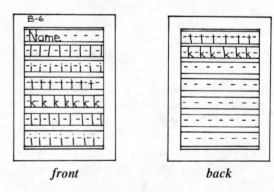

front   *back*

Copy-work models for lower case letters

Also make several copies of the following illustration, using full sheets of the students' handwriting paper. This provides drill on all of the letters of the alphabet, as well as numbers.

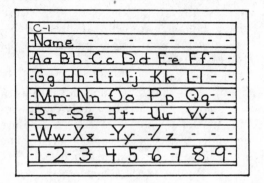

*Copy-work page of letters
of the alphabet and numbers*

The same system can be used effectively for teaching cursive. Only the sequence of letters needs to be changed, so that each letter builds on strokes previously developed.

1. *i*	8. *d*	15. *b*	22. *y*
2. *u*	9. *g*	16. *h*	23. *x*
3. *w*	10. *z*	17. *k*	24. *v*
4. *t*	11. *j*	18. *f*	25. *s*
5. *c*	12. *p*	19. *q*	26. *r*
6. *a*	13. *e*	20. *n*	
7. *o*	14. *l*	21. *m*	

*Sequence for cursive half sheet dittos
(with green arrows and beginning dots)*

All handwriting material should be coded for easy retrieval: A-1, A-2, A-3 for half-sheet dittos with green dots and arrows; B-1, B-2, B-3 for grouped letters written on students' handwriting paper as "model card"; C-1 for model card of all the letters of the alphabet and numbers 1-9. Continue to use this code or any code you choose for the materials which will be presented throughout the chapter.

B-1 . . . E, F, H, I, K, L, T
B-2 . . . C, G, O, Q, C, G, O, Q
B-3 . . . D, P, R, B, D, P, R, B
B-4 . . . A, X, V, W, Y, Z, A, X, V, W, Y, Z
B-5 . . . J, M, N, S, U, J, M, N, S, U
B-6 . . . l, i, t, k, l, i, t, k
B-7 . . . c, a, d, q, g, c, a, d, q, g
B-8 . . . j, q, g, y, j, q, g, y
B-9 . . . m, n, r, h, m, n, r, h
B-10 . . . x, v, w, y, z, x, v, w, y, z
B-11 . . . e, f, s, u, p, o, b, e, f, s, u, p, o

Coding for grouped model cards

J-1 . . . *i, u, w, t, i, u, w, t*
J-2 . . . *c, a, o, d, c, a, o, d*
J-3 . . . *g, z, j, p, g, z, j, p*
J-4 . . . *e, l, b, h, e, l, b, h*
J-5 . . . *k, f, g, k, f, g*
J-6 . . . *n, m, y, x, v, n, m, y, x, v*
J-7 . . . *s, r, s, r, s, r*
J-8 . . . *a, o, c, a, o, c*
J-9 . . . *P, B, R, P, B, R*
J-10 . . . *m, n, m, n*
J-11 . . . *T, F, T, F, T, F*
J-12 . . . *H, K, X, H, K, X*
J-13 . . . *U, V, W, U, V, W*
J-14 . . . *Q, Z, Y, Q, Z, Y*
J-15 . . . *S, G, S, G, S, G*
J-16 . . . *D, J, E, D, J, E, D, J, E*
J-17 . . . *L, I, L, I, L, I*

Cursive Model Cards

Instead of developing your own set of cursive dittos, you may prefer to use commer-

129

cial material, such as *Handwriting Hints from Harvey Hippo and His Horrible Henchmen,* by Susan Ryono (3). This book consists of black cursive worksheets with clever cartoon characters, appealing to students. (Permission is granted for reproduction for classroom use.) The contents of the book can be rearranged to follow the sequence suggested on page 129.

Sequence of Pages
Based on Illustration   *"Harvey Hippo"*
on Page 129   *Use book's*

1. (i) .... p. 8
2. (u, w) .... p. 14
3. (t) .... p. 7
4. (t, i) .... p. 9
5. (c, a, o) .... p. 2
6. (d) .... p. 10
7. Make a page or pages for g, z, j, p (Loops all go in same direction.)
8-9. (e) .... pgs. 3-4
10-11. (l) .... pgs. 5-6
12. (b) .... p. 16
13. (h, k, f) .... p. 13
14. Make a page for q (Loop goes the same direction as f's loop.)
15. (n, m) .... p. 12
16. (x, y, v) .... p. 15
17. (s, r,) .... p. 11

Pages 17 and 18 should be used at your discretion (f, g, p, q, j, z), as the loops go to the right and to the left.

The "Harvey Hippo" sequence for capital letters can be used, as is, with the exception of *D, L, E, Q, Z.* The various directions of the loops can be most confusing to children. This confusion can be eliminated by making four worksheets—one each for D, L, and E, and a fourth for Q and Z. Since these letters do not fall into a pattern, as do most of the other cursive letters, you may prefer to use these toward the end of the upper-case cursive sequence (rather than near the beginning of the sequence as indicated in the "Harvey Hippo" book).

Whether you decide to use "Harvey Hippo," or to make half-sheet dittos to work on cursive letters, it is best to have the students master the lower case letters, before beginning the cursive capital letter. The lower case letters are used much more frequently. Prior to learning upper-case cursive letters, students can use printed capital letters:

Susan Tommy

There are always some students who have an extremely difficult time making the transition from printing to cursive. These are generally the students who have poor visual-motor coordination, and all the "loops and curves" simply become too much for them.

There has been a great need in education for a special cursive alphabet which retained, as much as possible, the characteristics of printing, and eliminated unnecessary embellishments.

An alphabet which meets this criterion has been developed through the combined efforts of teachers, an optometrist, a graphic artist, and an occupational therapist. An article in *Journal of Learning Disabilities,* "A Handwriting Model for Children with Learning Disabilities," (4) describes the alphabet in detail.

Another description and sample of the alphabet can be found in a commercial student workbook, *Total Communication* (5). This workbook should be checked for accuracy.

Also note that its sequence is alphabetical rather than by stroke pattern.

The alphabet can easily be learned by students who are able to print, and research is being undertaken to determine whether it can be used as the "first and only" alphabet a child learns to write.

By obtaining a sample of this alphabet, you can make half-sheet or whole-sheet dittos for each letter. To help the student develop connecting strokes, include words on each of the worksheets, thus providing practice on the current and previous strokes. After i, u, and t have been introduced, the words till, lit, it, tutu, Tilli, and Tut can be used for practice, etc.

The following sequence of letters for the special cursive alphabet, based on building on previous concepts, is recommended.

1. i	8. b	15. q	22. y
2. u	9. k	16. j	23. q
3. l	10. p	17. v	24. s
4. t	11. c	18. w	25. r
5. h	12. a	19. x	26. z
6. n	13. d	20. e	
7. m	14. o	21. f	

To avoid any embarrassment for the children who need to learn the special cursive alphabet, it should be stressed to students that there are many ways to form each and every letter.

An excellent book to have on hand is *Lettering*, by Harry B. Wright (6). It contains many different styles of script, italic, and text. To make charts of the more practical and interesting alphabets, place the book on an opaque projector, project and image on poster board, and trace the projected letters. Students can be encouraged to experiment with some of the styles (good drill for refining small-muscle control). They begin to realize

that the exact shape of the letter is unimportant, as long as their writing is legible.

Often teachers who introduce students to cursive writing spend the entire year stressing and drilling on *the way* to form each letter. Yet if you look at the writing of these students a few years later, you would never know that they had all had the same instruction. Handwriting is individual. Everyone develops a personal writing style. It is the legibility that must be stressed from the beginning. The purpose of writing is communication!

A useful tool in conjunction with all dittos on handwriting is an acetate copyboard. These can be made from heavy-weight clear acetate or blank x-ray film. (This can often be procured free of charge by asking labs or hospitals for used blank x-ray film.)

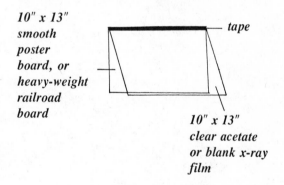

10" x 13" smooth poster board, or heavy-weight railroad board

tape

10" x 13" clear acetate or blank x-ray film

Acetate copyboard

Pieces of acetate and poster board are joined together at the top with masking tape, or heavy plastic tape. A worksheet can be inserted between the poster board and the acetate. Since the acetate is transparent, the worksheet is clearly visible. Prior to writing on the worksheet, the student can practice writing on the acetate with a grease pencil.

The writing can be erased with a piece of material, paper towel, or chalkboard eraser which is used only for erasing grease pencil. Label the top of the eraser, "GREASE PENCIL ERASER," so that it does not accidentally get used on the chalkboard.

After practicing with the grease pencil, the student can fill in the worksheet. This extra practice is often helpful for students who find cursive or printing difficult.

Copy Work for Beginning Readers

Once the mechanics of basic letter formation are mastered, copy work for continued practice on these skills should be provided. As mentioned in the introduction, this copy work for beginning readers should reinforce each student's current reading vocabulary. This can be accomplished by preparing a series of copy-work model pages.

If you are using a phonetic or linguistic reading series, the first set of copy-work model pages might contain vocabulary with the short "a." The next set might include short "a" and short "i" vocabulary. The entire series should parallel the sequence of the reader. The same principle should be applied to sight word readers.

The copy-work model pages are made on student writing paper. A brief story based on those in the students' reading books, six to thirteen lines in length, using current vocabulary, is written. When the students are first beginning to read, constructing the copy work pages is quite simple. Since the stories in most pre-primers are short, you often can copy them word for word. Condensing a five or six-page story in a reader into six to thirteen lines, without introducing words which are unfamiliar to the student becomes a little more tricky!

Since the copy-work model pages are designed for reinforcement, the student writes one of these pages approximately two to three weeks after reading the story in the reading book. This provides automatic review of vocabulary. The student is able to read the copy-work page without struggling with vocabulary. Because a few weeks have elapsed since the child originally read the story, when it crops up again as copy-work, it is like meeting an old friend.

As with the model pages of grouped letters, the copy-work pages are glued on larger pieces of construction paper. When these pages are glued to the construction paper, there should be at least a half-inch margin of construction paper around the edges of the handwriting paper. For durability, the pages should be covered with clear contact paper, or laminated.

The pre-primer and primer copy-work model pages may not be terribly exciting. But fortunately at the beginning reading level, the students are so thrilled about being able to read, that it carries them through the rather dull beginning phonetic or sight word stories!

If you include poetry in a copy-work page, indicate to the total class that these should be copied just as they are. Explain the difference between poetry and prose and the reasons for the special format. A code can be used to indicate a poem. (Colored adhesive stickers with the word "poem" written on them, work well.)

You may want students to illustrate some of their copy-work stories. This provides you with an added check on reading comprehension. A crayon, drawn at the end of the story, can be used as a code for this.

A series of ten to twenty copy-work model pages, which parallel each of the first-grade reading books, should be sufficient (10-20 for pre-primer, 10-20 for primer, etc.).

Stands to hold model cards are essential. Since primary writing paper is large, the resulting copy-work model pages are correspondingly large and can create a space problem.

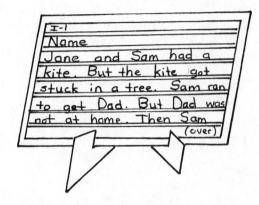

Copy-work page in stand

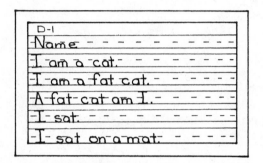

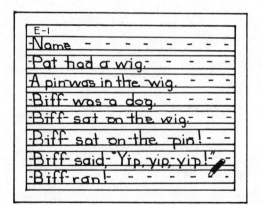

*Copy-work model pages
for beginning readers*

A stand can be made by using heavy plastic tape to hinge two of the following patterns, cut from heavy poster board.

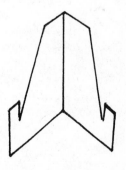

Copy work stand

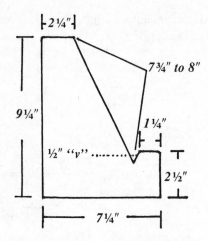

Pattern for stand

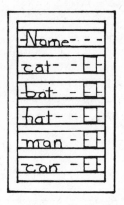

Copy-work word page

Marilyn Austin and Marian Hickman (7) developed a series of writing booklets for students in their classrooms. These can be used effectively for beginning writing practice.

Supplemental Material for Beginning Readers

When working with beginning readers, it is sometimes necessary to have supplementary writing material, especially for those students who are progressing slowly. One possibility is to develop copy-work pages from quarter-sheets of writing paper. These list words from the student's reading vocabulary, which are to be copied and illustrated. A rectangle at the end of each word can be used to indicate that the student is to draw an illustration of the word. Like the other copy-work pages, these are mounted on construction paper, and covered with contact paper or laminated.

Book 1

The first booklet involves comprehension and overwriting (tracing). Two dittos and a booklet made, (by folding four pieces of 9″×12″ paper in half and stapling on the fold), are given to the student.

Dittos for Book 1

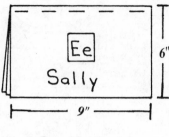

Cover for Book 1

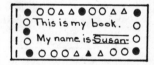

This is my book.
My name is ------

See my three green ------

Look at the one red ------

See my four purple ------

See my two yellow ------

I have five orange ------

Dittos for Book 2

The student first cuts out the rectangle with "Ee" on it, pastes it on the front of the book, and writes his or her name. The child then carefully overwrites, or traces on top of the letters in the first sentence, "See my pet hen." The student cuts out this sentence and pastes it on the first page inside the booklet. Then the child finds the picture which illustrates this sentence, cuts it out, and pastes it above the sentence. The student continues in this fashion with each sentence.

Ditto #3 . . . I have six brown _____
I can see seven black _____
I see eight yellow _____

Ditto #4 . . . I can make nine blue _____
I can make ten pink _____

The student writes his or her name on the cover of the booklet and colors a patterned border around the edges.

See my pet hen.

Inside of Book 1

Book 2

This booklet requires the child to write one word. Four dittos are duplicated, cut into thirds, and assembled in a small booklet.

This is my book.
My name is Susan.

Cover for Book 2

To fill in the blanks in the sentences, the student either refers to picture-word cards, or a picture dictionary, or an aide or the teacher writes the word on a slip of paper. The child then copies the word and illustrates the sentence.

135

Inside of Book 2

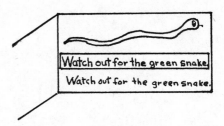

Inside of Book 3

Book 3

This booklet (ten pieces of 6″×9″ paper stapled together) requires overwriting and illustrating. Underwriting may also be included. The child cuts out the top section, and pastes it on the cover of the booklet. The student then decorates the cover with a picture. Next, the child over-writes each sentence, cuts them all out, and pastes them on separate pages, and illustrates them. If able the student finally rewrites the sentence.

Book 4

"A Book About Animals" is made from six pieces of 9″×12″ construction paper. The student cuts out the title from the first ditto and pastes it on the cover of the booklet. The child then over-writes each sentence on the ditto and copies it on the line below, cuts these out, pastes them on the pages in the book, and illustrates them.

Ditto for Book 3

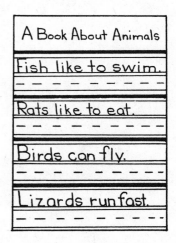

Ditto for Book 4

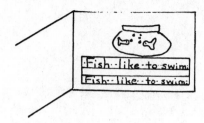

Inside of Book 4

This same format was also used for a book about Christmas.

Ditto #1 . . . My Christmas Book.
              Toys are fun.
              Snow is white.
              I like jingle bells.
              Santa has a red hat.

Ditto #2 . . . My stocking is red.
              I like Christmas.
              Christmas trees are green.
              Rudolf has a red nose.

Book 5

The days of the week, and information about each, are the subject of another booklet. It contains a folder made from a piece of 12″×18″ construction paper, folded in half with a record page stapled to the front. Other supplies include ditto paper with two lines for writing at the bottom and space at the top for illustration, and seven tagboard cards, 4″×12″, with the following information:

Sunday is a fun day.
Sunday   Sunday

Monday is back to school day.
Monday   Monday

Tuesday is a good new day.
Tuesday   Tuesday

Wednesday is the middle day.
Wednesday   Wednesday

Thursday is another work day.
Thursday   Thursday

Friday is bye bye to school day.
Friday   Friday

Saturday we play all day.
Saturday   Saturday.

Folder for Book 5

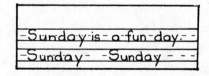

Tagboard card for Book 5

137

The student copies each card on to the ditto and illustrates it. Next, the child colors or decorates the corresponding square on the front of the record sheet. The completed page is then put in the folder. When the student has completed all of the cards, the pages are sequenced and stapled inside the folder, making a book about days of the week.

The same procedure can be used for months of the year. For example:

In January it is cold outside.
We have a lot of rain (or snow).

In February we tell people
that we love them.

In March the wind blows.
We can fly kites.

In April the flowers are pretty.
They have blossoms on them.

In May the days are getting
warmer. The flowers are pretty . . .

When a student is working with a stapled booklet and one or more separate ditto sheets, the best procedure is to store all loose material inside the booklet. When the child comes to the center the following day, all of the material will be together. Work can then get off to a quick start.

Diagnosing and Planning for Individual Student Needs and Record-Keeping

For students who have already had instruction in basic printing and/or cursive, it is necessary to administer a diagnostic test to determine what they have mastered.

A simple test of this nature is to have the students copy a short story from the chalkboard, or in the case of non-readers, copy Aa

Bb Cc. . . from the board. By analyzing these handwriting samples, the student's writing strengths and weaknesses are apparent. An individualized handwriting program is then planned for each child.

Students who have minimal writing skills will be started in the half-sheet dittos, progressing sequentially through these sheets. If certain letters have been mastered, these are marked on the student's record folder.

A student's assignment can be indicated by using the following record page.

STUDENT RECORD

John			Writing		
9/15 Watch out for tall letters. Be sure they touch the blue line.					
B-1		G-6			
B-6					
C-1					
G-1					
G-2					
G-3					
G-4					
G-5					
9/28 Tall letters much better. Watch your "e"s.					
A-26					
C-1					
G-4					
G-5					
G-6					
G-7					
G-8					
G-9					

B-1:	E, F, H, I, K, L, T
B-6:	l, i, t, k, l, i, t, l
C-1:	Aa Ba Cc Dd . . .
G-1 to G-9:	Model-card stories which reinforce the student's reading vocabulary
A-26:	e, e, e, e, e, . . .

Other children may need a brief review of certain letters, but perhaps you find that their writing as a whole seems satisfactory. In this case assign the necessary half-sheet dittos, and/or the grouped-letter model cards. They then move on to the copy-work story pages.

A record/storage folder should be made for each student by stapling a record page to the front of a piece of 12″×18″ construction paper, folded in half.

Student record and folder

After analyzing a sample of each student's writing, the teacher fills in the record page for each child, and spends part of the following day at the writing center, meeting with the students individually. (A thirty-minute center is sufficient to meet with each of the seven or eight students to discuss assignments.)

Prior to meeting with individual students, the storage and code system for all of the writing materials and the record page should be explained to the whole class. Show them where the materials are kept. Also let them know the procedure for handling the copy-work pages. (Young children sometimes inadvertently bend edges when putting away the materials. Therefore, you or an aide may want to handle the material.)

Explain that each student will have different assignments. You will meet with everyone at the writing center to discuss assignments. Stress that, as they complete each of their assigned pages, they should bring it to the person supervising the writing center to have it checked, before beginning another page. Tell them that, if the writing is not of the quality you expect from them, they will be asked to re-do the page. If only a few letters are poorly written, they will be asked to correct these before beginning the next assigned page. The emphasis should always be quality, not quantity, as long as they are not wasting time.

At the end of the center, papers are to be stored in their folders and placed in cubbyhole or desk, or in boxes provided for this purpose. The next day the children are to continue from where they left off. (Be certain to indicate that one copy-work page may take several days for them to complete.)

As each page is completed and corrections made as necessary, the person supervising the Writing Center checks it off on the student's record page and initials it. The paper should then be returned to the student so that it will be available when you take their folders home after a few weeks and go through all their written work.

Since you don't want them to run out of work, be sure they understand that you have assigned more pages than you expect them to complete. (This minimizes the temptation to rush through their assignments.) When you plan a conference at the Writing Center, for the first time, a "total-group" assignment should be given, perhaps copying from the chalkboard, so they will not be idle, thus disruptive, while waiting to meet with you.

With each student, explain any comments you have written on the individual folder. Illustrate what it is that you want the child to do. Then write several letters which are incorrect. Ask the student if these are all right, or if there is something wrong with them. If the child thinks that they are fine, a further explanation is called for. However, if the student says that they are incorrect, ask what is wrong. As soon as the child is able to analyze letters and verbalize observations about mistakes, ninety per cent of the problem is solved. Next have the student write several letters. Make certain that the child is able to write these correctly. Also be certain that the student understands the assignment page, and that it is necessary to show all work to the person supervising the center, as each assigned page is completed. Check to see if the child understands the procedure for storing material. The student can then proceed independently, while you go on with someone else.

After you have met with all of the students, you may wish to supervise the writing center for several days, to make certain that the children understand the system. Volunteers or para-professional aides can then supervise the center, spot-checking each child's work daily, and providing guidance as necessary. (See Chapter VII.)

After several weeks, take home all the student folders. As you go through a child's work, do not take the time to write in each and every correction. Instead, go through the pages looking for incorrect patterns, those which need further work. If there are several things on which the student needs to work, select the most obvious. Have the child concentrate on this during the next two-week period. Do not overwhelm the student by listing all errors!

As soon as you determine the next steps for a student, staple all completed pages together and write a brief note on the front, commenting on any improvement made, and mentioning the next assignment. Return the student's papers to the folder, and fill in the outside record page.

In the allocated space, write the date, and a summary of the comment you wrote on the student's pages—in the case of the sample record page on page 138, "Tall letters much better. Watch your e's." Then decide upon appropriate follow-up work. (This may necessitate skipping a large number of copy-work pages if the child is progressing rapidly in reading.)

This process for all students can be accomplished in one evening, provided you do not meticulously write in corrections on all pages. (This really does not help the student, as you are the one getting all of the writing practice!)

The following day is spent at the Writing Center, conferring with each of the students. Read your comment to them, and go through their papers with them, looking for examples to illustrate your comment. Once more introduce what you want the student to work on. Have the child demonstrate understanding by writing the necessary letters. The student's old papers can then be sent home. And the child can proceed with the next assignment.

Copy-Work Books for Grades 1-6

The procedures and material for students who have progressed beyond the beginning reading stage is somewhat different. They can begin using high-interest "copy-work books." The topics of these books should be selected on the basis of their appeal to students. (A wide range of materials appropriate for many ages is listed on pages 145-155.)

Each "book" is composed of eight to ten pages of related material. There are a series of 5″×8″ "mini-copy-work books" (10 pages each), with four to eight line poems, jump-rope jingles, etc., which use a limited vocabulary.

Another series of "larger copy-work books," (9″×12″) utilizes a wider vocabulary. Topics of these books include poems, tongue twisters, selections from the *Guinness Book of World Records,* riddles, etc. The material on each page is 8 to 15 lines in length, often covering the front and back of the page.

Each "copy-work book" has an attractively colored railroad board cover, whose title indicates the contents. The pages have holes punched in them, and are held together with binder rings. On each of the eight or ten pages, the teacher has carefully written model material that the student will copy to practice printing or cursive.

Cover of "mini-copy-work book"

Inside of "mini-copy-work book"

The lined inside pages are drawn on a ditto master, and duplicated on 5″×8″ index cards for the "mini-copy-work books," or 9″×12″ tagboard for the "larger copy-work books."

Or you may prefer to glue lined ditto papers to tagboard. The completed cards should be covered with clear contact paper or laminated.

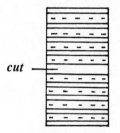

*Inside pages for
mini-copy work books*

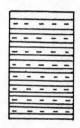

*Inside pages for
larger copy-work books*

The student's writing is assembled in a stapled booklet, which can be taken home, when completed, as a valued addition to the home library.

In the primary grades, it is helpful to have a supply of student stapled booklets. These are made by stapling together eight or ten sheets of student writing-paper, with construction paper covers.

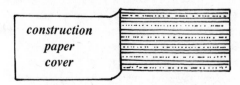

Inside of student booklet

141

If several sizes of writing paper are in use in the classroom, stapled booklets using the different sizes of paper should be made. Students should then have the choice of using whichever size paper they feel is most comfortable for them.

In order to identify which stapled booklets contain eight pages, and which contain ten pages, as each booklet is assembled, write a small "8" or "10" in the upper right-hand corner of the cover. Upper-grade students can easily assemble these for you if you are a primary teacher. In upper-grade classrooms, students can assemble their own.

Direct the student who is ready to make a copy-work booklet to the material you feel is most appropriate: mini-book with limited vocabulary, or larger book with expanded vocabulary.

The student should look through the copy-work books and select the one found most interesting.

It is helpful if students in the same center group use different copy-work books so that one book is not simultaneously in demand. If it is necessary to share books, this can be handled by having the students unclip the binder rings and remove one or two of the pages, and then re-assemble the book at the end of center time. They must be cautioned to check the number on each page and re-assemble the pages in correct order, or it will prove confusing to the next person who uses the book.

When the student has made a selection, the next step is to bring you (or assemble) an eight or ten-page stapled booklet. With a felt pen, write on the front of the stapled booklet the title of the "copy-work book" selected, and the student's name.

The student is to copy each page, and in most cases illustrate the individual pages.

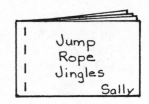

Cover of student booklet

Some students will complete all the writing first and then go back and do the illustrations. Others will copy one page, and illustrate it, then begin work on the next page. Both methods are acceptable.

When the entire copy-work book is completed and illustrated, it is handed in, and necessary corrections are made. The student then selects another copy-work book. The same procedure is repeated.

Copy-work books inspire personal interest on the student's part, unlike many handwriting papers which end up in the trash or worse as litter! The topic for the copy-work books has been selected by the student. The child has meticulously copied each of the pages, and illustrated them. The result is a real feeling of accomplishment when one is completed and taken home. Booklets containing poems, riddles, etc., will be read and re-read to anyone willing to listen. Quotes from the *Guinness Book of World Records,* tongue twisters, jump-rope jingles, etc., will find their way back to school and onto playground.

Years later students will appear with a tattered copy-work book and say, "Do you remember when I wrote this?"

In addition to having captured the students' interest through copy-work books, you will find that their writing improves immensely. You have involved them in something that has meaning to them.

Selecting Material for Copy-Work Books

It is often difficult to find limited-vocabulary, high-interest material, which covers only four to eight lines. The problem is somewhat lessened when you search for material for the larger copy-work books. The following sections of this chapter list material useful for copy-work books. In many cases the specific selection and page number are included, to save you the time of having to go through the books page by page.

Almost all books listed should be available in the children's section of your local or school library. If you are unable to locate exact titles, check the library's card catalogue for books under that heading: jump-rope jingles, tongue-twisters, etc. You will undoubtedly find substitute or additional materials.

If possible, keep some of the books in your classroom, which were used as your references for copy-work books. Students are delighted to discover something they have copied in a "real" book!

Generally eight to ten books will be ample for a center group of eight students. However, you can get by with less by sharing books. So, select from the following lists, according to the interests and ability levels of your students.

Mini-Copy Work Books

Materials for Students with Limited Reading Vocabulary (Late First/Second Grade Level)

Many rhymes have become part of our oral tradition, handed down from generation to generation. A group of these make an interesting copy-work book.

1. Old, Old Rhymes

See my finger,
See my thumb,
See my fist,
You'd better run!

Hickety-pickety,
My black hen,
She lays eggs
For the railroad men.
Sometimes one,
Sometimes two,
Sometimes enough
For the whole blamed crew.

Fuzzy wuzzy was a bear.
Fuzzy wuzzy had no hair.
Fuzzy wuzzy wasn't fuzzy,
Was he!

Red sky at night,
Sailor's delight.
Red sky at morning,
Sailors take warning.

It's raining, It's pouring,
The old man's snoring.
Bumped his head

And he went to bed,
And couldn't get up in the morning.

I had a little pig,
I fed him in a trough.
But he got so fat
That his tail dropped off.
So I got me a hammer,
And I got me a nail,
And I made my little pig
A brand new tail.

A wise old owl
Lived in an oak.
The more he saw
The less he spoke.
The less he spoke
The more he heard.
Why can't we be

Like that wise bird?

Baby Bobby in the tub,
Mama forgot to put in the plug.
Oh, what sorrow,
Oh, what pain,
There goes Bobby,
Down the drain.

See a pin and pick it up,
All the day you'll have good luck.
See a pin and let it lay,
Bad luck you'll have
All that day.

I asked my mother for fifty cents
To see the elephant jump the fence.
Jumped so high, he touched the sky
And never came back
Till the Fourth of July.

2. Mother Goose Rhymes

Diddle, diddle, dumpling,
My son John
Went to bed,
With his britches on,
One shoe off
And one shoe on,
Diddle, diddle, dumpling,
My son John.

Little Miss Muffet
Sat on a tuffet,
Eating her curds and whey.
There came a big spider,
Who sat down beside her
And frightened
Miss Muffet away.

Old Mother Hubbard
Went to the cupboard,
To fetch her poor dog a bone.

But when she came there,
The cupboard was bare
And so the poor dog had none.

Little Jack Horner
Sat in the corner,
Eating a Christmas pie.
He put in his thumb,
And pulled out a plum,
And said, What a good boy am I!

Once I saw a little bird
Come hop, hop, hop.
And I cried, Little bird,
Will you stop, stop, stop?
I was going to the window
To say, How do you do?
But he shook his little tail,
And away he flew.

One, two, buckle my shoe;
Three, four, knock at the door;
Five, six, pick up sticks;
Seven, eight, lay them straight;
Nine, ten, a big fat hen.

Pease porridge hot,
Pease porridge cold,
Pease porridge in the pot
Nine days old.
Some like it hot,
Some like it cold,
Some like it in the pot
Nine days old.

To market, to market,
To buy a fat pig,
Home again, home again,
Jiggety-jig;

To market, to market,
To buy a fat hog,
Home again, home again,
Jiggety-jog.

Jack Sprat could eat no fat,
His wife could eat no lean,
And so between them both, you see,
They licked the platter clean.

Ladybug, ladybug,
Fly away home,
Your house is on fire
And your children all gone;
All except one
And that's little Ann,
And she crept under
The warming pan.

3. More Mother Goose

Bow, wow, wow,
Whose dog art thou?
Little Tom Tinker's dog,
Bow, wow, wow.

Baa, baa, black sheep,
Have you any wool?
Yes, sir, yes, sir,
Three bags full;
One for my master
And one for the dame,
And one for the little boy
Who lives down the lane.

Higglety, pigglety, pop!
The dog has eaten the mop.
The pig's in a hurry.
The cat's in a flurry.
Higglety, pigglety, pop!

Hickory, dickory, dock,
The mouse ran up the clock.
The clock struck one,
The mouse ran down,
Hickory, dickory, dock.

Hot cross buns!
Hot cross buns!
One a penny,
Two a penny,
Hot cross buns!

Humpty Dumpty sat on a wall,
Humpty Dumpty had a great fall.
All the kings' horses,
And all the kings' men,
Couldn't put Humpty
Together again.

Here am I,
Little Jumping Joan.
When nobody's with me,
I'm all alone.

Jack and Jill
Went up the hill
To fetch a pail of water.
Jack fell down
And broke his crown,
And Jill came tumbling after.

Jack be nimble,

Jack be quick,
Jack jump over
The candle stick.

Little Bo-peep
Has lost her sheep,
And can't tell
Where to find them;
Leave them alone,
And they'll come home,
Wagging their tails
Behind them.

If you have ever been around a child who is a "jump-rope addict," a natural outcome is a collection of jump-rope jingles. The jingles listed in this chapter are the result of my daughter being bitten by the jump-rope bug!

4. Jump-rope Jingles

House to rent,
Inquire within,
When I move out,
Let _____ move in.

Lady, lady at the gate,
Eating cherries from the plate.
How many cherries did she eat?
1, 2, 3, . . .

Bread and butter,
Sugar and spice,
How many boys
Think I am nice?
1, 2, 3, . . .

Up the ladder,
Down the ladder,
A-B-C.
Up the ladder,
Down the ladder,
H-O-T!

Mabel, Mabel,
Set the table.
Don't forget the
Red hot pepper!

Apples, peaches, pears and plums,
Tell me when your birthday comes,
January, February, March, etc.
(Run out when you say the month
of your birthday.)

Piggy on the railroad
Picking up the stones,
Along came a train
And broke Piggy's bones.
Oh, said Piggy.
That's not fair!
Oh, said the driver,
I don't care.

Grace, Grace,
Dressed in lace,

Went upstairs
To powder her face.
How many boxes
Did she use?
1, 2, 3, . . .
———————

Red, white, and blue,
The cat's got the flu,
The dog's got the chicken pox

And so do you!
———————

Last night, the night before,
A lemon and a pickle
Came knocking at my door.
I went down to let them in,
They hit me on the head
With a rolling pin!

Young students are always excited about writing fingerplays which they have previously learned in the classroom. Often they cannot actually read all of the words, but can recall them from memory. Fingerplays are also interesting for older students who enjoy helping in the kindergarten classroom. They will copy the fingerplays and memorize them, giving them a new skill to use with the kindergartners.

5. An excellent source is: Marion Grayson, *Let's Do Fingerplays,* Robert B. Luce, Washington, D.C., 1962. The following list will make a mini-copy book of ten short fingerplays. This same book will be referred to later for an additional eight fingerplays for a larger copy-work book.

6-8. Short and easy-to-read poems can be found in Louise Binder Scott's, *Phonics in Listening, in Speaking, in Reading, in Writing,* Harper and Row, New York, 1962. (This is currently out of print, but copies can be found in college libraries or county and district teacher-professional libraries.)

6. Poems for Fun

7. Poems with Pictures
(Very simple illustrations accompany each of these poems.)

5. Fingerplays

8. Hide-And-Go-Seek Riddles

In the previously mentioned book, *Phonics in Listening, in Speaking, in Reading, in Writing,* there are a total of eighteen short easy-to-read, riddle-poems which involve the child in the process of discovering the hidden vowel or consonant. These can be found on pages 86-87, and 243-244. You can make a copy-work book by using ten of the eighteen riddle-poems, or make up two more and then have a total of twenty, which will give you two copy books of "Hide and Go Seek Riddles."

Additional easy-to-read work books can be made by using *Time for Poetry* as a reference. This book will provide materials for two mini-copy work books. It is also the source for five additional longer copy-work books.

If you can't find this book in the children's section of your local or school library, check your school or county Instructional Materials Center, or college education department, or with your language-arts specialist or consultant. It is such a well-known and loved book, that you should be able to find a copy if you persist. You might even consider buying a copy for yourself. This is an excellent anthology of poetry for primary grades.

9-10. May Hill Arbuthnot and Shelton L. Root, *Time for Poetry,* Scott, Foresman and Company, Glenview, Illinois, 1968.

9. Poems, Poems, Poems

10. Poems for You!

11. One additional source for easy-to-read poems is *Father Fox's Penny-rhymes,* by Clyde Watson, (Scholastic Book Services, New York, 1971). This little paperback book is filled with cute short rhymes. Almost all are ideal for copy-work books for beginning readers.

Larger Copy Work Books: Material for Grades 2-6

The following jump-rope jingles are somewhat longer than those found in the short copy-work books. But, regardless of length, you can almost always be assured that students will enjoy them!

148

1. Jump-rope Jingles for You

Mother, Mother, I am ill.
Send for the doctor,
Over the hill.
In came the doctor,
In came the nurse.
In came the lady
With the alligator purse.
Doctor, Doctor, shall I die?
Yes you must,
And so must I.
Out went the doctor.
Out went the nurse.
Out went the lady
With the alligator purse.
How many pills did the
Doctor give her?
1, 2, 3, . . .

I woke up Monday morning,
I gazed upon the wall.
The spiders and the fireflies
Were playing a game of ball.
The score was ten to twelve,
The spiders were ahead.
The fireflies knocked a home run
And knocked me out of bed!

I went downtown
To the alligator farm.
I sat on the fence
And the fence broke down.
  (Squat down.)
The alligator hit me
By the seat of the pants
And made me do
The houchi-kouchi dance!

Down in the valley
Where the green grass grows,
There sat _____
As sweet as a rose.
She sang, she sang
She sang so sweet,
Then along came _____
And kissed her on the cheek.
How many kisses
Did she receive?
1, 2, 3, . . .

Teddy Bear, Teddy Bear,
Turn around.
Teddy Bear, Teddy Bear,
Touch the ground.
Teddy Bear, Teddy Bear,
Show your shoe.
Teddy Bear, Teddy Bear,
That will do.
Teddy Bear, Teddy Bear,
Go upstairs.
Teddy Bear, Teddy Bear,
Say your prayers.
Teddy Bear, Teddy Bear,
Turn out the light.
Teddy Bear, Teddy Bear,
Say goodnight.

Ice cream soda
And lemonade punch,
Tell me the name
Of your honeybunch.
A, B, C, D, . . . (When you
miss, that's the first initial
of your honeybunch.)

2. More Jump-rope Jingles

Down by the ocean,
Down by the sea,
Johnny broke a bottle
And blamed it on me.
I told Ma
And Ma told Pa,
And Johnny got a licking
So Ha! Ha! Ha!
How many lickings
Did he get?
1, 2, 3, . . .

Three little bad boys
Dressed in white,
Wanted to go to Harvard
On the tail of a kite.
The kite string broke
And down they fell,
They didn't go to Harvard,
They went to ---
Now don't get excited,
And don't turn pale.
They didn't go to Harvard,
They went to Yale.

I had a little brother,
His name was Tiny Tim.
I put him in a bathtub
To see if he could swim.
He drank all the water
And ate all the soap.
And almost died
With a bubble in his throat.

My mother is a butcher,
My father cuts the meat.
I'm a little hot dog
Running down the street.
How many hot dogs can
you eat? 1, 2, 3, . . .

Cinderella, dressed in yellow,
Went upstairs to kiss a fellow.
Made a mistake
And kissed a snake.
How many doctors
Did it take? 1, 2, 3, . . .

I'm a little sailor girl
Dressed in blue.
These are the things
I have to do.
Salute to the Captain,
Bow to the Queen,
And turn my back
To the submarine.

Lincoln, Lincoln,
I've been thinkin'
What on earth
Have you been drinkin'?
Looks like water,
Smells like wine,
Oh, my gosh!
It's turpentine.

My mother and your mother
Live across the way.
Every night they have a fight
And this is what they say:
Acka backa soda cracker
Acka backa boo
Acka backa soda cracker
Out goes you.

Fireman, fireman,
Number Eight,
Hit his head
Against the gate.
The gate flew in,
The gate flew out,
That's the way

He put the fire out.
O-U-T spells out,
And out you go.

Bluebells, cockle shells,
    (Sway rope.)

Eevie, ivy, over!
    (Make rope go all the way over.)
Doctor Brown is a very good man.
Teaches children all he can.
First to read and then to write.
Eevie, ivy I pop out!

---

3. *Let's Do Fingerplays* was referred to on page 147 as a good source of fingerplays appropriate for young children, or for older children to copy and memorize and then teach to young children. The following fingerplays are longer than the ones listed for the short copy-work book.

3. Fingerplays You Can Teach Others

4-8. The poems for the next five "copy work books" can be found in *Time for Poetry*. (See page 148.)

4. Poems About Animals

5. Poems About Children

6. Poems About Nature

7. Poems to Enjoy

8. Poems With Imagination

There Was An Old Man Named
Michael Finnegan .... p. 132
Jonathan .... p. 133
The Folk Who Live in
Backward Town .... p. 135

Another good source for verse for larger copy-work books is *Let's-Read-Together Poems.* Although this book was first published in 1949, it is still in print. It is part of a series designed for choral reading. However, many of these poems are also ideal for copy-work books. This particular book is intended for grades K-2. The series includes a book for each of the grades 3 through 7.

9. Helen A. Brown, *Let's-Read-Together Poems,* Harper and Row, New York, 1949.

9. Poems for Fun

A Coffeepot Face .... p. 5
Naughty Soap Song .... p. 45
Skyscrapers .... p. 53
Whistle .... p. 56
I Love Little Pussy .... p. 68
Catkin .... p. 96
The Dandelion .... p. 97
The Little Plant .... p. 99

Ten other poems which were previously listed in *Time for Poetry* can also be found in *Let's Read Together Poems:* My Dog, Mud, New Shoes, Hippity Hop to Bed, Mice, The Squirrel, The Little Turtle, First Snow, Rain, Snow, Clouds, and The Little Elf.

10. Lucia and James L. Hymes, Jr., *Oodles of Noodles and Other Hymes' Rhymes,* William R. Scott, Inc., New York, 1964. This is a delightful book filled with easy-to-read rhymes, some of which involve a play on words.

11. Ray Wood, *Fun in American Folk Rhymes,* J. B. Lippincott Co., New York, 1952. A book of short humorous poems, which are part of our American heritage. Students find them most amusing.

12. Margaret J. Olson, *Tell and Draw Stories,* Creative Storytime Press, P.O. Box 572, Minneapolis, Minn., 1963. Although you will probably not find this book in your public library, it has been included because of its particular suitability for copy-work booklets. The book presents a series of stories which are illustrated, step by step, with very simple drawings. Younger children are enchanted to learn and repeat the stories for others. Older students enjoy memorizing them and then going to a kindergarten class to present them to small groups.

13a. Duncan Emrich, *The Hodgepodge Book,* Four Winds Press, New York, 1972.

13b. Duncan Emrich, *The Nonsense Book,* Four Winds Press, New York, 1970.

These two books are filled with jokes, riddles, puzzles, superstitions, etc., which have been drawn from American folklore.

14. William Cole, *Pick Me Up: A Book of Short Short Poems,* Macmillan Co., New York, 1972. A collection of very short poems which cover a wide range of topics.

Cursive Copy-Work Books: Material for Grades 3-6

Many of the previous lists can be used for cursive copy books. In addition, selections from the following books are particularly appealing to third, fourth, fifth, and sixth-grade students.

Each of the following lists will provide sufficient material to cover both sides of eight or nine pages in a copy-work book. Some pages will be completely filled, others not, depending on the length of each selection. For cursive booklets it is generally better to ditto paper with the lines running across the widest part, eight lines per page. The same ditto can be used to run handwriting paper for the student's stapled booklets, or they can use regular handwriting paper.

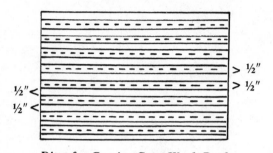

½" <   ½" <   > ½"   > ½"

Ditto for Cursive Copy Work Books

The following two copy-work books incorporate rhymes which are part of our American folk heritage.

1. The first group of rhymes are from *Rocket in My Pocket*, by Carl Withers, Holt, Rinehart and Winston Publishers, New York, 1948.

1. Rhymes and Chants

2. The next collection of rhymes is from *The American Mother Goose*, by Ray Wood, J.B. Lippincott Co., New York, 1940.

2. American Mother Goose

3. The *Guinness Book of World Records*, Bantam Books, New York, always fascinates students. That interest should be capitalized upon and used for cursive copy-work books. Many of the items will need to be slightly paraphrased or abbreviated, but you can be assured that your work will be rewarded with considerable excitement. The following selections are ideal for your first cursive "Guinness Book."

3. Selections from the Guinness Book of World Records

Hair, longest
Fingers, longest nails
Humans, tallest man
            tallest woman
Hiccoughing, most persistent
Moustache, longest
Bread, longest
Cake, largest
Hamburger, largest
Ice Cream Sundae, largest
Speeds, land speed record
Walking, endurance record
Cycling, duration record
Apple Peeling
Balancing on One Foot
House of Cards
Sports, Games and Pastimes, oldest
Bowling, origins
Sports, youngest record breaker
Track, men's world records—running

4. Since tongue twisters are a great challenge to students, a tongue twister copy-work book is always in great demand. The following selections can be found in two books, *Tongue Tanglers*, by Charles Francis Potter, Hale Publishers, Eau Claire, Wisconsin, 1962, and *More Tongue Tanglers*, by the same author and publisher. By using the selections from both books, listed below, you will have one 8-to-9-page copy-work book, with both sides of each page filled.

4. From Tongue Tanglers

From More Tongue Tanglers

5. If your students want more tongue-twister copy books, an excellent source is *A Twister of Twists, A Tangler of Tongues*, by Alvin Schwartz, J. B. Lippincott Co., New York, 1972

6. Gerald L. Wood, *Animal Facts and Feats: A Guinness Record of the Animal Kingdom*, Doubleday and Co., Inc., Garden City, New York, 1972. If the students enjoyed the *Guinness Book of World Records*, they should be delighted with this book of animal records.

7a. Lillian Morrison, *Remember Me When This You See: A Collection of Autograph Verses*, Thomas Y. Crowell Co., New York, 1961.

7b. Lillian Morrison, *Yours Till Niagara Falls: A Collection of Autograph Verses*, Thomas Y. Crowell Co., New York, 1950.

These books provide a wealth of chuckles for students who have been bitten by the "autograph book bug."

8a. Marguerite Kohl and Frederica Young, *More Jokes for Children*, Hill and

Wang, New York, 1966.

8b. Marguerite Kohl and Frederica Young, *Jokes for Children*, Hill and Wang, New York, 1963.

Ideal copy-work booklets for those students who never tire of jokes and riddles.

9a. Sara and John E. Brewton, *Laughable Limericks*, Thomas Y. Crowell Co., New York, 1965.

9b. Edward Lear, *The Complete Nonsense Book*, Dodd, Mead, and Co., New York, 1912.

Some limericks are quite sophisticated. Be certain to take into consideration the level of sophistication of your students as you make the selections to include in your copy-work book.

10. William Cole, *Beastly Boys and Ghastly Girls*, World Publishing Co., New York, 1964.

How delighted students are to read about boys and girls who do not always behave as they should! A marvelous collection of poems! You may wish to include only one, two, or three of these lengthy poems in a single copy work-book.

11. William Cole, *Humorous Poetry for Children*, World Publishing Co., New York, 1955.

A collection of poems, filled with humor and sufficient sophistication to entice fourth, fifth and sixth grade students.

12. Fred Ferretti, *The Great American Book of Sidewalk, Stoop, Dirt, Curb, and Alley*, Workman Publishing Co., New York, 1975.

This is a marvelous reference book of children's games: variations on hopscotch, marbles, jump rope, jacks, four-square, etc., etc., etc. The students can use their copy-work book to learn new games, review rules, etc. The book can also serve to refresh your memory of some of the games you played in your own childhood. You may wish to teach some to your students. In return they can show you some of the more popular games they enjoy. Later you might want to make a copy-work book containing the rules of their games. (A note of caution: a few of the games in this book could prove to be dangerous, so use discretion.)

13. Maria Leach, *Noodles, Nitwits, and Numskulls*, World Publishing Co., New York, 1961.

A series of absurd and hilarious short folktales, which make a delightful copy-work book.

14. Bring in a collection of poem books, and encourage students to compile a collection of their favorites. Helen A. Brown, *Let's-Read-Together Poems*, Harper and Row, 1950, would be good to use in this way.

15. Ask students to bring copies of the lyrics of current popular songs. Write these in cursive. You will have an "instant success" copy-work book.

Notes

1. Louise Binder Scott and J. J. Thompson, *Phonics in Listening, in Speaking, in Reading, and Writing*, McGraw-Hill, New York, 1962, pp. 289-304.
2. Louise Binder Scott, *My First Writing Book*, McGraw-Hill, New York, 1968.
3. Susan Ryono, *Handwriting Hints from*

Harvey Hippo and His Henchmen, Frank Schaffer Publishing Company, Palo Verdes Peninsula, California, 1975.

4. June Mullins, Florence Joseph, Caroline Turner, Robert Zawadzski, and Larry Saltzman, "A Handwriting Model for Children with Learning Disabilities," *Journal of Learning Disabilities,* May, 1972, 5: 305-311.

5. Florence Joseph, Beate Vogel, Caroline Turner, and June Mullins, *Total Communication,* Mafex Associates, Johnstown, Pennsylvania, 1973.

6. Harry B. Wright, *Lettering,* Pitman Publishing Company, New York, 1962.

7. Marilyn Austin and Marian Hickman, Teachers, Novato Unified School District, Novato, California.

CHAPTER X

Creative Writing

Introduction

The intent of this chapter is to provide detailed information about materials and methods for one component of the language-arts program, often neglected but very important: creative writing. It is hoped that this information will help you structure a successful creative writing center, enabling students to develop many necessary writing skills. A further aim is to provide a format for the other language-arts components (letter writing, poetry, oral language, reference work and reports, etc.)

There has been much concern voiced about students' lack of basic writing skills. If students are to become adept at putting their thoughts on paper, it is important that they have frequent creative-writing experiences. When students write every day, or every other day, creative writing simply becomes an extension of thinking and speaking. It is not perceived as a threatening experience but instead as an enjoyable one. Concomitantly, the development of basic-writing skills takes place because of this practice.

In many primary classrooms students seldom have the opportunity to write. Then they are suddenly expected to write quality reports and creative stories in the upper grades. This can be extremely difficult if not impossible, if their exposure to writing has been limited. Compounding the problem at the upper-grade level is the students' self consciousness and concern about peer relations. The enthusiasm and spontaneity which could have been tapped so easily a few years earlier are now somewhat dampened. Creative writing becomes a threat.

Another factor which often inhibits successful creative writing experiences is a limit on the time a student may spend on a story. The child is given a topic on which to write—one which may be of little interest.

Then the student is told to complete a story on this topic in the next 45 minutes. Is it any wonder that students do not get involved in their stories?

Speed only comes from a sound base after many years of practice. Thus, at the elementary school level, when we are attempting to build initial writing skills, speed and time limitations generally are unwise. This is not to imply that one sentence a day will be considered acceptable. The standards set should apply to the circumstances and the individual students.

Through on-going assignments at the Creative Writing Center, the student is encouraged to become involved, and to take the time and effort to do the best work of which he or she is capable. In most cases a student should choose a topic of strong personal interest and begin to write the story. When the allotted center time is completed, the child should continue to work until reaching a comfortable stopping point. The story is continued for as many days as is necessary for the student to feel satisfied.

In addition to having students write frequently (every day or every other day), and providing flexibility in the time a student spends on any given story, a successful Creative Writing Center demands that the teacher have at hand a wide variety of techniques and materials. These make creative writing an exciting subject which children enjoy and through which they can acquire many necessary skills.

The material which follows in this chapter is intended to help fill this need.

Readiness Activities

At the readiness level it is extremely im-portant for children to become aware of the relationship between spoken words and the corresponding written symbols. A weekly dictated newspaper is a vivid demonstration of this relationship. It is meaningful to children and an experience they greatly enjoy.

Monday is an excellent day for this. Most students can report on a weekend activity. It may be nothing more than having played with a friend. But to them it is important.

This center should initially be supervised by the teacher. Once the students are familiar with the procedure and are comfortable dictating, the center can be turned over to an aide.

Explain to the children that they are going to make a newspaper which they may take home to their parents. Within reason, they may tell you anything that is important to them. You will record what they say on a ditto master. If they wish, they may add accompanying illustrations. Later you will duplicate the ditto masters. (Show them how the ditto master works, and let them see a duplicating machine in action if possible.) The newspaper will then be stapled together so that each person will get a copy of what everyone said. You will read them the newspaper, and then they each may take a copy home to share with their families.

As soon as one child has finished dictating, ask if the student would like to draw a picture to go with the story. If so, allow a space on the ditto master for the picture. Then draw a line. Tell the student to draw a picture in the allocated space, but to leave the rest of the ditto blank, as that will be used for someone else's story. While the student draws a picture, use another ditto master to record the next child's story. (You will usually have space for two to four stories and illustrations on each ditto.)

If kindergarten students are dictating

newspapers early in the year when the centers are free-flowing, keep a class list and check off the names of those who have dictated. When you run out of children who have come to you to dictate, circulate about the room. Ask those who have not dictated if they would like to tell something to go in the newspaper. If a student seems hesitant, do not coerce! Instead you can ask leading questions. See if you can help the child to discover something to include in the paper even if it's only a brief sentence.

If it is possible to have an aide duplicate and collate the newspaper that day, it is particularly nice to be able to read it to the children and send it home with them on the same day that they wrote it. If this is done each week, parents will comment on various events they have been following in the newspaper, such as a trip a child may be taking.

Each week a little more information is added. Then the big day comes. You get a report of where the student went, what was seen, etc. Many families will keep the entire year's collection of newspapers. The students will bring a copy to you a year later and say, "Look, now I can read the newspaper we wrote! Do you remember when I wrote this?"

Because the student is talking about and sharing with others experiences which are of great personal interest, this is a popular activity.

Another dictating experience which the children enjoy (and which helps keep parents informed about the current activities in the classroom) is a daily log. At the close of each day, take large heavy chart paper and ask the students what things were new that day, which things they most enjoyed, etc. Write the date on the chart paper and a brief account (experience story) of their remarks about that day.

> Kindergarten Newspaper
> October 26
>
> Marilyn - We're going fishing to Clear Lake and we're going to go camping and spend the night.
>
> Will - Yesterday we went to go get our pumpkins. We got three. My dad is the only one that gets to cut them. For Halloween I'm going to be a ghost whose name is Gus.
>
>
>
> John - I slept over at my friend's house. My two brothers slept over too because mom and dad were going some place. We ate over there. John

Kindergarten-dictated newspaper

At the end of the week this information can be transferred to a ditto master, duplicated and included in Monday's newspaper as a summary of the preceding week's activities.

If you save the chart stories, then, prior to Open House in the spring, these can be assembled into a large book. It becomes a record of the entire year. Both parents and students enjoy reading this over-sized book.

Students are also delighted if someone will type their dictated stories. They may want to tell about personal experiences. Or they may prefer to select a picture and then make up a story about it. If the person typing begins the story in the middle of the page, the student can use the top half for illustrations. Each student's stories can be compiled into a book. Or they can be sent home as individual stories.

In addition to this type of experience, young children enjoy making simple books about related material. A fun book to start at the beginning of the school year is one about seasons. As the leaves turn into the beautiful fall colors and the weather turns crisp, it is an ideal time to discuss seasons with the students. Have them talk about the signs of fall they are currently observing. Then have the class take a "fall walk" through the neighborhood. Take the time to have discussions, regarding their observations during your walk.

When the students return to the classroom, each should be given a stapled book which consists of five 9"×12" pages. The cover should read, "My Book About Seasons," with the student's name on the front. The student should be directed to turn to the first page, and draw a picture of something which has to do with fall. The child should then dictate to a helper a sentence or several sentences about fall. This can be handled quite effectively by having four or five fifth or sixth-grade students take dictation. Or you can take a walk at the beginning of the day and then have dictation as one of the centers for that day.

After the "fall" dictation, the books are put away. The same procedure is repeated in the winter and spring. At the end of the school year, discuss summer and then have them finish their book. This is a particularly interesting book, since it reflects the student's growth during the entire school year.

An "All About Me" book can be made by following the same general format. Each student draws pictures and dictates about family, house, pets, friends; things which are easy to do, things which are hard to do, etc.

Another book, which can be quite successful early in the year, is about shapes. One shape should be discussed and the children should then make observations. This is followed by drawing a picture which incorporates the shape, and then dictating: . . . "A door is a rectangle". . . "Windows are rectangles . . ." Additions can be made to this book once or twice each week. In a few weeks the book is compiled and can be taken home. Somehow, a book is much more interesting to take home than a series of single pages.

The book about shapes leads into classification and class booklets, discussed on pages 176-177.

Introducing First-Grade Students to Creative Writing

An excellent time to introduce first graders to writing their own stories is when the students return to school after Christmas vacation. They are bursting with excitement to talk about what they received for Christmas or Hanukkah. This is the ideal moment to capture that enthusiasm and begin having them put their thoughts on paper.

Creative writing should be introduced in as simple a format as possible, so that it does not overwhelm the children. This can be accomplished by writing on the chalkboard:

"My favorite Christmas (or Hanukkah) present was _____." Instruct the students that, instead of telling you about their favorite present, they are going to write about it.

When they get to the Writing Center, they are to copy the sentence on the board and fill in the blank. Then they are to write a sentence telling why this was their favorite gift, what they can do with it, etc.

Be certain to supervise the writing center that day so that you can provide the necessary assistance and support. Have small slips of paper available. When students need a word, they bring a slip of paper for you to write the word. This is always a successful first-writing experience.

The same day, at a different center, the students should be introduced to their individual dictionaries. (See the following section in this chapter.)

The next day, the following is on the board:

"If I were an animal, I would like
to be a _____ because . . ."

Once more they copy from the board, fill in the blank and then complete the statement.

A fun assignment for the next day is to have them draw an imaginary animal:

"My name is _____"
"I make a noise that goes _____"
"I live in a _____"
"I like to _____"

With this longer assignment, the on-going work can begin. Tell the students that some will finish the work today, while others may want to continue the story for a day or two—particularly if they expand on the subject "I like to _____."

The next day introduce the first short creative writing story-starter ditto. (See pages 178-180.) Follow the suggestions for "brainstorming" (described throughout this chapter). Then tell the students that they may continue on their story from the day before. Or, if that is finished, they can begin working on the story-starter ditto.

Over the next several days, introduce other story-starter dittos, mounted pictures, several of the beginning phrases from the Creative Writing Chart, etc. (See pages 180-181.)

It should be stressed at this point that all the materials will remain available. Tell them it is much better to spend several days on one story and do a good job than it is to rush through an assignment so they can begin a new one. Soon, the students realize that there will be a variety of material for them to choose from, when they finish one story, and that there is no need to rush. The Writing Center is now on-going.

Individual Student Dictionaries

Often when students are required to use commercial dictionaries during creative writing, the process of finding the needed word is so long and tedious, that by the time the children locate the word they have forgotten what they wanted to write! The result is that dictionaries become a barrier to effective creative writing.

Recognizing the importance of developing dictionary skills, specific assignments, using commercial dictionaries, should be given. However, these assignments should not be associated with creative writing.

Later, with increased skills, the student will be able effectively to use a commercial dictionary as an aid during writing. In the meanwhile, if the students are to have success in creative writing, they need to be able to locate the correct spelling for needed words easily and quickly. Individual dictionaries make this possible. Therefore they are one of the most important ingredients of a successful Creative Writing Center.

Two separate lists which are appropriate for individual dictionaries follow. One is intended for use with primary students, and the other for upper-grade students.

Words For First-Third Grade
Individual Dictionaries

The following word list is a combination of the first 254 words of highest frequency used in children's writing as determined by Henry D. Risland (1), and the 220 Basic Sight Vocabulary Words selected by Edward W. Dolch (2).

a	before	come	far	grade	is	man	once
about	best	coming	fast	great	it	many	one
after	better	could	father	green	its	may	only
again	big	country	few	grow		me	open
all	black	cut	find		jump	men	or
along	blue		first		just	milk	other
also	book	daddy	five	had		more	our
always	both	day	fly	happy	keep	morning	out
am	boy	days	for	has	kind	most	over
an	boys	dear	found	have	know	mother	own
and	bring	did	four	he		much	
another	brother	didn't	friend	heard	large	must	people
any	brown	do	from	help	last	my	pick
are	but	does	full	her	laugh	myself	place
around	buy	dog	fun	here	let		play
as	by	doll	funny	him	letter	name	played
ask		done		his	light	never	please
asked		don't	gave	hold	like	new	pretty
at	call	door	get	home	little	next	pull
ate	called	down	getting	hope	live	nice	put
away	came	draw	girl	hot	long	night	
	can	drink	girls	house	look	no	ran
	car		give	how	looked	not	read
baby	carry	each	glad	hurt	lot	now	red
back	cat	eat	go		lots		ride
ball	children	eight	goes	I	love	of	right
be	Christmas	every	going	if		off	room
because	clean		good	I'm	made	old	round
bed	close		got	in	make	on	run
been	cold	fall		into			

162

said	sit	sure	there	today	upon	way	why
Santa Claus	six		these	together	us	we	will
saw	sleep	take	they	told	use	week	wish
say	small	teacher	thing	too		well	with
school	snow	tell	things	took	very	went	work
see	so	ten	think	town		were	would
seven	some	than	this	tree	walk	what	write
shall	something	thank	those	try	want'	when	
she	soon	that	thought	two	wanted	where	year
should	start	the	three		warm	which	years
show	started	their	through	under	was	while	yellow
sing	stop	them	time	until	wash	white	yes
sister	summer	then	to	up	water	who	you
							your

Words For Upper-Grade Individual Dictionaries

This word list combines the first 260 words from the Kucera-Francis word list (3), composed of words most used in newspapers, magazines and books, and the words on the previous individual dictionary list (Rinsland and Dolch). After the lists were combined, the easier words were omitted as well as words which might be associated with younger children (Santa Claus, baby, ball, etc.).

about	asked	boys	clean	door	face	funny	hand
after	away	bring	close	down	fact		happy
again		brother	cold	draw	far	gave	have
against	back	brown	come	drink	father	general	head
all	being	business	coming	during	few	getting	heard
almost	because	buy	could		find	girls	help
along	become	by	course		first	give	her
also	been		country	each	fly	given	here
always	before	called		early	for	goes	high
American	best	came	days		form	going	himself
among	better	car	dear	eat	found	good	hold
another	between	carry	didn't	eight	four	government	home
any	black	case	do	end	friend	grade	hope
are	blue	children	does	enough	from	great	house
around	book	Christmas	done	even	full	group	how
ask	both	city	don't	every	fun	grow	however
				eyes			

hurt	made	of	president	sleep	things	used	will
	make	off	pretty	small	think		wish
important	many	often	program	snow	this		within
its	may	old	public	social	those	very	without
it's	men	once	pull	some	though		work
	might	one	put	something	thought	walk	world
just	more	only		soon	three	want	would
	morning	open	rather	started	through	wanted	write
kind	most	or	read	state	time	war	
knew	mother	order	right	states	today	warm	year
know	Mr.	other	room	still	together	was	yellow
	Mrs.	our	round	such	told	wash	yet
large	much	out		summer	too	water	you
last	must	over	said	sure	took	way	young
later	myself	own	same	system	toward	week	your
laugh			saw		town	well	
left	national	part	say	take	tree	went	
less	need	people	school	teacher	try	were	
letter	never	per	second	than	two	what	
life	new	pick	set	thank		when	
light	next	place	several	their	under	where	
like	nice	played	shall	them	until	which	
little	night	please	should	then	united	while	
live	nothing	point	show	there	upon	white	
long	now	possible	since	these	us	who	
looked	number	present	sister	they	use	why	

Individual dictionaries can be made by assembling a stapled booklet for each child with twenty-six blank pages and a cover from wallpaper or construction paper. The student's first task is to write a letter of the alphabet in sequence on each page, e.g. "Aa" on the first page, "Bb" on the second page, etc.

Each student is then given a ditto on which the words for the dictionary have been written or typed, grouped according to the first letter in the words.

The block of "Aa" letters can be cut out and pasted on the "Aa" page, and so on through the alphabet.

For your convenience, pages of this type (for both dictionary lists) are available in the supplement to this book, in a black, large print, reproducible format.

An alternate method for constructing individual dictionaries consists of typing a ditto master for each letter of the alphabet, e.g., an "Aa" page with the corresponding "a" words, a "Bb" page with the corresponding "b" words. Duplicate the twenty-six dittos for each child, collate, cover and staple together.

Either of these methods will result in a dictionary composed of high frequency words for each student. Do not have students copy the entire list of words in the dictionary. If this is expected of them, by the time they finish the process you can be sure they will dislike dictionaries!

a	baby	call	daddy
about	back	called	day
after	ball	came	days
again	be	can	dear
all	because	car	did
along	bed	carry	didn't
also	been	cat	do
always	before	children	does
am	best	Christmas	dog
an	better	clean	doll
and	big	close	done
another	black	cold	don't
any	blue	come	door
are	book	coming	down
around	both	could	draw
as	boy	country	drink
ask	boys	cut	
asked	bring		
at	brother		fall
ate	brown	each	far
away	but	eat	fast
	buy	eight	father
	by	every	few
			find

Duplicated page for cut and paste student dictionary

Additional words the students need for writing are written in their individual dictionaries throughout the year. This results in each child having a personalized dictionary. These are taken home at the end of the school year as an encouragement to continue writing over the summer.

It is extremely helpful if the dictionary is divided into thirds, using a different color paper for each section. By assembling the dictionary in this way, you can continuously reinforce the dictionary concept, "Is the word in the beginning, middle, or end of the dictionary?"

There should be an alphabet strip displayed near the Writing Center. To help the student learn to find words easily in the personalized dictionary, place colored paper borders behind the three sections of the alphabet strip. These colored borders should correspond to the colored sections of the dictionary. When a student wonders where the "Ss" page is in this dictionary, a glance at the displayed alphabet strip will quickly show that "Ss" is bordered with pink. Therefore the "Ss" words will be in the pink section, the final third of the dictionary. Before long the students find the correct page in their dictionaries with little or no trouble.

If colored paper for the dictionaries is not available, the same thing can be accomplished by using white ditto paper or a composition book. The color-coded sections can then be indicated by having the students use a ruler and crayon to draw a colored line along the right hand edge of each page. This creates a ¼" to ⅓" margin. (One color should be used for the first third of the dictionary, a different color for the middle third, etc.)

The individual dictionaries can effectively be introduced to seven or eight students at a center. The center may either be supervised by a teacher or an aide. The following procedure should be used.

1. The students should discover how the dictionary is assembled (Aa page, the Bb page, etc.).
2. The three colored divisions of the dictionary should be pointed out, along with the correlation to the colored borders around the displayed alphabet strip. The students should then practice applying this knowledge:
   a) Where would you find "m?" (in the middle blue section.)
   b) Where would you find a word that began with "f?", etc.
3. Practice should then be given on actually finding designated pages in their dictionaries:
   a) Find the "o" page.
   b) Find the "t" page in your dictionary, etc.
   (Be certain to watch for any students who take a long time to locate the page, and provide help as needed.)
4. Next direct them to find given words:
   a) Find the word "because" in your dictionary.
   b) Find the word "something," etc.
5. Finally, ask each child to find a different word.
   a) Sally, find the word "want." Tom, find the word "your," etc.

The purpose of this introduction is to acquaint students with how to use their dictionaries so that the following day the individual dictionaries can become an integral part of the Creative Writing Center. After this initial introduction, the rule at Creative Writing should be that the student first turns to the correct page to see if the word needed is listed. If not, the child should bring the dictionary, turned to the correct page, to the person supervising the center, who will then write the word for the student.

By insisting that the student have the dictionary turned to the correct page when asking for a word to be written, automatic practice on alphabetizing skills and facility with the dictionary is provided.

If a student is experiencing difficulties or generally needs a great deal of support at the Writing Center, you should help in any way possible. (This may include helping the child find the correct page.)

It is interesting to observe the words which accumulate in each student's dictionary. You can almost determine to whom a dictionary belongs by looking at the words which have been written in it. One child may have words like dinosaur, Brontosaurus, monster, etc., while another one has race track, motorcycle, engine, etc. The individual dictionary makes it possible for a student to accumulate those words which are personally important and which are frequently used. You will also find that students are a great help to each other. One will say, "Do you have the word 'Tyrannosaurus Rex' in your dictionary?" and the other student will reply, "Sure, let me find it for you."

Many teachers have stated that the introduction of individualized dictionaries proved to be a real stimulus for creative writing. This helped get their Creative Writing Centers off the ground.

Class Booklets

Mentioned earlier in this chapter was the avoidance of threatening or overwhelming assignments for primary children. This same rule applies to upper-grade students. It is important to remember that they may have had unpleasant prior experiences and, as a result, dislike creative writing.

The first step in this case is to convince them that creative writing can be interesting and fun. It does not have to be overwhelming. As always, assignments which assure success initially augur well for the future. Although little writing may be involved, call these assignments "Creative Writing." The students' reaction will be positive: "Oh, if this is Creative Writing, I can do it. This is different than what I thought it would be." Gradually you can take advantage of the students' growing sense of self-confidence and make assignments more challenging.

Class booklets are ideal for these beginning high-success experiences. Because each student is required to complete only one illustrated page, with minimal writing, the experience is non-threatening.

All of the students' pages are assembled and stapled into a book. It is read to the entire class and becomes part of the class library. Each student has a sense of accomplishment as the completed book is there for all to see!

After several class booklets have been made, you should begin other creative writing assignments, such as those suggested in the next section, "Materials and Methods." Too much of anything can get tiring, but the booklets are ideal as a starter and are fun to return to periodically during the year.

If the students are to have successful experiences, it is important that you take the time to introduce thoroughly each writing experience. This should be followed by a brainstorm session with the children. Extract ideas and suggestions and more ideas and suggestions from them, until everyone is excitedly waving a hand with an idea. At this point, stop the brainstorming and tell them to save the idea. They may want to use it for Creative Writing. Or they may think up something completely different.

What is important is for the students to feel secure when they go to the Creative Writing Center. Their problem should not be "What am I going to write about?" but instead, "I have so many good ideas, it's hard to decide which one to write about!" This is the beginning of success!

Have a stack of 6"×9" paper at the Creative Writing Center. Prior to putting the paper at the center, fold a margin of approximately ¾ of an inch. Tell the students not to write in the folded margin, which will be used to staple the pages together. If they write in the margin, some of their words will be hidden.

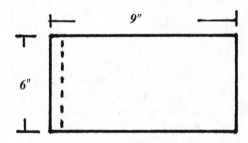

Page for class booklet
with folded margin

In addition to the 6"×9" paper, you should have tagboard markers, approximately 1¼"×8". These can greatly assist students in writing in a straight line. The child lays a marker across the page and uses it as the equivalent of a bottom line, on which all letters stand. As each line of writing is completed, the marker is moved downward on the paper.

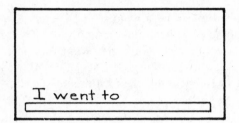

Using a marker for writing

When writing a letter which has a tail (y, g, j, etc.), the student slides the marker out of the way, in order to complete the tail stroke, and then replaces it and continues writing.

Often the stimulus for a class booklet will come from a book. In this case read several pages so that the students can discover the basic repetitive format. Then suggest that they try to write a book, using the same type of format.

If you want the students to start their writing with a particular phrase, be certain to write it on the chalkboard so they can refer to it as needed.

After they have written their books, you will find the students are greatly interested in hearing the original book read in its entirety. In addition, the book becomes of high interest if left in a place where the students have access to it.

The following illustrates the basic procedure for introducing and making class booklets.

A Good Thing to Be . . . and A Good Thing Not To Be

Get a copy from the library of the book, *Open House for Butterflies,* by Ruth Krauss

(4). Many of the pages in the book begin with the phrase, "A good thing to be _____," "A good thing not to be _____," or "A good thing to know _____." Mark these pages so you can easily find them. Also write these three phrases on the chalk-board. Read four or five examples from the book to the students. Then suggest that they try to think up some things starting with one of those phrases. Typical responses will be, "A good thing not to be is a tooth, because you might get lost." Or, "A good thing not to be is an ant, because you might get stepped on." Continue brainstorming until everyone has the idea. Tell them that, when they get to the Creative Writing Center, they should write their ideas near the bottom edge of one 6″×9″ paper, and use the upper portion to illustrate. You will be in for some surprises. The following are from a second grade class:

A good thing to be is a rotten egg,
because you won't get eaten.

A good thing not to be is a tree.
You might end up a two by four.

A good thing to know is when you'll die,
so you can start praying.

Everyone should make at least one page for the class booklet, and more if there is time. The entire time at the Creative Writing Center should be spent on contributions for the class booklet. It is important to stress that you would rather have one page done neatly than four sloppy pages. Inform them that the book will become part of the class-room library, so others will be reading it. Therefore it is important that people can read the writing!

At the end of the centers, collect all of the pages and staple them together with a front and back cover of construction paper or wallpaper. Proof-read the booklet to make certain that each page is legible. Read the book to the entire class at the end of the day. There will be many chuckles of delight, and you will have had a successful beginning "Creative Writing experience!"

In summary:

1. Introduce the idea and format and give examples, preferably both verbal and visual.
2. Brainstorm.
3. Write beginning phrase or phrases on chalkboard.
4. Have each student make at least one page.
5. Assemble pages into a booklet.
6. Proof-read.
7. Read booklet to students.
8. Add booklet to classroom library.
9. If stimulus was a commercial book, display the book where students have access to it.

If students are inclined to copy ideas, assemble the booklet so several pages of the same idea come one after another. Then ask students if that makes an interesting book. They will almost always say that it's more interesting if all the pages are different. Tell them that, in the future, if there are two or more of the same page, you will select only one for the class booklet. Generally this solves the copying problem.

Our Topsy-Turvy Book

Fold a ¾" margin in pieces of 9"×12" white construction paper. Then fold the paper in half. Have the students make a silhouette picture by putting some black tempera near the center of the paper and then folding the other half of the paper over the paint. A "blob" type of picture should result. You do not want the paint to spread into thin, wavy lines. Therefore, you will need to experiment to determine the correct consistency.

The student should look at the picture and decide what it seems to be. The child should write this underneath the picture, then rotate the paper a quarter turn, decide what the picture looks like from that angle, and write this underneath. The student should continue rotating the picture, deciding what it looks like from all four angles.

Topsy-turvy picture

Tell students if they rotate the picture to one side and it doesn't look like anything, to ask several of the other students around them if it looks like something to them. (This is a good way to stress helping each other.)

If no one can figure out something for the picture from that angle, they should just leave that side blank and not worry about it. It's amazing how many different shapes the black paint forms on the paper, and how much each silhouette changes as it is rotated.

The students always enjoy making, reading and re-reading this book, regardless of age level.

Happiness Is . . .
Being Sad Means . . .
Anger Is . .

Use 6″×9″ paper with a folded margin for each of these. Students always have definite ideas ready to be tapped for any one of these books!

Lucky/Unlucky Book

If possible, buy a copy of *Ziggy's Lucky/Unlucky Book,* by Tom Wilson (5). You may be able to find this at a stationery store which carries a wide selection of greeting cards.

Read several pages to the students so that they become aware of the pattern. One page starts, "Lucky is ____," and the following page begins, "Unlucky is ____." Point out that sometimes words and pictures are used to illustrate the situation. Other times, only pictures are needed. Use 6″×9″ paper. Have the students write and illustrate their "Lucky is ____" comment on one side of the paper. On the reverse side, they should write and/or illustrate their "Unlucky is ____" situation. This makes an especially amusing class book!

Our Alphabet Zoo

Send for a copy of *Alphabet Zoo,* by Hugh A. Wayne (6). This book is composed of imaginary animals for each letter of the alphabet with an accompanying zany rhyme.

Read the entire book to the students and then suggest that they make their own Alphabet Zoo Book. Have each student select one letter of the alphabet. (If you have more than twenty-six students, some letters can be used twice: "E is also for ____.") Students should illustrate their animals and write their rhymes or explanations on 9″×12″ construction paper. These are then alphabetized, and assembled into a hilarious class booklet.

The next five class booklets are particularly suited for primary grades, or they can be made by upper-grade students for primary grade classes. If done in the upper grades, have several of the students take the booklet to one of the kindergarten or first-grade classrooms, read it to them, and then leave it for their enjoyment.

The Hole Book

Linda Rowe and Marilyn Schaffer (7), have their students make "Hole Class Booklets" by giving each student a piece of 9″×12″ construction paper with a hole. (The holes can be cut in the same place on each piece, resulting in a hole which goes all the way through the book when the pages are assembled. Or the holes may be cut in different places.) The students are to draw pictures which incorporate the hole in some way. The hole may be a wheel, a balloon, a porthole on a ship, etc. Then they are to write a story about their picture, ending with the phrase, "____ and that's my hole story."

A Hole Is to Dig

Read several pages of Ruth Krauss' book, *A Hole Is To Dig* (8), to the students so that they perceive the pattern. Words are defined by their function, or what they are for. Then suggest that they try to tell what some things are for. That word "for" seems to help them get underway. Delightful responses will follow:

Buttons are to hold on your shirt
so your stomach doesn't show.

An umbrella is to keep the rain
out of the way.

A wig is to wear on your head
if your hair looks ugly.

Babies are for changing diapers.

This format of writing comments on the lower part of the paper and then illustrating on the upper half of the paper should be followed.

This class booklet is even successful in Kindergarten. The students dictate their comments.

If I Weren't Me, I'd Like to Be . . .

Read several pages from *I Like to Be Me*, by Barbara Bel Geddes (9) so that the children can discover the pattern. In this case the children think about a series of things they would like to be if they were not themselves.

Use 6"×9" paper. Have the students draw a picture of themselves on the front of the paper and write, "If I weren't me I'd like to be." Then they should turn the paper over, complete the statement (what and why) and illustrate it.

If I weren't me, I'd like to be a baby
so I could drink out of a bottle.

(Guess who had a new baby
in the family!)

If I weren't me I'd like to be a gopher,
so I could dig under the ground.

What Are Colors For?

Have students write sentences naming things they associate with a specific color. Encourage them to use at least one descriptive word.

Red is for a crunchy apple
Red is for Rudolph's shiny nose.

If I Were _____ , I Would

Have the students start their sentences with the phrase, "If I were _____ , I would." You may want to use 6"×12" paper for this book, for a change of pace.

If I were a door, I would slam.

If I were a turkey, I would run away
on Thanksgiving Day.

If I were Santa Claus, I would go
through the window.

If I were a house, I would keep
the people warm.

Word Balloons

A word-balloon class booklet is great fun for students of all ages. Explain to the students the main components of cartoons.

*Someone is
talking.*

*Someone is thinking or dreaming. This can be
indicated by words or pictures.*

*The person
has an idea.*

*The person
is sleeping.*

Often students have seen these symbols, but have not really understood them. Have them draw a picture on a piece of 6″×9″ paper. Include a word balloon as part of the picture. These can be mounted on colored construction paper and used as a bulletin board in the classroom. Later they can be assembled into a booklet to become part of the class library.

Facility with this skill becomes especially valuable when students begin illustrating their own stories and books.

Riddles

Although riddles aren't creative writing, they are appropriate for class booklets.

Several days before the booklet is to be made, tell each of the students to find a riddle that they particularly like. Have lots of riddle books available in the room and encourage them to talk to their friends about their favorite riddles, etc.

When riddle day arrives, you should have large 12″×18″ colored construction paper, smaller pieces of colored construction paper, paste, paste brushes, scissors and pencils at the Creative Writing Center.

Students each choose a riddle, and write it on the top of a piece of 12″×18″ construction paper. They illustrate their riddles by making cut-and-paste pictures. No crayons are allowed. Somewhere on each paper they should hide the answer to their riddle. (They become quite ingenious: doors open, drawers pull out, pull-out tabs, etc.) This is always a very popular class booklet.

After students have written some of the short class booklets, you can assign booklets which involve having the student write an entire page, but still in a simple format.

More Challenging Class Booklets

Fun Is . . .

This booklet consists of an entire page written by each student. The student is to begin each line, "Fun is . . .". The following two examples were written by second graders.

Fun is sliding down a big pile of snow!
Fun is having math corrections!
Fun is doing art like my big sister Paki!
Fun is calling someone!
Fun is having my arm around Brandy, Kim, Natty, Lexa and Crystal!
Fun is going into a big big big forest and woods!
Fun is going swimming!
Fun is getting presents for me!
Fun is love!
Fun is not hearing anything!
Fun is playing nurse!
Fun is having kittens and cats!
Fun is getting a new dog!
Fun is having lots of toys!
Fun is having fun!

—Juneko Robinson

Fun is catching lizards and snakes.
Fun is doing Math.
Fun is playing soak 'em.
Fun is going home from school.
Fun is riding my bike.
Fun is playing cops and robbers in the night.
Fun is going to my friends.
Fun is Mark!

—Mark Gregory

A Friend Is . . .

Use the same format as *Fun is . . .* You will get some introspective and observant statements.

The Important Book

Read several pages of *The Important Book,* by Margaret Wise Brown (10). The students discover that each page begins by describing the most important characteristic of something. It continues by telling many other things about the object. Then the final statement is a repetition of the first statement.

Write on the chalkboard, "The important thing about . . ." Leave quite a lot of space, and then write, "But the important thing about . . ."

Have the students brainstorm several of these with you before they are asked to do one by themselves. "Let's make up one about a tree. What do you think is most important thing about a tree?" They may decide that the most important thing is that it provides shade when you are hot. Or an argument may erupt. Some will feel that it is more important that the wood from trees can be made to build things. This is the ideal time to say that different people will think differently about what is more important. This can be translated into: "When you are doing the writing, you should choose whatever is most important to you!"

The important thing about hair is that it grows long. It is curly. It is straight. It can be blonde. It can be black. It can be red. It can be brown. It can be brushed. It can be combed. It can be pulled! It could be cut into a shag. It can be a pony tail. But the most important thing about hair is that it grows long.

Kim Drummond
Second Grade

Point out the phrases on the board, which they are going to use for their assignment at Creative Writing. To avoid repetitions, each student should write a topic title on the chalkboard. As new groups rotate to the Creative Writing Center, the board should be checked to make certain that a topic has not already been chosen.

Classroom Newspaper

The section in this chapter, which dealt with readiness activities, described the process of making a weekly class newspaper in which students reported on their activities. (See pages 158-159.)

The same process can be used with the students doing the actual writing on ditto masters. To help them write neatly, make the following ditto master.

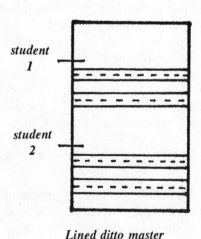

Lined ditto master
for newspaper

This should be duplicated on other ditto masters. The lines provide a frame of reference for writing, but will not show up when the ditto is duplicated.

I Used to Be . . . But Now . . .

An excellent source for ideas for class booklets is Kenneth Koch's book, *Wishes, Lies, and Dreams* (11). One fun example in the book is having students start a line, "I used to be ___." The following line begins "But now ___." The following were written by second grade students.

I used to be dry diapers,
But now I am wet diapers.

I used to be in a house
But now I am in the dump.

I used to be a weinersnitzel,
But now I am a hot dog.

I used to be a mouse
But now I am a rat.

Steven Masterson

I used to be a puppy
But now I am a dog.

I used to be a tooth
But now I am a cavity.

I used to be a car
But now I am a truck.

I used to be an ocean
But now I'm a lake.

I used to be a classroom
But now I am a teacher.

Craig

After students have written humorous "I used to be" pages, return to the topic later. This time ask them to write a true page of "I used to be ＿＿. But now ＿＿."

Students become aware of their own growth through this exercise, making it a valuable creative writing assignment.

I used to have a sore throat
But now I have no sore throat.

I used to think I was short
But now I am tall.

I used to be slow
But now I am fast.

I used to think calendars told years
But they tell the month.

I used to think 20 was 50, and 50 was 20.
But now I know.

Paul Jakobsen
Second Grade

Individual Booklets

To bridge the gap between class booklets in which a student contributes a page, or more lengthy creative writing, the individual booklet requiring minimal writing serves the purpose well.

One example of such a booklet is "Thumbprint Books." *This Thumbprint,* by Ruth Krauss (12), is a delightful book in which a thumbprint is turned into a cat, a person singing, a witch, sun, bird. . . . by drawing legs, arms, ears, etc., to the basic thumbprint. Thumbprint characters can easily be made by kindergarten children. But the idea appeals equally to sixth graders.

Read part of the book to the students, showing them all the illustrations. At the writing center, have available 3"×4½" booklets with fourteen pages, made from seven pieces of 4½"×6" paper, folded in half and stapled along the folded edge.

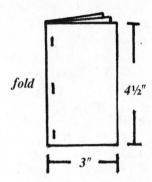

Small thumbprint booklet

In addition to the little booklets, you will need pencils and approximately three commercial ink pads. Green ink seems to be the most attractive. The student should write, "My Thumbprint Book" on the front page and decorate the cover with a thumbprint character, stamp a thumbprint on the next page, and turn it into something, by adding eyes, mouth, hair, etc. The child then writes one sentence describing it, and continues this way throughout the entire booklet, making a series of interesting thumbprint characters.

Pages from Thumbprint Books

Students of course end up with "green thumbs" . . . not the gardening kind, but green from ink! To avoid inky thumbprints while they search Krauss's books for ideas, replicate some of the thumbprint characters on a piece of tagboard or railroad board approximately 2½"×22". Covered with contact paper, the students can freely refer to it without concern about the book getting soiled. Some students will copy several of the thumbprints from the demonstration strip, then suddenly devise their own creations. Others immediately have ideas of their own. They have no need to refer to the demonstration thumbprint strip. But the strip is important for those students who would have difficulty getting started otherwise. It serves the same function as brainstorming prior to creative writing. It is a resource of available ideas, to be used as needed.

Keep a copy of the book available even when the ink pads are put away, as it is a work that children love to read. This initial experience of making a thumbprint book filled with a variety of characters often inspires some students to write a story about one of their thumbprint characters, along with thumbprint illustrations.

Another similar book, *Fingerprint Owls and Other Fantasies* (13), encompasses a variety of characters using fingers as well as thumbs!

Classification Booklets

Classification booklets are another popular individual book assignment for young students, kindergarten through second grade. Sample booklets should be made as starters. Each of these should have six 6"×9"

pages stapled together. The title should be written on the cover, followed by several pages of illustrations.

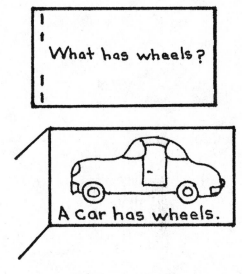

Classification booklet

An example of a sample classification booklet is "What Has Wheels?" The first page shows a car, with the caption printed underneath. "A car has wheels." The next page is a bicycle with the caption, "A bike has wheels"; a third illustrated page, "A truck has wheels." When introducing the sample booklet to the students, explain that they should use the ideas to get started on their own. Since several pages are left blank in the sample booklet, the class can begin by brainstorming about other things which have wheels. After this, introduce several other classification booklets.

Put the sample booklets at the Writing Center, along with stapled blank booklets (approximately fifteen to twenty blank 6″×9″ pages, stapled together, with construction paper front and back covers). They can choose one of the topics from the sample classification booklets. The title and the student's name are written on the front of one of the blank books. The child then makes an entire book on that one topic.

The purpose of the classification booklets is twofold: One is a writing exercise, the other a classification exercise. Students begin by naming the obvious, in the case of what has wheels: truck, car, bicycle, motorcycle. To complete the remaining pages, they begin to develop sub-categories, enumerating different types of trucks, cars, etc.

When students run dry in a particular category, they should be encouraged to check with other children at the center for their suggestions. This encourages verbal interaction as well as a sense of cooperation.

Periodically, the original six to eight booklets should be supplemented to provide more categories for children.

Ideas for classification booklets include:

What I Saw On My Way to School
What Has Wheels?
Foods I Like to Eat
Colors
Things That Fly
Tall Things
What Can You Hear?
Things That Walk
What Has Hair?
Animals
Opposites
How Do Things Feel?
Good Things and Bad Things
Rough Things and Smooth Things

What Has Bells?
Stores
Fruits and Vegetables
Tools
What Is Pretty?
Hot Things and Cold Things
Things You Could Put In Your Pocket
Things For the Kitchen
Things That Grow
Things That Swim
Things That Are Sweet
Things in the Forest
Scary Things
Things That Are Light
Big Things and Heavy Things

These booklets work well at a kindergarten center. The student selects a topic, draws a picture, and dictates the sentence to an aide. The students need a little time to decide what they are going to draw, discuss other possibilities and draw the illustrations. In this situation, one adult can manage six to eight students.

Maya D'Anjou (14) adapted these classification booklets as a beginning creative-writing experience for her first-graders. They began with descriptive words, e.g., "dump truck," rather than sentences. At the center were placed copies of Richard Scarry's *Best Word Book Ever* (15). Since words and pictures in this book are arranged by category, the students learned how to find the pages they needed for reference. They became quite self-sufficient.

After making several books by writing only identifying words on each page, the students transformed these into sentences, adding articles, verbs and their classification topic.

Shape Books

Individual booklets, made in the shape of what students are writing about, (e.g., if the topic is snakes, the booklet is cut in the shape of a snake), are also successful with young children. A good source for well-designed shape covers is *Shape Book,* by Elisa Gittings (16). This book includes black reproducible shapes for book covers for a variety of topics. These can be used for class booklets as well.

Materials for Stimulating Creative Writing

There are several important components in structuring successful creative writing experiences: (1) material which captures the student's interest and stimulates the imagination, (2) "brainstorming" during which time a myriad of ideas pour forth, and (3) readily available assistance.

Unfortunately, it is often difficult to find material which captures the child's interest and provides a springboard for successful creative writing experiences. The following illustrations are a representative sample from forty 8½"×11" black reproducible story starter pictures which are available in the supplement to this book. These story starters have been found extremely helpful in providing the stimulus for successful creative writing. Many of the story starters in the supplement were originally drawn by Averil Anderson (17). Others were drawn by Anne Drummond (18), Florence Moon (19), and Darlene Dinelli (20). They have been used by many teachers with excellent results. Children seem to immediately relate to them, quite possibly because they have a certain informality about them.

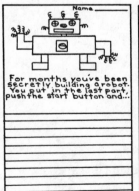

178

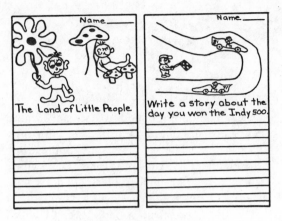

Story starters

Continuation ditto

Some of the story starters in the supplement are geared to younger children. However, many teachers have used them effectively with older students who are having difficulty with creative writing. They have asked these students to write "pretend" stories to be shared in book form with younger children. (See the next section in this chapter.) Upper grade students often find it difficult to write "sophisticated" stories appropriate for other students their age, but can relax and let their imaginations roam while writing stories for younger children. Success at this type of writing leads to more difficult writing experiences. You might have the students write four or five pretend stories, choosing the best one for a book.

If you already have a good selection of story starters of this type, you may prefer to use these rather than purchasing the supplement. In either case, duplicate the story starters you wish to use, so that each student may have his or her own copy. (Having an individual copy of their very own greatly ap-

peals to students.) In addition, duplicate a large quantity of the "continuation ditto" for stories which extend beyond one page.

Since the Creative Writing Center is on-going, a story can be written over several days, or even weeks, if a student is so inspired.

The story-starter ditto should be introduced slowly; two dittos the first time and then one or two at intervals. When introducing a new story-starter ditto allow time for brainstorming: What do you think is happening? — Why do you think it happened? — What might happen then? — What else might happen?

Using this type of questioning try to get the children to volunteer many possible versions. Be careful however, not to give any clues as to what you think, or the students will perceive this as the right answer, which will abruptly end the brainstorm session. Use phrases such as, "That's an interesting idea. What else could have happened?" Or, "I can't decide what's happening here. What do you think?" When many ideas have been verbalized, assure the students that they may use any of the ideas suggested. Or they may employ a completely different thought. Even if several students start with the same idea, they will develop stories in different directions. Confidence in knowing that there are plenty of ideas for starting a story is all-important for the students.

Tell the students they may write about the brainstormed story-starter dittos, make up a story of their own, or write about something they have done, something they are going to do, etc. For students who elect to make up their own story or write a true story, you should have available two initial-page dittos, one with, and the other without space for illustrations.

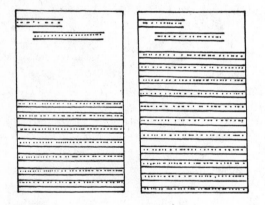

Initial-page dittos

As students reach the bottom of the first page of their story, they attach one of the previously illustrated continuation dittos and continue writing.

Helping Students Begin a Story

Students often have difficulty starting stories. They are inclined to state only what they see. This puts an end to their story in short order: "The big elephant is pulling the little elephant." You say, "Fine. Then what happened?" The child replies, "That's all. The big elephant pulled the little elephant."

To elicit more from a child, a chart with examples of beginning phrases for starting stories is helpful. These phrases automatically lead the student into a story format. Seldom will a child write, "Once upon a time a big elephant pulled a little elephant," and then come to an abrupt halt. The "Once upon a time" phrase sets the stage for action: "Once upon a time there was a big elephant and a little elephant. The big elephant wanted the little elephant to . . ." The child is now on the way to writing a story rather than a single statement.

Provide two beginning phrases initially. "Once upon a time," and "One day" are familiar to most children so they will feel comfortable. Gradually introduce other beginning phrases: "A long time ago," "There once was," "There lived . . ." The beginning phrases should be added to the chart and displayed in a prominent place at the Creative Writing Center. The top half can be used for beginning phrases for imaginary stories and the bottom devoted to starters for true, or experience, stories. Students will rely less on the chart after a time and begin their stories in a variety of ways. But the chart is invaluable for helping students over the beginning hurdles to creative writing.

Beginning-Phrase Chart

Once upon a time
A long time ago
There once was
One day
There lived
Yesterday
There was
Once there was
It happened

Last night
Yesterday
Today I'm going
Tonight I'm going
This afternoon I'm
Tomorrow I'm going

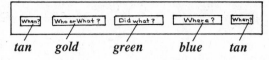

tan   gold   green   blue   tan

Back side of story board

Story boards which Alma Briggs (21) designed for her students are the next step in encouraging writing.

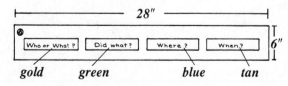

gold   green   blue   tan

Front side of story board

A piece of railroad board, 6″×28″, with four 2″×6″ pieces of colored tagboard for pockets are attached with glue along the bottom edge. Use different colors for the pockets, and label as illustrated. On the front, a small star should be drawn or glued in the upper left-hand corner.

The back of the story board is very similar, except for the first and last "When" card, which is only 2″×2½″ and is completely glued to the piece of railroad board, so no pocket is formed. The other three cards are attached to form pockets. Both sides of the story board should be covered with clear contact paper to hold the pockets in place. The top of each pocket is slit with a razor blade and reinforced with a piece of plastic tape.

A series of color-coded cards, consisting of statements to be placed in the pockets should be made. (See pages 182-183 for list.) The colors of the cards should be the same as the pockets, e.g., the "Who or What" pocket on the diagram is gold. Therefore, all the "Who or What" cards are gold.

The student first uses the front side of the board and selects one of the colored cards, "a big green caterpillar," and inserts it in the "Who" pocket. The next card selected, "stood as still as a stone," is then placed in the "What" pocket. This procedure continues until cards containing phrases have been matched with each of the pockets.

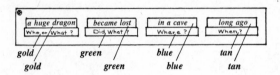

Story-board example

This forms the beginning of the student's story. Later, the child uses the back side of

the story board. and begins to experiment with changing the placement of the "When" card. Once more the student selects the four colored cards. All but the "When" card are inserted in their matching pockets. This card is first laid on "When" on the left-hand side of the story board. The beginning sentence is read. The tan card is then moved to "When" on the right hand side of the story board. Once more the sentence is read. This type of experimentation helps the student discover the different uses of phrases to begin a story.

A list of the phrases to be written, or typed on cards to go with the story board, follows.

Who or What? (Gold Cards)

a beautiful princess	five funny faces	an empty house
a piece of lace	two large raindrops	many mixed up mice
a pair of dull scissors	a juicy strawbery	twelve polka dots
a puffy pillow	George the Giant	three flying kites
a pair of mittens	an enchanted castle	a naughty puppy
a flying saucer	Mr. Hoot Owl	a sinking submarine
a lady bug	a spotted monster	a friendly snake
a pack of wolves	an ugly witch	a fluffy white cloud
a gooey candy bar	a grandfather clock	Brother-Big-Bones
a fuzzy animal	a sly old fox	a sweet smelling rose
a warm blanket	a giant flower pot	a swarm of bees
a clumsy grown-up	Buzzy Bee	beautiful flowers
a pair of shoes	a magic key	three sleepy kittens
a bunch of bananas	a bundle of packages	a huge dragon
a stranger	a piece of pie	ten tired turtles
a cozy cushion	eight kangaroos	two noisy bongo drums

a big yellow truck
a lazy lizard
six swift swallows
a stubborn mule
a spider named _____ ?
a magic bean-stalk
a big green caterpillar
a set of false teeth
a jumping bean
a big parachute

a talking zebra
King Cross of Angryland
a smiling dentist
two dancing bears
a gaggle of geese
a slurpy ice cream cone
a clever _____ grader
a squishy squash
two helicopters
an ancient dinosaur

Hoodle the Poodle
a large envelope
a full moon
a dish of pudding
a wonderful walrus
a lonely lion
a haunted house
a wild wolf

Did What? (Green Cards)

dreamed he was
baked a pie
bit me
pointed to me
burst into a thousand pieces
looked down a long hall
waited
was frightened
pushed a door open
splashed
followed a jet
watched T.V.
crowded
frightened me
bit a big pig
whistled a tune
knocked over a _____?
became a hero
moved fast
painted a picture
rumbled noisily
kept hopping
rolled over and over
puffed and puffed
inched his way
kept hearing noises

tumbled down
blew bubbles
came to life
boiled over
disappeared
whined and whined
put out a fire
stood as still as stone
folded up
screamed loudly
listened to a record
growled angrily
climbed up
covered his eyes
slurped six sodas
rowed a boat fast
hopped like crazy
shook his fist at me
heard a noise
floated lazily
flew aimlessly
grabbed a bat
fell quickly
broke into a million pieces
wrote a poem
was watching all alone

kissed his mother goodby
spent all his money
lived happily
danced a jig
couldn't stop crying
felt sick
became frightened
breathed fire
worked slowly
scared my brother
growled at me
pouted and pouted
snapped its finger
coughed loudly
whispered a secret
grumbled and grumbled
licked a lollipop
spied on his friend
rattled
became lost
swam
stamped and stamped
boxed my ears
unlocked a tiny door
sat on a curb
ran pell-mell

Where? (Blue Cards)

in a big barrel keg
at the North Pole
in a nearby yard
into the oven
on a bumpy ride
under an umbrella
on a ranch
on a magic carpet
around his neck
on a huge platter
at a Wild-West movie
in a big red box
deep in the forest
in a crowded school bus
by the ice cream store
around a big circle
on a log
in the jello salad
on the sidewalk
over the school
inside a large pumpkin
behind the home plate
in the deep ocean
at a peanut stand
in a cave
on a green toadstool
over in the corner

in a tree house
at a barber shop
in a park
past a haunted house
up on a high ladder
in the tiny kingdom of _____ ?
under a purple stone
in a dark tunnel
in a glass factory
among some rocks
in an old leather shoe
in the rain
at the pizza shop
out in the darkness
in your science book
in a glass shoe
all around the world
in my pocket
on a marble throne
in a far away land
in our fort
past an empty house
up the street
under the table
at the grocery store
beside a quiet lake
in a tin can

over my head
under a polka dot
on a mountain
over the fence
on the 50-yard line
at the aquarium
on a door
on a pincushion
above the clouds
on the swings
along the beach
behind the house
at the piano keys
in church
in a mud puddle
on a stormy sea
in a noodle factory
along the freeway
in the mirror
in a purse
in a castle
through the gate
out of the darkness
into the cookie jar
around his desk

When? (Tan Card)

for quite a while
late in the evening
in the winter

for a long time
a little earlier
one day

yesterday
at first
for an hour

when the wind blew
at lunch time
when a whale whistled
for Christmas
for many months
next week
long ago
all day long
a long time ago
when it was dark
finally
in January
after dark
after school
a few minutes later
forever and ever
several months ago
in the summer
very soon
at noon
two weeks ago
on a windy day
never again
too late

next year
tomorrow
this afternoon
in an instant
at sunset
many days ago
at bedtime
while some were asleep
early in the morning
when his or her mother called
this afternoon
in late December
suddenly
right away
presently
years ago
when the wind blows
on a stormy night
on a rainy day
today
in a few days
at dawn
one evening
much later

after _____ got up
many moons ago
never again
long ago
once in a while
after breakfast
when the moon came up
at last
for a couple of hours
all night
before dinner
on a gorgeous day
from sunup to sunset
when all was quiet
for just a second
in the fall
once a long time ago
while the bell rang
when no one was looking
until his mother called
for a hundred years
once upon a time in the spring

Providing Assistance at the Creative Writing Center

For students who are beginners at creative writing, or those who have had unpleasant experiences in creative writing, it is often helpful to subdivide the children at the Writing Center. While half the students work on the mechanics of basic printing or cursive, the other three or four engage in creative writing. This enables the teacher or aide to concentrate attention on the creative writing group, providing the needed assistance, encouragement and support.

As the students' self-confidence grows and less assistance is needed, you can supervise all of them at the center in creative writing. Sub-groups are no longer necessary.

Sub-groups can be identified by numbers or letters written by each student's name on the coded group charts.

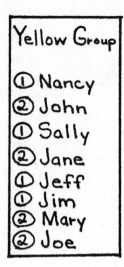

Chart indicating sub-groups

Students should be divided evenly. There should be approximately the same number who need help with creative writing, and the same number who find creative writing easy. Announce which sub-group will do what, reversing the rolls each day.

Writing ① creative writing
       ② copy work
↓
Independent
↓
Math
↓
Spelling — choose words for this week

*Daily center schedule
incorporating sub-groups*

After a month, or when you sense students have become secure with creative writing, let them choose between it and copy work. If almost all the students select creative writing, you will know you have succeeded in building their feeling of success and accomplishment. Creative writing has become an enjoyable experience for them. In this case you may continue almost every day, giving them a choice at the Writing Center and knowing that they will spend most of their time involved in creative-writing activities. Confer individually with those students who choose a steady diet of copy work, and perhaps require that they spend at least three days a week on creative writing. The more creative writing they do, the sooner their skills and confidence will develop.

If the majority of students choose copy work, this is an indication that they have not yet developed sufficient skills to be at ease with creative writing. In this case, continue to assign creative writing activities at least three days a week—preferably every day.

Periodically, students get stuck at midpoint in story-writing. When they ask for help the teacher or aide will often say, "Why don't you say . . ." Invariably the child will reply, "No, that's not what happened." This can go on and on, and become exasperating for all concerned. The student seems to resent the fact that someone is dictating the direction the story is to take. Yet the child knows help is needed.

This can often be remedied by re-phrasing suggestions into questions. "Did the boy run home and tell his mother? Or was he so frightened that he ran and hid? Or did his dog or best friend come along just then? What did his mother say when he got home?" Questioning stimulates the child to think about various possibilities. Often in the middle of your questions the student will say, "Oh, I know what happened," and will go off to continue the story. The student may have picked up directly on one of your comments. Or your question may have been a springboard to another idea. But it is still the child's very own story.

If the inquiry process does not work, suggest that the student sit and think about it for a few minutes. Perhaps an idea will come. You have provided the child with many possible directions. If the student takes the time to sit quietly and think, it may become possible to continue the story. Do check back to be certain the child is not still floundering.

Drawing a picture to accompany the student's story can also be suggested. Often while involved in drawing, the child's mind will wander creatively, exploring various possible continuations for the story. You may find that, part way through drawing the picture, the student stops and returns excitedly to the story.

If a child's story begins to ramble, with no visible buildup to a climax, ask what is the most exciting or interesting part of the story (climax). Explain that, once the most exciting part of the story is reached, it should be brought to an end in order to hold the reader's interest.

The system Darlene Dinelli (22) uses to call her upper-grade students' attention to the process of building a story (and the importance of building a relationship between the elements within the story) can be useful in this context.

Cover five small boxes (all the same size) with contact paper. Then label the boxes: (1) setting, (2) characters, (3) problem (adventure), (4) climax (exciting part), (5) ending.

Give students slips of paper and have each student write at least one sentence for each box:

1. Two boys are walking home from school on the railroad tracks, on the outskirts of town.
2. Billy and Bobby, who are both ten years old, are best friends.
3. Billy's shoe gets caught in one of the tracks.
4. The boys hear the whistle of an oncoming train.
5. Bobby grabs Billy and pulls him out of his shoe just as the train whizzes by.

When all students have contributed a sentence to each box, pass around one box at a time. Each student takes a slip from each box and decides whether it describes the setting, characters, etc. (The slips should not be labeled.)

Write on the chalk-board:
1. setting
2. characters
3. problem (adventure)
4. climax (exciting part)
5. ending

Each student now reconstructs perhaps a silly or funny story by arranging slips in the above order. The child writes this on a separate piece of paper and shares it with the other students.

This helps the student to be aware of irrelevance. At the same time it emphasizes

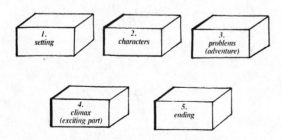

Building a story boxes

187

the necessity for continuity throughout a story.

In addition, the boxes can then be stacked in order and displayed at the Writing Center as a reminder of the components and process of building a good story.

This same system can be used with second and third grade students, by using only three boxes: beginning (setting), middle (exciting part), and ending (what happened).

Additional Materials for Stimulating Creative Writing

In order to maintain interest and involvement in creative writing activities, the materials used for stimulating this writing need to be changed frequently. If students are faced only with story-starter dittos day after day, before long the novelty wears off. On the other hand, students can become overwhelmed if too much material is introduced at any given time. Introducing one, or at the most two dittos and thoroughly brainstorming these, is much wiser.

Coffee cans covered with contact paper make neat space savers, and can be used to hold the various dittos.

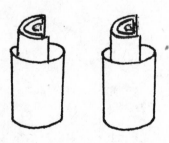

Story-starter storage in coffee cans

The students should be assured that these story-starter dittos will remain available to them. There is no need to rush through their current stories in order to get copies of the new dittos. (At first students may tend to "hoard" copies of all new material. But once they realize that this is not necessary they will discontinue the practice.)

You will need four or five cans for the newest story-starter dittos. The old material should be stacked nearby. Tell students that, if they can't find what they are looking for, you will gladly duplicate additional copies.

Once a few story-starter dittos have been introduced, wait a few days and then put out a set of eight to ten pictures which you have cut from magazines mounted on construction paper and covered with contact paper or laminated. These should be equally divided between child-oriented subjects and fantasy-oriented subjects. Fantasy pictures are particularly helpful to students who are convinced that there is only one right story to be written about a picture. You can dispel this notion, by using fantasy pictures and saying, "I haven't the faintest idea what is happening here. What do you think?" This can often encourage the inhibited student.

A particularly good source for fantasy pictures is medical magazines. The advertisements in medical magazines are unlike anything seen in regular news-stand magazines! Doctors subscribe to a variety of these and most will be glad to save their old issues for you if you but ask.

The magazine section of Sunday city newspapers is often an excellent source for people-oriented pictures. *National Geographic, Teen Magazine, People Magazine, Sixteen Magazine, Psychology Today* and *Sesame Street Magazine* are equally good resources.

As always, when displaying something for

the first time, either brainstorm or ask a leading question about some or all of the pictures.

A shallow box or a potato bin can be used for storage. As a space saver, a stand (see diagrams, pages 133-134) can be used by the child to hold the picture.

Continue to introduce small amounts of new material once or twice each week. After three or four weeks or when you see interest waning in the mounted pictures, ask if there are any pictures someone wants to remain available. Then put the others away and substitute a new activity, perhaps story-starter sentences or situations typed on 3″×5″ cards dealing with the student's thoughts and feelings: "What do you think about?" "Which of these things would you rather do on a Saturday morning?" "What would you do if?" Topics for feelings and thoughts can be found in Sidney Simon's *Value Clarification* (23). Although the topics are designed for discussion, many of them work equally well for writing assignments. These ideas can be adapted so that young students copy a partial sentence from the chalkboard, fill in a blank, and then briefly expand on the idea. (See pages 160-161.) Older students can be asked what they think or feel about a situation. They should explain why or how they perceive the pros and cons. Questions about pets, families, favorite experiences they can remember, happy experiences, sad experiences, television programs, how they like to spend their free time, frightening or emergency situations, etc., are all suitable. Prior to writing, hold a discussion with the students about these topics.

If the story-starter ideas are written on 3″×5″ cards it is helpful to make a holder so that the cards can be displayed attractively. Hinge together two pieces of 11″×14″ colored railroad board. On the front, draw a picture of a person or cartoon character asking, "What do you think?" Inside this folder, glue eight library pockets with edges outlined by a felt pen. Stickers or pictures can be glued to each of the library pockets to make the folder more colorful.

Put some of the brainstormed cards in the pockets and periodically change them. For students who want to write a real story, or a story about what they think or feel, this folder always has ideas for them.

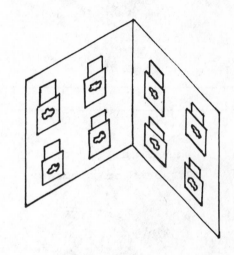

Holder for story cards

It is fun to have students make up story-starter titles. Those shown on pages 190-191 resulted from a discussion with a group of second-graders. After reading a collection of possible story titles to them, one of the students said, "We could make up some titles like that. I have an idea already!" What ensued was a barrage of titles which were hastily jotted down. Some of these were selected, and Anne Drummond (24) then

ILLUSTRATED STORY TITLES

The Cat Walk On Who Could His Tail

The Ghost, the Boy, and the Girl

The Worm Who Got Stuck

The Lizard That Was 20,000 Feet Long

The Dog Who Couldn't Bark

The Cat Who Couldn't Climb

The Time Santa Claus Didn't Come

wrote the titles and drew the delightful illustrations on pieces of colored construction paper. They were then laminated for protection.

If you use some of these, introduce only a few at any given time, for maximum interest. They then can become part of a display at the Creative Writing Center.

Upper-grade students enjoy a session of making more sophisticated illustrated story titles. Read these titles and explain that they were written by primary students. Challenge them to see what titles they can write of interest to students their age: mad scientists, sports, etc.

Another day, try brainstorming various combinations of characters for a story: a baseball player, a magic bat, and an umpire; a witch, a magic broom which doesn't follow orders, and a cat; a monstrous dinosaur, a tiny dinosaur and an egg, etc. These can be written on cards and placed as a resource at the writing center. Or each person can think up one or more of these character cards and list them on a piece of 6"×9" construction paper or tagboard, and then illustrate the card with pictures of the characters. These stimulate much interest in the classroom. Students are delighted when others select "their" character cards.

Dittos made from pages in coloring books can also be used to stimulate creative writing for students of all ages. Select child-oriented and action-packed coloring pictures, and number each one for retrieval purposes. Duplicate these. A 10"×12" manila envelope, with the flap and top ½" cut off, makes a good holder.

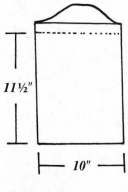

Cut top ½" off
10"×12" envelope

Staple the top of one of the duplicated dittos to the top edge of the envelope. You should then glue the bottom of the ditto to the bottom edge of the envelope. Place the remainder of the duplicated dittos inside the envelope.

Storage envelope for creative-
writing color-dittos

Make eight to ten sets of coloring dittos. You can brainstorm several of these in depth, and briefly discuss the others. These can be stored in a potato bin, or propped up in a box at the Creative Writing Center. The ditto is used as the "cover" for the student's story. To this the child staples one of the initial page dittos, illustrated on page 180. Some students will choose to color the cover page. Others will simply use it as a stimulus to creative writing. To make additional copies, refer to the number on the manila envelope in order to locate the ditto master.

Discarded book-jackets also make delightful material for stimulating creative writing. These can be mounted on railroad board in such a way that a student's story can be inserted between the covers. Cut two pieces of colored railroad board approximately 10″×12″. In order to hinge the front cover, cut a 1¼″ strip from one of the pieces. Then cut off approximately ⅜″ more and discard this piece.

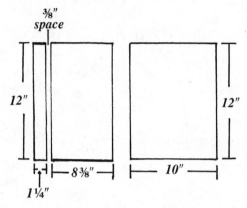

Constructing a jacket cover

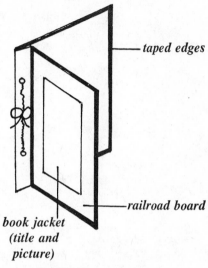

Book jacket cover

Lay the 1¼″ strip and the remaining large piece on top of the back cover. Leave a ⅜″ strip between the two front pieces, so that they are the same size as the back cover. Tape the two front pieces together with colored plastic tape.

Glue the front of the book jacket to the railroad front cover. Cover with clear contact paper. Then cover all exposed edges with plastic tape. Punch holes in the left-hand side of both front and back cover. Hold together with heavy yarn.

A series of these book-jacket covers can be made. Holes are punched in the student's story, and it is inserted between the covers. It can then become part of the classroom library. Later it can be removed and stapled together with a construction paper cover. The same book jacket cover can then be made available for others.

An additional use for book-jacket covers at the primary level is for stories dictated by a group of students or the entire class. Or each person can make up a one-page story about the picture and title on the cover. All of these can be inserted in the book jacket cover.

Another idea which appeals to primary students is a colorfully decorated box, with a special set of materials to be used for story starters. It is helpful if this box is rather large, perhaps 10″×10″×3″ for versatility. Cover the box with bright-patterned contact paper. Tape the sides and bottom edge of a piece of clear acetate (approximately 4″×7″) to the inside of the lid. This forms an acetate "pocket." Directions typed on 4″×6″ colored cards are slipped into the pocket. Materials are placed in the box. Periodically, the materials and direction card can be changed.

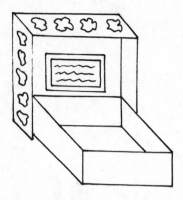

Creative writing special material box

Direction cards and related materials which can be placed in the box include:

Stuffed Toys

1. Choose one of the stuffed toys.*
2. Write a story about what your toy might do if it came to life during the night.

Contributions or purchases

A Shell For A Home

1. Take one shell* and glue it on your paper.
2. Who lives here? . . . Or is someone hiding? . . . Or has someone moved out of his shell? Why?

3. Draw the rest of the picture.

Dyed macaroni shells. (Directions for dyeing macaroni can be found on page 97.)

Little Things

1. Look at all the little things.*
2. Choose one and write a story about it.
3. Be sure to put it back in the box when you leave the writing center.

Small toy boats, dinosaurs, animals, a shell, a small doll, etc.

A Special Bow

1. Take one bow* and glue it on your paper.
2. Is the bow on an animal?
     on a present?
     on a little girl?
     on something else?
3. Draw the rest of the picture.
4. Write a story about it.

Dyed macaroni bows.

Pick A Gift

1. Look at the pictures* in the toy book.

2. Pretend it's your birthday. Cut out a picture of what you'd most like to get for a present. Paste the picture to your paper.
3. Write a story about your gift. What will you do with it? Who will you invite over to play with it?
4. Start your story . . . I could hardly wait to open my birthday present. I tore off the paper, opened the box, and there was . . .

Christmas toy-catalogue books.

A Little Lost Hat

1. Take a paper with a little hat* on it.
2. Who lost the hat . . . an animal?
                          an elf?
                          a person?
3. Draw a picture showing the person or animal looking for the little hat, or with the hat on.
4. Write a story about how the hat became lost.

9"×12" papers with little paper hats or acorn caps glued to them.

Upper-grade students are delighted with assignments in which they make up an explanation for how a product got its name. The book *Why Did They Name It . . .?* by Hannah Campbell (25), reveals the story behind many well-known products: Jell-O, Log Cabin Syrup, Wheaties, Potato Chips, etc. Students can invent their own explanation of how the product was invented and named, and then compare this with the actual circumstances. Fun for all!

The book *Fortunately,* by Remy Charlip (26) is also excellent for upper-grade students. Read part of the book to the students, so that they discover the pattern of one line starting with "Fortunately," and the next line starting, "Unfortunately." Stories built on this format can be quite amusing. But the students writing them need to have sufficient sophistication to be able to think two steps ahead. While they are writing an "unfortunately" sentence, they need to have already figured out how they will be able to save the situation with a "fortunately" sentence, etc.

Middle and upper-grade students also find Title-Twister (27) an interesting addition to the Creative Writing Center. By placing the inner wheel and outer wheel in various positions, it is possible to arrive at 400 different titles!

Commercial story-starter task cards make another pleasant change of pace at the Writing Center. The same rules of thumb apply. Introduce a few at a time, and brainstorm or ask questions about them. Otherwise, students will use a few of them and then say they can't find anything else they want to write about. Part of the reason for this is that, after having looked through the cards quite a few times, they seem "old." Two sets of commercial story-starter task cards which are exceptionally good, are "Story Starters, Set 1: Intermediate Level" and "Story Starters, Set 2: Primary Level," published by Creative Teaching Press (28).

Regular creative-writing activities, such as those described in this section, will develop writing skills, positive attitudes about writing, and imagination. From this sound base, it is possible to move on to more formalized writing assignments, analysis of plots, reference work, and report writing.

Writing and Illustrating Books

Teachers are well aware of the interest generated when students have the opportunity to write and illustrate books. Unfortunately, most of the methods previously used for making books have required so much teacher time and effort that students were fortunate to be allowed to make one book during the entire school year. This section describes a method for making student books which has proven highly successful, with both primary and upper-grade students. It requires little teacher time. As a result, students can make many books throughout the year.

The following book, *The Bunny Who Went to the Mushroom,* was written and illustrated by Karen Stuber, a second-grade student. The example includes the illustrations for the first and last two pages of the book, and the writing from the intervening pages. (In the actual book, illustrations accompany each page.)

Page 2

Student Book

Page 1

p. 3	On the way to the farm there were two hunters hunting for rabbits.
p. 4	The hunters heard Mr. Rabbit. And Mr. Rabbit was too TERRIFIED to move!
p. 5	Then the two hunters saw Mr. Rabbit and chased the poor thing to the farm.
p. 6	But the hunters lost him,
p. 7	and Mr. Rabbit went on walking to the farm.
p. 8	Then Mr. Rabbit bumped into a pole.
p. 9	But it really wasn't a pole. It was Mr. Horse.
p. 10	Mr. Rabbit said, "Oh, excuse me! And oh, by the way, do you have a mushroom seed?"
p. 11	"No, but my master has one."
p. 12	"Oh, thank you!"

p. 13 "You're welcome, Mr. Rabbit."

p. 14 And so Mr. Rabbit went to Mr. Farmer and said, "Do you have a mushroom seed?"

p. 15 Mr. Farmer said, "Yes."

p. 16 Mr. Rabbit said, "May I have it?"

p. 17 and Mr. Farmer said, "O.K. You may have it."

p. 18 So Mr. Rabbit planted it.

The following story was written by a first-grader, Jim Kassenbrock, and has a rhythmic feeling which makes it particularly appealing. The cover is entitled, *The Lion Who Didn't Have a Friend.*

Student Book

Page 19

Page 1

Page 20

p. 2 And he did not have a single friend in the jungle.

p. 3 But he was happy, because he was the king of the jungle.

p. 4 And then one day there was a fight against a tiger,

p. 5 and a leopard

p. 6 and a gorilla

p. 7 and a monkey

p. 8 and an octopus.

p. 9 Then the lion came along and said, "Break it up, boys."

p. 10 Then the monkey,

p. 11 and the gorilla,
p. 12. and the octopus
p. 13 and the tiger,
p. 14 and the leopard,
p. 15 all went home.

These books were originally creative-writing stories, and then were rewritten and illustrated as books.

The main problems for students making books are: 1) How much should be written on each page; 2) how to provide the correct amount of space, not too many lines or two few lines, for the writing which is to be placed on each page; and 3) how to assemble the books.

The teacher should solve these problems for younger children. But you may want to work with older students, helping them discover how to solve each of the problems so they can independently assemble their own books.

The step-by-step process involved in segmenting a story is illustrated below.

Student's Creative-Writing Story

Once there was a worm. His friend went into a cave. Then a snake came and pushed a rock where the hole was. The snake went home and told his mom and then he got some Kool Aid. Then he went back to the cave and said, Do you want out? No answer. Then an ant came and said, Do you want out? Yes! The ant went to get his 74 cousins, 89

---

friends, 100 grasshoppers, a frog, a rabbit, a polly-wog, and a train too! They pushed and pushed and he got out! And they were friends again.

Lori House
Second Grade

Ask yourself how much is needed on the first page in order for the student to be able to draw a picture? The first sentence would be sufficient—"Once there was a worm." (The student could draw a picture depicting the worm.) To indicate to the student that this is all that should be written on the first page, two slash marks are placed at the end of the first sentence. (See below.)

The next sentence can be illustrated on the second page, "His friend went into a cave." Two more slash marks are placed at the end of this sentence. Continue reading and marking the story in this fashion. (In some cases, as little as one word will be written on a pages.)

Once there was a worm.// His friend went into a cave.// Then a snake came and pushed a rock where the hole was.// The snake went home and told his mom,// and then he got some Kool Aid.// Then he went back to the cave and said, do you want out?// No answer.// Then an ant came and said, do you want out?// Yes!// The ant went to get his 74 cousins,// 89 friends,// 100 grasshoppers,// a frog,// a rabbit,// a polly wog,// and a train too!// They pushed// and pushed,// and he got out!// And they were friends again.//

By dividing some sentences mid-way, you can help build a rhythmic feeling: "And they pushed// and pushed// and he got out," is more rhythmic than "And they pushed and pushed and he got out." Look for the poetry as you divide the story into segments.

Count the total number of slash marks, write this number at the beginning of the story, and circle it. This indicates the number of pages in the book. Accumulate three to five stories and then assemble these into books at one time.

Use the illustrations below as guides, copy on ditto masters and duplicate a stack of each.

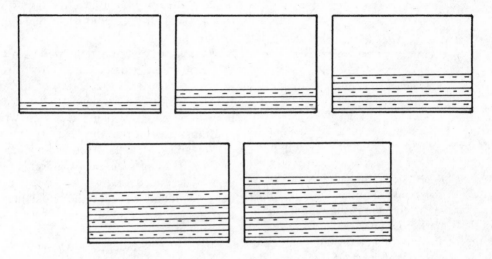

Pages for student books

These are the pages for the student's books. Set these along a counter. Then select the ditto with the correct number of lines to accommodate the number of words between slash marks. Place these in order, one behind the other. Count the ditto pages to make certain the number matches the number you wrote and circled at the beginning of the story (number of slash marks).

To form a cover (both sides) use two pieces of colored 9"×12" construction paper. Staple the assembled book together along the left hand side. Near the bottom of the front cover, write with felt pen "by" (and the student's name). Do not write the title of the story at this point. By the time the student has recopied the book and illustrated it, a different title may appeal! Insert the child's original copy of the story, marked with slashes.

*Assembled student book
and original story*

When introducing the individual book format to the students, stress that all they write on any given page is the amount *up to* the slash marks. Otherwise they are apt to fill the entire page, negating all your careful calculations! Watch while they copy the first several pages to be certain that they understand the procedure. From this point on, they can independently do the copying and illustrating.

The student should copy the entire story, writing as neatly as possible. To reinforce the concept of neatness, remind them that the book will be read to the entire class and then will become part of the classroom library. Others will therefore be reading *their book*. Mention that past experience has shown that, if a book is not neatly written, other people do not want to read it. (As a result, you will be amazed at the effort students make in seeing to it that their books are neatly written.)

After the story is re-copied, the original draft may be taken home. Each page of the book is re-read and illustrated. Help from others, or from available resources if they are having trouble with their illustrations, should be encouraged. (A list of such materials can be found on pages 257-258.)

When the book is completed and you have proof-read it, it should be read to the entire class and then added to the classroom library. Students should have the opportunity to make many of these books throughout the year.

In addition to stimulating interest in creative writing, they make an effective display for Open House in the spring of the year. Several tables can be pushed together. The myriad of books which have been written and illustrated during the year are arranged on the tables. Parents will spend a great deal of time, reading their own children's books as well as the books written by other students. Students can take the books home at the end of the school year for continued enjoyment.

Upper-grade students enjoy writing books of this type which can then be shared with younger students. After writing and illustrating several books like the ones previously described, you may want to have them choose their favorite book to be typed, illustrated and bound. (The pages are sewn to a cardboard cover which has been covered with wallpaper or fabric.) These books then become part of the school's library and are checked out the same as any other book.

The following photographs were of a book written by two fourth-grade students. (Note the clever illustrations: doors which open, a telephone which can be taken off the receiver, etc.) This book, *The Surprise Party*, by Dana Torres and Laura Duckworth (29), is now part of the school library.

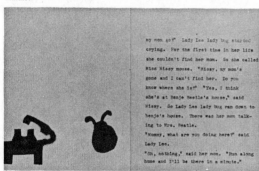

On the first day of Spring, Lady Lee lady bug jumped out of her bed. "I'm going to ask my mom if I could go over to Flubber's house." But she couldn't find her. "Where did my mom go?" Lady Lee lady bug started crying. For the first time in her life she couldn't find her mom. So she called Miss Missy mouse. "Missy, my mom's gone and I can't find her. Do you know where she is?" "Yes, I think she's at Benje Beetle's house," said Missy. So Lady Lee lady bug ran down to benje's house. There was her mom talking to Mrs. Beatle. "Mommy, what are you doing her?" said Lady Lee. "Oh, nothing," said her mom. "Run along home and I'll be there in a minute."

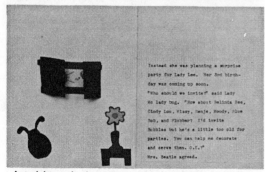

Instead she was planning a surprise party for Lady Lee. Her 3rd birthday was coming up soon. "Who should we invite?" said Lady Mc lady bug. "How about Belinda Bee, Cindy Lou, Missy, Benje, Moody, Blue Bob, and Flubber? I'd invite Bubbles but he's a little too old for parties. You can help me decorate and serve them. O.K.?" Mrs. Beatle agreed.

***Sample pages from book written
and illustrated by fourth-grade students***

Correcting Student Work

"To correct or not to correct" has been the teacher's dilemma for years. There are two opposing views on this subject. On one side red pencilling the student's entire paper inhibits creativity. The child quickly learns that it is much safer to write a short composition, as there will be less to re-copy. The other side of the coin: misspelled words, incorrect punctuation and grammer left uncorrected, will rob children from learning these important skills. If these skills are covered only in formal grammar assignments but not applied, what is reinforced are the student's errors! The arguments on both sides are valid. A compromise has to be struck.

A learning center's environment is ideal for the resolution of this problem, particularly if the center is supervised by an aide or the teacher.

Once the students become involved in writing, you can circulate around the center and proof-read individual student's work. A student can continue writing while you read over his or her shoulder. Or you can have the child hand you the work underway. When you spot an error, say to the child, "This word is misspelled. If you will turn to the correct page in your dictionary, I'll write it for you." "Somewhere in these two lines you need to place a period (or comma, semi-colon, etc.). See if you can discover where it is needed." As soon as the student finds what looks like the correct place, a quick check with you serves to verify it. Or you can discuss it with the child if necessary. You may also need to remind the student about capitalization. "What happens to the next letter after a period?" Or, "On this page there are three words which need to be capitalized. See if you can find them." The student makes these corrections while the story is in progress. Thus the child is the one doing the thinking and correcting. If you make corrections with your red pencil, the wrong person is getting the practice! When you write in the corrections, the hope, of course, is that, as the students recopy their work, they will notice the errors they made. Unfortunately, what usually happens is that the student recopies without assimilating.

The secret to continuous corrections is to proof-read the student's work frequently enough so that there will only be one or two errors which need correcting at any given time. If you work with seven or eight students at a center, this can easily be handled. Often, as one student is looking up the correct page in the dictionary and checking to see if the desired word is listed, you can proof-read another student's work.

This method of correction results in the student's continuously seeing correct spelling, correct punctuation and correct grammar as they re-read their stories. Soon these skills become automatic. The need for correction decreases. In addition, a student is encouraged to use the dictionary when in doubt or to check with you on the correct punctuation, capitalization and grammar. The child realizes that corrections will have to be made within a short time, anyway. Helpful hints on content and style can be given in the same context.

If you look over a student's shoulder, there is no need for the child to stop writing while you proof-read. If there are no errors, a word of encouragement is in order.

Occasionally, a student will be bothered by your over-the-shoulder reading or having a train of thought interrupted. This is valid and should be respected. The student can bring work to you at the conclusion of each page. Put your initials or a check to indicate how far you proof-read, to be certain the student is following through with frequent "check-ups."

By using this system of continuous correction there will be few errors by the time a story is completed. More importantly, the students develop a feeling of success. They will tell you that they enjoy creative writing and seldom make mistakes. In addition, parents are impressed with the quality of the work sent home. And you are able to see to it that students practice spelling, punctuation, capitalization and grammar on a regular basis.

Record Keeping

Each student should have a creative writing folder made from a piece of 12″×18″ construction paper, folded in half. An individual record page should be stapled to the front of each student's folder.

Each day, as the student leaves the Writing Center, the current story is placed inside this folder. The child then puts the folder inside his or her dictionary. The following day when the student comes to the Writing Center, all of the necessary materials are together: the dictionary, story and record page. The student's record page (see page 203) is always available whenever work is done on creative writing, for your easy reference and commentary.

Completed stories are placed in the children's folders and put into a box designated for completed creative writing. (The student does not hand work in daily, as on-going corrections keep the checking up to date.)

Since students generally work several days or even a week on the same story, you

Creative Writing					Jane		
[1]Date	[2]No. of pages	[3] Book	[4]Content	[5]cap., punc...	[6]Comments	[7]Instruc. needed	[8]Spelling
9/15	½		✓		*much concentration!*		✗ *where* ✗ *never* ✗ *what* ✗ *upon* *looking* *they*
9/17	½		✓				
9/20	1		✓		*Beginning to get the idea of a story!*		
9/25	2		✓		*much better! Discuss using too many "ands"*	AMD ✗	
9/30	2		✓	*discussed periods*	*(Some humor)*		
10/10	3	✓	✓	"	*Great!*		
10/12	1		✓				
10/19	3		✓		*Thoughts are wandering. Read over with her and help her clear it up.*	✓	

Note: Most information is filled in as you check the student's completed story.

1 and 2   *Columns one and two enable teacher to compare the length of time that the student worked on the story, with the number of pages written. (Fill in at completion of story.)*

3   *Check indicates story was made into an illustrated book.*

4   *Placement of checks indicate quality of work. Far right equals poor quality. Middle equals staisfactory. Far left, excellent. (Placement of checks should not be obvious as in sample.)*

5   *Column five is filled in when teacher or aide discuss mechanics, content and/or style with the student.*

6   *Comments are written when the teacher or aide work with the student, make observations and/or when completed story is corrected.*

7   *Check indicates that follow-up instruction is necessary. When this is completed, the aide or teacher's initials are written. A slash mark is drawn through the check.*

8   *Spelling: See explanation below.*

will usually have only four to ten stories to correct in any given evening.

After you have corrected the student's work, you should determine whether 1) this would make a good story to turn into a book; 2) whether the story is satisfactory and can be returned to the student "as is"; 3) whether some corrections need to be made, or the story has sections which need to be reworked; or 4) whether you want to hold the story until you are supervising the center so you can work with the student. Under the first two circumstances, the student's empty record folder is placed in the stack of material to be returned to children the following day. Whoever hands out papers prior to school the next morning should be directed to place the folders inside each student's dictionary, so all personal working materials are together.

If you want the aide to work with the student, indicate on the record what is to be done. Place the folders in the area reserved for stories which the student and aide need to go over together.

If you would prefer to work with the student yourself, return the story to the folder. You can put it aside then until you supervise the Creative Writing Center.

The record and comments which accumulate on each student's record/folder provide a wealth of information as well as a complete profile of the student's creative-writing work.

The Spelling column is used for many purposes. If a student frequently misspells a word while at the Center, the teacher or aide records the word on the student's record page. When correcting the completed story, you can indicate the troublesome word(s) on the front of a child's folder. If students become annoyed because they have to always look up certain words, they can write those particular words on their folders.

When the students select their individualized spelling words for the week (see Chapter VIII), they should check their creative writing folder to determine whether there are any spelling words which should be included on the current list. As a student copies each word from the creative writing folder on the individualized spelling list, a small check is put by the word. The child brings the two spelling lists (the blue book and the list to go home) and creative writing folder to the teacher to be checked. The teacher places a slash mark through each of the checks, indicating the folder has been checked.

Once the word is written on the student's individualized spelling list, it will remain there as many weeks as necessary for the child to be able to spell it correctly. If at a later date the student has problems spelling the same word, it may reappear on the front of the personal creative writing folder, and would once more be included as one of the individualized spelling words. This system helps the student understand the relationship between spelling and writing.

This record page requires little teacher time. Yet it provides a great deal of information about each individual student. This is helpful to you as well as to others who supervise the Creative Writing Center. It is also invaluable at report card time or for parent conferences.

Notes

1. Henry D. Rinsland, *A Basic Vocabulary of Elementary School Children,* The Macmillan Company, New York, 1945.

2. Edward W. Dolch, *Teaching Primary Reading,* The Garrard Press, Champaign, Illinois, 1960.
3. Henry Kucera and W. Nelson Francis, *Computational Analysis of Present-Day English,* Brown University Press, Providence, R.I., 1967.
4. Ruth Krauss, *Open House for Butterflies,* Harper and Row, New York, 1960.
5. Hugh A. Wayne, *Alphabet Zoo,* (write to author to acquire book), 72 E. Third Avenue, San Mateo, California, 1970.
6. Tom Wilson, *Ziggy's Lucky/Unlucky Book,* American Greetings Corp., Cleveland, Ohio, 1973.
7. Linda Rowe and Marilyn Shaffer, Teachers, San Anselmo School District, San Anselmo, California.
8. Ruth Kraus, *A Hole Is To Dig,* Harper and Row, New York, 1952.
9. Barbara Bel Geddes, *I Like To Be Me,* Viking Press, New York, 1971.
10. Margaret Wise Brown, *The Important Book,* Harper and Row, New York, 1949.
11. Kenneth Koch, *Wishes, Lies, and Dreams,* Random House, New York, 1970.
12. Ruth Krauss, *This Thumbprint,* Harper and Row, New York, 1967.
13. Margorie Katz, *Fingerprints, Owls and Other Fantasies,* M. Evans and Company, New York, 1972.
14. Maya D'Anjou, Teacher, Mark West Union School District, Santa Rosa, California.
15. Richard Scarry, *Best Word Book Ever,* Golden Press, New York, 1963.
16. Elisa Gittings, *Shape Books,* Activity Resources, Haywood, California, 1974.
17. Averil Anderson, Teacher, Petaluma School District, Petaluma, California.
18. Anne Drummond, Parent Volunteer Aide, Novato Unified School District, Novato, California.
19. Florence Moon, Teacher, Petaluma School District, Petaluma, California.
20. Darlene Dinelli, Teacher, Kentfield School District, Kentfield, California.
21. Alma Briggs, Teacher, Sausalito Unified School District, Sausalito, California.
22. Darlene Dinelli, Ibid.
23. Sidney B. Simon, Leland W. Howe and Howard Kirschenbaun, *Values Clarification,* Hart Publishing Company, New York, 1972.
24. Anne Drummond, Ibid.
25. Hannah Campbell, *Why Did They Name It . . . ?,* ACE Books, New York, 1964.
26. Remy Charlip, *Fortunately,* Parents' Magazine Press, New York, 1964.
27. Teachers Exchange of San Francisco, *Title Twister,* San Francisco, California.
28. *Story Starters,* Creative Teaching Press, Monterey Park, California, 1972.
29. Dana Torres and Laura Duckworth, Students of Claire Molencamp, librarian Jean Hill, Novato Unified School District, Novato, California.

CHAPTER XI

Computation Math Center

Overview

Designing and making all the necessary materials for an individualized computational mathematics program can be overwhelming. However, if you start with a commercial text, adapt and add to it as necessary. Much less work in involved, and an individualized math program still results. The student text can be divided into mini-units. Each covers one skill. These can be supplemented as necessary with additional dittos. Or, if you are using a non-consumable text, mini-units can be made by listing the appropriate pages a student is to work. When students complete one of these mini-units, they are given a check-up page which checks their mastery of the current skill and previous skills.

If the check-up page indicates the student needs further work on the current skill or needs to review a previous skill, additional practice can be provided through the use of extension pages. (See page 210-211.) Once a child has passed a check-up page, the next mini-unit can be begun under your direction.

(This may be either in a small group situation or on a one-to-one basis.) The student works as many problems with your guidance as necessary to feel secure. The child then can continue working independently in the mini-unit, since it only contains problems on the current skill.

This system works successfully as part of your learning center's time block. Or with slightly less individualism, it can be implemented during a separate self-contained math time period, during which all of the students work on math. (See "Classroom Organizational Strategies," page 220-227.)

Sequencing Skills

The first step in setting up your individualized math program is to determine a sequence of skills. Before making any of the materials, you should carefully examine the sequence in the math text you use, in order to determine whether it meets your teaching style. Almost all teachers have certain preferences for the order in which they teach skills. One teacher will say, "Once I teach carrying, I find it is quite easy to teach the concept of borrowing." Another teacher with equal determination says, "Oh no. I find it is much easier to teach borrowing first. Children are familiar with the idea of borrowing from someone if they don't have enough of something . . . then I teach carrying."

Since there is no one "right way," make the changes as necessary in the math text sequence to reflect what works for you.

To determine the number of levels in the sequence, ask yourself, "If everyone in this class were exactly on "grade-level," which skills would I want to teach? Which are essential?" List these. Realistically, you know that everyone is not on grade level. Think of which essential skills students should have mastered before coming to your grade level. List these. By the same token, some of the students will complete all the skills on the original "grade-level" list. List those advanced skills which could be helpful to have them learn and/or confer with a teacher of the next grade level.

Now you have an idea of the scope of levels you will eventually need. Fortunately, you will not need all the material at one time. It is often possible to stay just ahead of the fastest-moving students.

Making Mini-Units From Consumable and Non-Consumable Textbooks

The next step is to assemble stapled booklets or mini-units for each of the skills listed on your skill sequence. These mini-units are extremely popular with students. They know they can complete one in a few days' time, and are therefore continually rewarded with a sense of accomplishment.

Much of the material you will need in order to assemble the mini-units will be taken from the commercial textbook. To make a master set of mini-units from a student text follow this procedure:

1. Eliminate or cross off any page or partial page which is more confusing than helpful (expanded notation, etc.).
2. Remove all pages which include linear measurement, volume, clocks, money, etc. Staple these into mini-units to be taught at a time when you have all of the materials available which correlate with the particular unit.
3. Note the first skill listed on your sequence. Remove all pages from the text which deal with this skill, and staple them into a mini-unit. Continue this same procedure, preparing mini-units for each skill listed on your sequence. (If no material is included in the text for a skill you have listed, make a note indicating that you will need to make material for this skill.)
4. Count the number of pages in each stapled booklet. Is it sufficient for students to master the skill? If you feel more practice will be needed, make a note at the top of the mini-unit, indicating how many supplementary pages will be needed.
5. Make a master of the facts which can appropriately be included in each skill lesson. You will find this bank of facts a tremendous time-saver when making supplemental pages.

To make a master list, recopy your skill

sequences. Next to each skill, list sample problems:

A. If the unit is a *Process Unit* (two and three-place addition and subtraction without regrouping, borrowing, carrying, two or three digit multiplication or division, etc.), write a few sample problems with a reminder of what should be included or excluded. (E.g., for two-place addition without regrouping, your note would serve as a reminder to be certain not to include any problems which require carrying.)

B. If the unit is a *Basic Fact Unit* (addition, subtraction, multiplication, division) it is necessary to write all of the problems related to that specific skill. E.g., for "Addition Combinations with Sums of 7", you would list the following facts:

$$\begin{array}{cccccccc} 0 & 1 & 2 & 3 & 4 & 5 & 6 & 7 \\ +7 & +6 & +5 & +4 & +3 & +2 & +1 & +0 \end{array}$$

Now that you have a sample set of mini-units and a master list of facts, you or an aide (many parents are willing to do this type of work at home) can assemble the materials for the entire class. Each student's text needs to

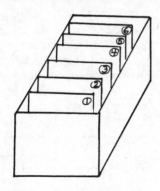

Storage of Mini-Units

be marked and stapled into mini-units according to the format previously described. (Use the materials you assembled as "master samples.") All of the copies of the same mini-unit should be kept in a labeled folder. (This can be $12'' \times 18''$ construction paper or tagboard folded in half.) The folders should be placed in a large cardboard box, covered with construction paper or contact paper.

If you want to be fancy, you can store the booklets in hanging file folders, available in stationery stores. These are quite sturdy. They literally "hang" from runners inside a storage box or file cabinet.

The core of your math program is now assembled. The next step is to add supplemental pages to those mini-units which do not contain sufficient work for the students to master the skill. Since you obviously cannot make all of these at once, you need to determine a priority list. This priority list will greatly depend on the organizational plan you intend to use for individualizing math (see pages 220-227) and on the results of a diagnostic skill inventory.

Diagnostic Entry Skill Inventory

Before students begin working on the mini-units, it is necessary to determine whether they have mastered the entry skills. (They are those you listed on your sequence as being essential for children to master before beginning the list of grade-level skills.) Make a Diagnostic Entry Skill Inventory by writing four or five problems for each of the *process* skills which you feel are essential for the student to have previously mastered. (Refer to your skill sequence.)

Also make lists of the *basic facts* the student should have mastered. Give timed tests on these. (See pages 216-217.) Children may understand the concept of addition, subtraction, multiplication or division facts. But they may not have developed speed and accuracy. In this case, it would be important to work on building speed and accuracy with these facts before introducing new skills.

The results of these tests can now be used to help you determine your priority list for making supplementary material.

Priority List for Making Materials

The first priority should be to make mini-units for entry skills which students haven't mastered. The provision of appropriate material for these students is the beginning of your individualized math program.

If math is one of your daily centers, the remainder of the children work on the first mini-unit assembled from the student text. Self-pacing can now begin. The students can proceed at their own rates through the various mini-units (with you or an aide staying just ahead of them, making supplemental pages, check-up pages and extension pages). Although at this point the program is not completely individualized, since many of the students started at the same place, individual differences will soon become apparent, creating a wide range of levels.

The following year you will be able to individualize your program completely. (See page 227.)

Check-Up and Extension Pages

A check-up and extension page follows each mini-unit. Each check-up page should contain problems on the current skill, as well as review problems. Four or five problems on each concept will provide sufficient diagnostic information. Check-up pages are used to determine whether a student needs any review. E.g., a check-up page following the mini-unit on borrowing might indicate that the student had mastered this concept, but was uncertain about the process of carrying, which had been taught earlier. In this case, you would review carrying with the child and then assign one or two extension pages. The extension pages should contain only problems related to the specific skill.

Check-up page

210

Extension Page for Mini-Unit 5 (Carrying)

Name _____

57 +19	36 +28	48 +13	26 +24	16 +66
37 +15	51 +19	54 +37	22 +39	59 +13
45 +15	37 +46	39 +42	47 +17	56 +28
45 +38	32 +19	35 +56	27 +49	78 +13
28 +45	17 +56	35 +59	15 +18	22 +68
21 +19	34 +47	15 +16	18 +54	25 +35
64 +19	13 +27	27 +64	72 +18	64 +16

Extension page

Although one extension page for each mini-unit will suffice, two extension pages allow more flexibility in the amount of review work you assign a child.

Check-up and extension pages can be kept in a vegetable bin or box. Store each set of pages in a labeled folder (12"×18" construction paper folded in half).

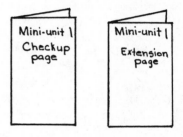

Storage folders for check-up and extension pages

Storage of check-up and extension pages in vegetable bin

Teaching New Skills

Now you're ready to think about teaching! It is important to keep in mind that students learn in different ways. There are three main methods you can use to teach mathematical concepts and processes to children:
(1) Through the use of concrete materials (discovery approach).
(2) By stressing relationships ("new math").
(3) By memorizing the process (how most adults learned math).
Experiment with various methods of introducing new concepts which you have

found successful. By insisting on only one approach, many young children who are not developmentally ready to understand that particular concept end up disliking math, not only in school but for life. Whenever possible, use manipulative materials so students have a concrete frame of reference.

Until society changes what it expects a child to know, for example, in second grade—facts to twenty, borrowing, carrying; third grade—multiplication and division with regrouping, etc., you are left with the responsibility of seeking ways that will help the student live up to these standards. At the same time you have to try to avoid turning off the students. In some cases this will mean teaching the step-by-step process for working math problems. ("This is how you get the answer. . . .")

For instance, a child may have worked for some time on basic addition and subtraction problems, using counters to derive the answers slowly and tediously, and still not have memorized any of the facts. At this point you might introduce the process of using fingers as a quick means of determining the answer. To work the addition problem 8+2, the student would say the larger number, regardless of whether it was the first or second number in the problem, and then count on from that number.

"eight"   "nine"   "ten"

Using fingers to work addition problems

Using fingers to count is not necessarily an evil. In the June 1975 issue of the medical magazine, *MD,* (1) there was an article about the former child prodigy, Norbert Wiener. Before he was 12, he was a college freshman. By the age of 14 he had earned his Bachelor of Arts. By 18 he was a Harvard Ph.D. Today he is considered one of the masterminds of science, although he is primarily a theoretical mathematician. Now here, one would think, is someone who would not have counted on his fingers! Yet that is precisely what he did, well into adolescence!

Using fingers as counters can be a tremendous help or an equally tremendous handicap. If, in order to work the problem 8+2, the child first slowly counts off eight fingers, then an additional two fingers, and then *goes back* and recounts all of the fingers he has used, it is a slow cumbersome process.

When a child has difficulty understanding a concept, it is important to provide the necessary tools to be able to work the problem, whether it is simple addition, borrowing, carrying, multiplication, etc. In time, understanding may develop and the student may continue into higher mathematics. If, however, the child never reaches this level of understanding, at least he or she possesses the basic skills that society demands.

Be certain, however, not to neglect the student who can learn by understanding relationships, discovering concepts and applying old concepts to new situations. It is important for you to see that this child has every opportunity to learn in these exciting ways.

It is also of utmost importance to ask questions as you work on new skills. This questioning process is best accomplished by explaining one new problem to the student. The child then explains how to work the next problem. You should intervene only if a mistake is made or the student seems uncertain. This enables you to find out what the child understands and does not understand. Then, instead of re-teaching everything, you teach to the specific needs of that particular child. This becomes a tremendous time-saver.

Correcting Completed Work and Parent Communication

When children work at an appropriate skill level, understand what they are doing and feel successful, it is amazing how much work they complete daily! However, if you or a classroom aide has to correct all the completed mini-units, the correction time can become all-consuming.

An alternative is to make a quick daily check of each student's work. This can easily be accomplished at the math center by glancing over each child's shoulder and spot-checking several problems. As has been previously stated, a child does not begin working independently in a stapled booklet until you feel that he or she understands how to work problems involving the current skill. Since the only problems encountered in the unit are those involving the current skills, a daily spot-check suffices, provided that the student completes a check-up page at the end of each new unit. The check-up page is the child's proof of having mastered the current concept, as well as the teacher's record.

If this procedure is used, a completed mini-unit is only spot-checked. It is important that you explain to the child that the purpose of the mini-unit is to provide practice so that facility with the current skill can be developed. If the student has made a few mistakes along the way, it is all right, pro-

vided that the check-up page indicates current mastery of the skill.

Obviously you should not send the completed mini-unit home if it is not corrected. Instead, attach the check-up page to a Parent Communication Form.

date _____

This signifies that _____

has completed the required work _____

Your child's knowledge of the current skill, as well as of skills taught at an earlier time, has been checked on the attached page.

Please sign here. _____

Date _____

Parent communication form

When the parent signs and returns the form, it becomes a record of the information you have sent home. An explanatory letter should be sent along with the first Parent Communication Form, indicating that instead of sending home all of the required work the child has completed, you are sending a page which checked mastery of the current and previous skills. You may also want

213

to attach the last page (corrected!) of the mini-unit as a sample of the work the child completed. The letter should also explain that in addition to the check-up page there have been daily informal checks by the teacher.

Should you decide that you want all of the students' work corrected, several strategies are possible.

If you teach at a school in which parents are actively involved, frequently parents will say that they would like to help at school but are unable to because of baby-sitting problems, etc. These parents are often willing to work at home, however. Correcting math mini-units is made to order!

List the parents who have offered to check work at home and the days they are available. The completed mini-units can then be slipped into a plastic bag and sent home with the proper child for the parent to correct. On the following day they are returned, corrected, and ready to be distributed.

Be certain to work out a system with the parents which assures that you are notified if it appears a child is having a problem. One such system involves having the volunteers divide the corrected mini-units into three groups: (1) Those in which students have missed a minimal number of problems (these can be sent home if you wish); (2) Those where___?___ or more problems have been missed (these should be returned to the students for the necessary corrections); (3) Those in which the students have made sufficient mistakes that you need to review some of the problems missed with each of those children.

The relationship between the exact number of problems missed on a given page and whether follow-up or corrections are necessary will need to be determined by you. You will have to take into consideration the difficulty of the material and the number of problems on the page.

Another method for correcting completed work is to have each student correct the top two lines on each page, and you correct the remainder on the page. This can easily be facilitated by making tagboard answer-cards for each of the mini-units. The student lays the answer cards on top of the completed math page.

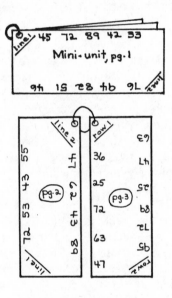

Tagboard answer cards

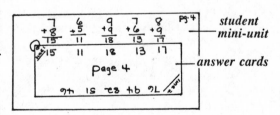

Using tagboard answer cards for correction

Explain to the children that they will only be making more work for themselves if they copy the answers, since the check-up page will reveal whether they have mastered the skill. All their time copying will have been wasted since they will have to re-do the work. Students quickly see the futility in copying under these circumstances.

One additional advantage of answer cards is that the children can check their own progress, discover for themselves if they are making mistakes and ask for help if needed.

Record-Keeping

It is extremely helpful to have the student keep his or her math materials in a file folder at the math center. By attaching a dittoed math record to the front of the file folder, the student automatically has the record at hand

whenever working at the math center. Hence it is readily available for reference.

Teachers often intend to get a child's record and add a note to it. However, the end of the day comes and goes and the note doesn't get written. By having the record with the student, you will be amazed at how much more information you actually do write down.

The record should be filled in as a child completes a check-up page, and you determine the next step. While this information is fresh in your mind, filling in the Parent-Communication Form and the child's record takes only a few minutes. Be certain to discuss with the student what you are writing. These little notes and discussions become so important to students that they will remind you if you neglect to fill in their record when they have completed a check-up page! Additional observations should be written under "Other Comments."

Multiplication and Division (with and without regrouping)					Name _____		
date start	finish	Mini-unit	Example	No. of pgs.	Comment	Instruction needed	Additional Comments
		① 1 place x 2 place (no regrouping)	24 x 2	3			
		② 1 place x 3 place (no regrouping)	232 x 2	3			
		③ 1 place x 2 place with regrouping	35 x 3	6			

Sample record page

215

Student math file folders and record pages are a marvelous asset at report card time. In addition during parent conferences, you can show the parents the child's folder. The record stapled to the front of the folder presents a complete picture of the work the student has completed in computational math during the year. Inside the folder the parent will find the material on which the child is currently working. This is a very effective way of communicating with parents about their children's progress.

Checking Mastery of Facts

The mini-units at kindergarten and beginning first grade should be used by the child in conjunction with counters or manipulative materials. The student should compare numbers and discover what happens when one adds to a number or takes away from a given number. The emphasis at this level should not be on memorizing facts.

Towards the end of first grade, however, you should begin having the students work for speed and accuracy with basic facts. Mastering facts (addition, subtraction, multiplication and division) should be stressed at each of the succeeding levels.

Time Tests

To check fact mastery, you can give periodic time tests which cover the facts in the mini-units. To make time tests, refer to your master list of facts in each booklet and include on each time-test current facts and review of previous facts.

Facts to ten time test

A graph of the results of the time tests should be kept in the math file folders as a record of each child's growth. This enables the child to see his or her progress, and at the same time eliminates the competition with everyone in the class.

Three Minute Time Test

Name Jim

Date	May 10	May 12	May 13			
30						
29						
28						
27						
26						
25						
24						
23						
22						
21						
20						
19						
18						
17						
16						
15						
14						
13						
12						
11						
10						
9						
8						
7						
6						
5						
4						
3						
2						
1						

*Individual graph of results
of three minute time tests*

Students may work time tests at the math center. Or you may prefer to plan time tests as a total group activity.

It is best to give a time test at the end of each of the multiplication and division basic fact mini-units. Administering time tests at the end of the more advanced addition and subtraction basic fact mini-units, is also effective.

An alternate method for checking mastery of facts is for the teacher to make sets of flash cards which correspond to individual mini-units. Each set of flash cards should have the facts for that unit. You may also wish to include review of previous facts.

To make the flash cards, cut 3"×5" index cards in half. Write a fact on each card. Label the top card with the corresponding mini-unit. Punch holes in each of the cards, which can then be kept together with a ring. (This eliminates many potential mix-ups.) Code the cards so you can easily tell which cards belong to each set. (Use different colors of ink to write the problems. Or put a colored dot in the corner of each of the cards which belong to a specific set.)

*Flash cards for
testing fact-mastery*

The teacher, an aide or an upper-grade student can test students with the set of flash cards. While testing, the cards should be separated into two piles: those mastered, and those the student doesn't know or seems uncertain about.

You should write the facts the child doesn't know under "Comments" on the record page attached to the math file-folder.

In addition, most students enjoy keeping an on-going record of the facts they have mastered. This can be arranged with a minimum of teacher time. Besides, it is a good ego builder!

Temporarily retain the flash cards the student did not know. The flash cards that were known are put back on the ring and given to the student. The child then marks or colors in the facts already known on the Fact-Mastery Record. (This can be attached to the math file folder.)

Fact-mastery records should list the new facts covered in each mini-unit. (Once more, refer to your "master list.")

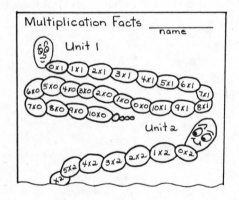

Fact-mastery record

When the student has finished marking the fact record, you can easily double-check to make certain there has been no accidental (or otherwise) marking off any of the facts not yet mastered, by referring to the flash cards you kept. These flash cards can then be returned to the ringed set.

Practicing For Fact Mastery

If the time test or ringed flash cards indicate the child needs additional work on basic facts, additional drill should be provided. This can be accomplished by having the children practice with individual sets of flash cards.

Flash cards are often threatening to a student because there are a large number to master simultaneously. To avoid a feeling of being overwhelmed, the child should be asked to take only two new facts each day and to add these to the pile of already mastered facts.

You can have a designated time each day when all the children make their next two flash cards, put answers on the back of the cards and then practice with partners. This could be done the first thing in the morning or after lunch.

Discarded computer cards are free, and excellent for flash cards. These can be procured from many companies which use computers.

An alternate method is to have the students make their flash cards at the math center. You can start the center some days by having the students make their next two flash cards and practice with partners. Other days, they can make their next two flash cards and then take a time test as a means of practicing for speed.

In addition to practicing on their flash cards at school, they can be assigned as home work each evening.

If the mini-units are being used in an individualized, self-pacing format, the children will be using different booklets. Therefore, their stacks of flash cards will also be different. Determining which two facts a student should write each day can be handled by having the child refer to the Fact-Mastery Record.

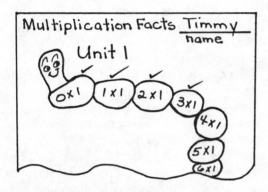

Indicating which flash cards have been made

While making a flash card, the child checks off that specific fact on the Fact-Mastery Record.

By referring to the above record, the child would know that the next two flash cards to make are 4×1 and 5×1. By the time the student completes a mini-unit, all facts for that unit should have been made.

Another way to handle flash card-making is to have the child make all the flash cards

for a particular mini-unit when the unit is first begun. These cards can then be stored in an envelope attached to the inside cover of the math folder. Each day two flash cards are removed and added to the pile of mastered facts.

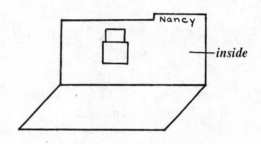

Storage of flash cards in the student's math folder

You may wish to point out that, when facts come in "pairs," such as 6×2 and 2×6, students may want to take two "pairs" (four facts) instead of just two facts.

A less individualized approach to making flash cards, but one which nevertheless provides the needed drill, consists of having a time each day when all of the students make the same two flash cards. Announce the two facts for that day. Then, write them on a chart of "Mastered Facts."

The students add these to their previous flash cards, and take the entire stack of flash cards home each evening for practice.

You may also want to have the students chant the facts from the chart as an added means of reinforcement.

To avoid too much paper-and-pencil drill, skill games can be assigned for added reinforcement, according to the individual child's needs, or can be group-assigned.

Classroom Organizational Strategies

Thirty minutes a day is generally sufficient for the type of individualized math program which has been described in this chapter. The children are actually involved in working on math problems the entire time, rather than copying problems or struggling through concepts they do not understand.

In addition to the computational math program, time should be planned for instruction and experiences with fractions, linear measurement, volume, telling time, geometry, balance scales, area, money, symmetry, story problems, etc. These are excellent for Discovery Centers. (See Chapter XIII.)

The ideal situation for this program is a learning center's environment with three or four centers, two of which are supervised by the teacher and an aide (volunteer or para-professional). However, the individualized math program can be incorporated in a variety of environments.

Because teachers are often concerned about ways to schedule an individualized math program, this section describes several organizational plans. Some include the use of aides (volunteer or para-professional). Others are designed for classrooms without aides.

When Teacher and Aide Supervise Three or Four Learning Centers, Heterogeneously Grouped

With an aide in the classroom, two centers are supervised. New skills can then be introduced at the math center on a one-to-one basis, by you or your aide. As you work with one child, the other children at the math center carry on independently in their own mini-units. Children proceed at their own pace. Your time is spent introducing concepts and spot-checking each child's work daily.

Check-up pages are given as each student finishes a mini-unit. Immediately correct the check-up page. Assign extension pages if necessary. If the check-up page indicates the student does not need any review work, introduce the next skill.

In this organizational plan, with two adults in the room (one at the writing center and one at the math center), the demands on the person at the math center and the amount of time available balance to perfection!

When you introduce skills on a one-to-one basis, it will take only 5 to 10 minutes, as opposed to 30 to 45 minutes for even small group instruction. Because you are working with only one student, it immediately becomes apparent when the child is confused. Therefore you teach to his or her specific needs. Time is not wasted trying to teach to everyone's needs, re-teaching and again re-teaching! (Re-teaching is always much harder for both the child and the teacher.)

One-to-one teaching also allows you to interact with a child. You get to know the student, and become acquainted with that child's special style of learning. In addition, because of the one-to-one instruction the child is always successful in learning new skills/concepts.

Seldom will two students simultaneously need your help. In the few cases when this does happen, ask one of the students to work on the flash cards, other reinforcement activities or in a supplemental math book or kit while waiting for help or instruction.

When Teacher Alone Supervises Three or Four Learning Centers, Heterogeneously Grouped

As in the previous plan, the children rotate to three or four centers daily. Math is one of the centers. Because there is no teacher aide, your time needs to be divided between the math center and the writing center. Plan to spend three days each week at the math center and two days each week at the writing center. On the days you work at the math center, it is important that the assignments for the writing center involve activities which the students can accomplish with a minimum of teacher help. (See pages 252-253.)

Since the students are grouped heterogeneously, there are "high" math students, "middle" math students and "low" math students in each group. The best plan is for you to work at the math center with the two or three students in that group who are at the same level. The remainder of the children at the center work independently in their mini-units.

The following charts are an example of four heterogeneous groups, and three levels of math ability within each group:

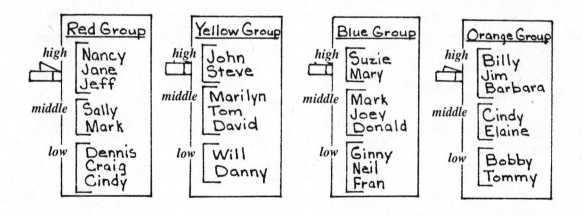

Scheduling instructional sub-groups

221

Each of the three days you are at the math center, work with one of the math levels within the color-coded groups, introducing a new skill or reviewing a previous skill.

A clothespin attached to each of the color-coded charts indicates the level of instruction for that day. (In the above illustrations, you would be working with the "high" level math students.)

The students should work under your direction as many problems as necessary until you feel they are secure with the new skill. Because you work with only two or three students, you are able to give much individual attention. (Although one-to-one instruction is the ideal, it is not always possible without extra hands.)

The second day you work with the "middle" math students, and the third day with the "low" math students.

Instead of using mini-units, you can use single dittos and pages from the student's textbooks.

List the students in each of the three math levels. Attach these lists to three coffee cans. Fasten a "work with me today" sign to one of the cans to indicate the students you will instruct that day. Have a ditto prepared for them which is the equivalent of the first page of a new mini-unit (problems involving a new skill). In the other cans, put the required work for the other groups (one or two dittos or text pages which review current and previous concepts).

*Indicating math material
for each student*

As the students complete the required work, they can then work with their flash cards, other reinforcement activities or in a supplemental math text.

Each day as you correct the students' work, determine assignments for the following day. If the students at one of the levels have completed the equivalent of a mini-unit and check-up page, and it appears they have mastered the current skill, introduce a new skill to this group the following day. How-ever, if you wish to work at a different center on the following day, flash cards, other reinforcement activities or supplemental math texts or kits would be appropriate.

This plan necessitates making three or more dittos each evening, so assignments can be placed in each of the cans daily. Gradually you can build up your supply of dittos. In the future these can be assembled into mini-units if you decide you prefer that method.

An Alternative Method: When Teacher Alone Supervises Three or Four Learning Centers, Heterogeneously Grouped

The preceding organizational plan can be adapted in the following manner. Instead of putting daily assignments in coffee cans, you can give the students the entire mini-units when you introduce them to a new skill. The length of time to complete a mini-unit would be determined ahead of time. This would vary from level to level and from mini-unit to mini-unit. The date of completion of the unit is assigned. With younger children or children who have a difficult time budgeting their time, it might be necessary to have them mark how much should be completed each day in order for them to finish the assignment on time. Children who fall behind can use their Independent-Center time to work on math, or take their mini-units home as many nights as necessary in order to complete the assignment.

Since your goal is to build positive attitudes toward math, it is extremely important to assign an amount of work daily which you feel the students will actually be able to complete during their math center.

Some skill units may take longer than a week to complete. These will enable you to spend more time at the other centers.

As in the previous plan, if students finish a skill unit ahead of time, they should work at the math center with flash cards, other reinforcement activities, or with a supplemental math textbook or kit.

When Teacher Alone Supervises Entire Class in Math Period, Grouped by Ability

Set aside a time block each day for the entire class to work on math. Extend the skills covered on the Entry Skills Diagnostic Inventory to include grade-level skills. You can then use the results of this inventory to divide the students into four math ability groups. Each day introduce a new skill. Or review a previous skill with two groups. Work with each of these groups of students for approximately 20 minutes. Meanwhile, the other two math groups work independently.

A sample schedule follows:

	Day 1		Day 2		Day 3		Day 4	
	20 min.	*20 min.*	*20 min.*	*20 min.*	*20 min.*	*20 min.*	*20 min.*	*20 min.*
Group 1	*with teacher*	← *assignment* →			*with teacher*	← *assignment* →		
Group 2	→	*with teacher*	← *assignment* →			*with teacher*	← *assignment*	
Group 3	*assignment* →		*with teacher*	← *assignment* →			*with teacher*	←
Group 4	← *assignment* →			*with teacher*	← *assignment* →			*with teacher*

The following is a typical schedule for three centers which follow or precede the total group math period.

	Mon.	Tues.	Wed.	Thurs.	Fri.
1.	*writing (mechanics and creative writing)*	*writing*	*writing*	*writing*	*language arts assignment*
2.	*individualized spelling*	*manipulative math or science*	*individualized spelling*	*manipulative math or science*	*spelling tests*
3.	*independent*	*language arts assignment*	*independent*	*art*	*independent*

This schedule allows you to spend three or four days each week at the writing center.

An alternate plan for the learning center time-block consists of four centers in the room, with each child attending only two centers each day. (See pages 21-23.)

When Teacher, Alone or with Aide, Supervises Entire Class in Math, Employing Flexible Groups and/or Student Contracts

Set aside a time block each day for the entire class to work on math. (Students using contracts will work on math throughout the day.) Your time will be spent introducing new concepts to small groups. As a student understands the concept, he or she leaves the center. This allows you to continue working with children who need extra help.

In order to organize the flexible groups, you will need to prepare a large chart, using library pockets mounted on chipboard. Each pocket should be labeled to correspond with one of the mini-units. If the unit provides review or for some other reason requires little explanation, the pocket should be labeled "See me." If, however, the mini-unit covers a more complex concept (borrowing, carrying, multiplication or division with regrouping, etc.), the pocket is labeled "STOP."

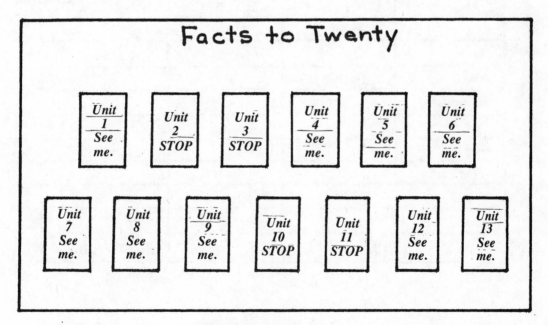

Using a pocket chart to schedule instructional groups

225

The children have individual name-cards. As a child completes a mini-unit and passes the corresponding check-up page, the card is moved to the next pocket. If the pocket is labeled "See me," give the student the next mini-unit. You can then briefly explain whatever the child needs to know in order to start successfully on that unit.

However, if the pocket says "STOP," the student waits until you call an instructional group for that skill. While awaiting instruction the child works with individual flash cards, on other reinforcement activities or in a supplemental math text or kit.

Determine instructional groups by checking the "STOP" pockets on the chart. An instructional group may be one or two children, or as many as seven or eight.

You should also keep a class record indicating when you work with each child. This enables you to see at a glance who has not had instruction for a while.

	Nov. 9-16	*Nov. 16-23*	*Nov. 23-30*
Anne	Un. 1 / Un. 2	Un. 3	Un. 4 / Un. 5
Betty	Un. 4		
David		Un. 6	Un. 7
Dolly	Un. 3		
Eileen	Un. 1	Un. 2	
Fred		Un. 6	Un. 7
Ginny	Un. 4		Un. 5
Hank	Un. 11	Un. 12	
Helen		Un. 2	Un. 3
Karl	Un. 5	Un. 6 / Un. 7	Un. 8
Kevin	Un. 2 / Un. 3	Un. 4	Un. 5 / Un. 6

Math record

Using this organizational plan in a daily math period works well for the teacher without aides. Obviously, the children will not get as much individual attention, as if there were two adults in the classroom. However, there is still a considerable amount of individualization and self-pacing.

Determining Original Placement in the Second Year of The Program

After using this self-pacing format for a year, you will have assembled a wide range of mini-units, extension pages and check-up pages. You can now use the program in a completely individualized format, determining individual placement for each child.

In order to use the program in this way, you will need to make a diagnostic inventory for mini-units on *processes* (addition and subtraction with and without grouping, multiplication and division with and without re-grouping, etc.). Refer to your master list of problems included in each booklet: entry skills, grade-level skills, advanced skills. Write four or five facts which are representative of each of the processes covered in the mini-units. Tell the students that they will know how to work some of the problems but will not know others. It should be explained that you do not want to give work that is either too hard or too easy. Students should work as far as they can. When they come to problems they do not understand, they should stop. The inventory helps you discover what they already know and what they need to learn.

A child may not need to work each of the mini-units at any one level. For instance, a student may have forgotten how to borrow, but may be secure on all of the other processes covered in "Addition and Subtraction of Two and Three Digit Numbers, With and Without Re-grouping." In that case the only mini-unit the child would need at that level would be the one about borrowing. Note on the record stapled to the front of the student's math folder each skill mastered, so these will not be duplicated.

Your diagnostic inventory will also need to include time tests for mini-units on *basic facts* (addition, subtraction, multiplication and division).

The results of these inventories will allow you to design an individualized math program for each student, geared to specific personal needs throughout the year.

Notes

1. "Master Mind," *MD* magazine, pp. 139-146, June 1975.

CHAPTER XII

Discovery Center
(Manipulative Math/Science)

Introduction

The list of possible manipulative math/ science experiences, which can be used at a Discovery Center, is limitless. Each item suggests additional possibilities! Your problem should not be, "What can I plan for a Discovery Center?" but instead, "With so many exciting possibilities, what shall I choose!" For starters, consider the following:

1. Science units which actively involve the student and/or reference work
2. Telling time
3. Ordinal numbers
4. Fractions
5. Odd/even experiments
6. Place value
7. More than/less than
8. Money
9. Estimation
10. Symmetry
11. Map making
12. Linear measurement ⎫
13. Volume (sand and   *Standard and*
    water measurement)   *non-standard*
14. Area and shapes   *units of*
15. Geoboards   *measurement*
16. Classification ⎭
17. Attribute blocks
18. Balance scales
19. Mobiles
20. Building structures (straws, tooth-picks, bridges, etc.)
21. Co-ordinates
22. Working with various size scales: 1 inch scale, ½ inch scale, ¼ inch scale, etc.
23. Tangrams
24. Geometry concepts (line segments, points, "closed and not closed")
25. Solid shapes

Teachers often involve students with a

manipulative math/science experience in one area of the curriculum, followed by a completely unrelated task. This results in an endless series of unconnected experiences. This type of approach fragments learning. It discourages student involvement. Instead, a series of experiences should be designed, each of which builds on the knowledge gained in the previous tasks. This allows students the time to reflect on what they have discovered and an opportunity to become involved in the subject matter.

When planning and implementing a series of experiences of this type, a learning centers environment is a tremendous asset. Less materials are needed than if the entire class were involved simultaneously. And students don't have to be rushed.

Because of the disparity of entry levels in student understanding of fractions, telling time, money, etc., you may wish to have a diagnostic center in order to determine the individual student's current level of comprehension. You can then re-group children for appropriate follow-up instruction and assignments. (See page 21.)

For other manipulative math/science topics you can introduce the concepts and materials required at a center. This is necessary for experimental science units and for some manipulative math units, such as geoboards, tangrams, etc. After the initial introductory center, you can structure follow-up work which the students can do independently, or with a minimum of teacher assistance.

Many manipulative math/science units only require a brief introduction and discussion with the total group in order for students to proceed independently with their work at the Discovery Center.

If there are only enough materials for two

or three students (water measurement, balance scales, etc.), subdivide the group into two or three sections. Write a one, two, or three after each student's name, taking into consideration the students who would work well together. Each sub-group works on a different activity. Make a chart indicating the three different activities. Use numbered clothes pins as markers. (These can be rotated when the assignments are completed.) The clothes pins indicate the new assignment for each sub-group.

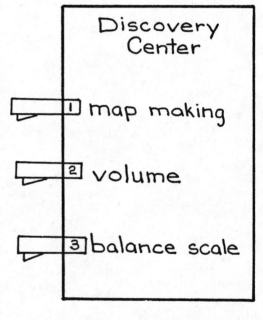

Assignment chart

When scheduling different assignments for subgroups at the Discovery Center, it is important to design the assignments so that they require approximately the same length of time to complete. They can take one day, or extend over a week or more. However, it is best to begin with one-day assignments, with the amount of work to be completed by the end of the center time clearly defined. The assignment should be such that the students can easily complete it in the allotted time, provided that they use their time well.

Daily assignments encourage students to develop good study habits, since it is immediately apparent if they have wasted time. Encouraging students to use their time effectively at the Discovery Center is important, since they will be working independently at this center. At the beginning of the year, check the center at the end of each time block to determine who may not have completed the assignment. Insist that it be finished during the Independent Center or recess. Once the students become aware of the fact that you know how efficiently they are using their time, and their study habits become established, you need only check the center at intervals.

As students become responsible, assignments can span three to four days. A series of experiences using the same material, and building on concepts developed in previous tasks falls into this category. One of the subgroups at the center might have a three-day assignment in map making. Another subgroup works on volume. And the third subgroup experiments with balance scales.

Tell the students that they will probably be able to finish their assignments in three days, provided that they use their time well. When they are finished and their work has been checked in terms of content and quality, they may spend the remaining days of the week during the Discovery time block either doing further experiments and investigations with the material, or may go to the Independent Center. (Don't schedule Independent as one of the four centers on these days, or it will become overcrowded.)

Other students may not apply themselves as much at the Discovery Center and will require the entire five days to complete their work. However, an assignment of this kind generally encourages students not to waste their time.

Assignments of this type should not be given until you have established your expectancies for quality work. The students must realize that rushing and handing in poor-quality work is not acceptable.

It is also essential, if students are to have independent time at the completion of their work, that the assignments not favor the more academically gifted students. The most gifted or least capable student in the class should be able to complete experiments with a balance scale in approximately the same amount of time. However, a research assignment would favor the more academically gifted students and penalize the less capable students if they were expected to complete the identical assignment in the same length of time.

Contracts can also be used at the Discovery Center. On the contract are listed various activities the student is to complete at that specific center within a given length of time. Each of the tasks requires approximately the same level of understanding, so the student may do the activities in any sequence. Later contracts will build upon the concepts developed in earlier contracts.

A sample manipulative math contract follows. Similar contracts can be made for language arts, science, social studies, etc.

Name _____ *Date started* _____

To be completed by _____

Use the box of measuring materials.
Work measurement task cards:

1	2	3	4	5	6

☐ *If you have a dog, use a string to measure the length of its tail.*
☐ *Tape the string to the graph on the wall.*

☐ *Listen to the tape, "How We Measure Things."*
☐ *Do the follow-up work sheet.*

☐ *Get someone to measure you. Color in the strip on the chart HOW TALL ARE YOU to show your height.*

Manipulative math contract

Contracts for upper-grade students can include detailed written directions. Picture symbols to indicate the various activities should be used on contracts for younger children.

When contracts are first introduced, be careful not to give students too many tasks or too many choices. This helps them to avoid indecision and confusion. Later, when you use longer contracts, you may find that these are difficult for students who have not developed the necessary self-discipline to budget their time. With these students it may be necessary for you to check their work daily and to specify the amount of work to be completed each day. Your hope, of course, is that in time they will learn to budget their

own time. Meanwhile it is important for you to provide structure and expectations.

When planning Discovery Centers for upper-grade students, bear in mind that they may have had limited concrete experiences on which to build. Often teachers ask students to deal with concepts on an abstract level before they have had time to develop an understanding by manipulating materials and discovering that abstract symbols and rules are the end product of actual experimentation with real materials.

Therefore, it is often necessary to begin with concrete experiences and slowly build to abstractions. As an example, the sample manipulative math unit in this chapter provides students with a thorough understanding of this symmetry. Students can then use this knowledge as the foundation for more advanced mathematical concepts.

Through careful selection and correlation of the units, Discovery can become an exciting center providing many worthwhile experiences for students. Use your imagination and professional sense, as there is no end to the possibilities!

Sample Manipulative Math Unit (Symmetry)

Students are always interested in "blob pictures," but often are unaware of the symmetrical properties of these pictures. Therefore, these are an ideal vehicle for introducing a unit on symmetry.

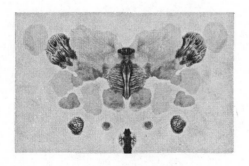

Blob pictures

Introduce the procedure for making blob pictures: (1) fold paper in half, (2) put some paint on one side of the paper, (3) carefully fold over the other side of the paper and gently press, (4) open.

Through observation and discussion, students should be led to discover if they drew a line down the middle of the picture, exactly the same thing would appear on both sides of the paper. ´

Tell them if they look carefully at their blob picture, sometimes it will look familiar. An added feature may be the key, in which case it is placed on one side of the picture, and the paper gently folded again.

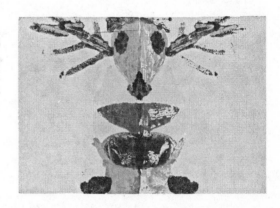

Blob picture which resembles something

After one or two Discovery Centers for experimentation, students will often discover that they can paint half of a picture, fold the paper and gently press, resulting in an entire picture.

If students have not yet discovered this, ask them to name symmetrical objects. They will generally name: butterflies, people, faces (animal, insects and people), leaves, flowers, insects—from a top view, etc. Ask what would happen if they folded a piece of

233

Symmetrically drawn pictures

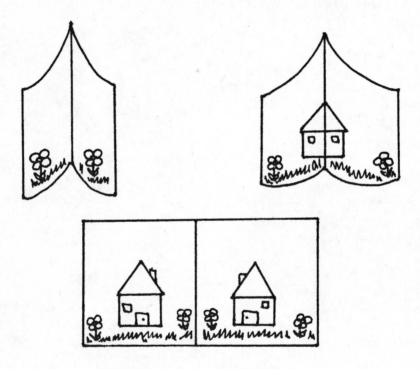

Checking a picture for symmetry

paper in half and painted half of one of these things near the center fold? Would there be a way they could get the entire picture without painting any more?

Students become fascinated with this prospect. Your Discovery Center is set for that day as the children experiment with "half-people, half-faces, half-animals . . ."

This is a good time to have students begin using crayons to draw symmetrical pictures.

Have available a stack of 4½″ by 9″ pieces of paper. Show the students several sample drawings such as the above. Ask if these are symmetrical. Then tell them a good way to check this is to fold the picture in half and then very slowly open it. If it is symmetrical, they should see exactly the same thing on both sides at the same time. Demonstrate this with your samples.

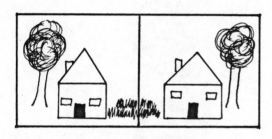

Non-symmetrical picture

In the above picture, opened slowly, students will discover that the chimneys are not symmetrical. Explain that if something is near the fold on one side of the picture, then for the picture to be symmetrical it must also be near the fold on the other side of the picture. The same rule applies to the edges of the paper. This provides a frame of reference as students draw their pictures. Encourage them to check their pictures using the fold-and-open-slowly technique. Students will need at least one Discovery Center to experiment with this concept.

Mirrors can be introduced effectively at this time. Help students discover that they can draw half a picture. The mirror will reproduce the remainder of the picture. *Mirror Cards* are an ideal supplement (1).

The experiences the students have had thus far involved mirror symmetry or bi-

lateral symmetry. Introduce this terminology and explain that, in Latin, *Bi* means two; lateral means side. Therefore, bilateral symmetry means two-sided symmetry.

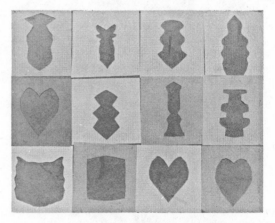

"Tiling" with symmetrical designs

The next project involves two sizes of colored construction paper. Each child will need one piece, 9″×12″, and enough 3″ squares to cover the large sheet. The little squares can be in a variety of colors, but the 9″×12″'s should be in a contrasting hue.

The student folds one of the 3″ squares and cuts out a shape. The square is then pasted on the 9″ by 12″ paper. The child continues this way until the entire page is covered or "tiled." (The small cut-out shapes can be put in a box and used for making greeting cards, etc.)

As the students cut out the shapes and then open the squares of paper, they are delighted to discover the symmetry in the resulting shape. This tiling experience leads to Discovery Centers investigating which shapes successfully cover a surface, and which shapes cannot be used for tiling. This in turn leads into study of area.

Flip-flop picture

The next experience is a logical outgrowth of the previous Discovery Center. For each student you will need one piece of 6"×12" construction paper and one piece of 3"×12" construction paper in a contrasting color. A thorough introduction and demonstration is necessary in order for students to understand the process.

They should cut out a series of shapes along one edge of the 3"×12" construction paper. These shapes should be saved. The 3"×12" piece of paper should be pasted to the 6"×12" paper so that the cut edge is in the middle.

Next, each of the cut-out shapes should be placed inside the corresponding shape on the 3"×12" paper, as if the student were working a puzzle.

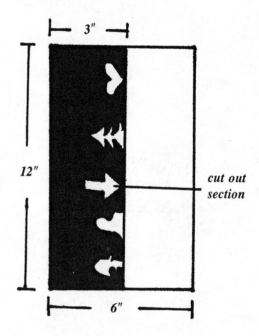

Step 1, Flip-flop picture

The student should then lift one of the pieces and turn it over, as if turning a page in a book. This piece should then be pasted in place.

The child should continue turning each piece over and pasting it in place until the picture is completed.

Students are always delighted with the results of these flip-flop pictures and intrigued by the positive/negative aspect of the symmetry.

Graph paper symmetrical picture

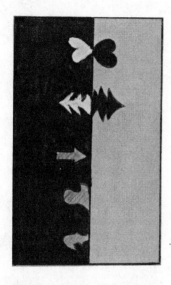

Step 2, Flip-flop picture

Drawing with crayons on 1″ graph paper is an ideal tool for further exploring their understanding of symmetry. Encourage students to discover symmetrical pictures which can be drawn on graph paper. They must continue to remember that what goes on one side must have a "twin" on the other side.

Up until this time most students will have used a vertical line of symmetry. Other lines

of symmetry can now be introduced. Experimentation can begin with letters of the alphabet. Have them write the alphabet in large capital letters, use a mirror, and discover which letters have mirror symmetry. Be certain to point out that the mirror may be turned vertically or horizontally. Have them draw in the line (or lines) of symmetry when they find it.

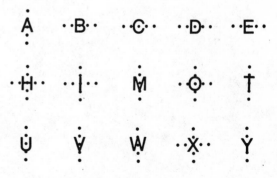

Children will be fascinated to discover that some letters have two lines of symmetry (H,

237

I, O, and X). Also, in some cases, differences in how the letter is formed will determine whether or not it is symmetrical. **K** is symmetrical. However, K is not symmetrical. Likewise U is symmetrical, but u is not.

Next, challenge them to see if they can discover a "mirror-image word"—

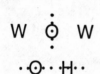

Folding paper and cutting out shapes, the way you used to make snowflake patterns, follows.

Start with two lines of symmetry, and introduce the following two variations.

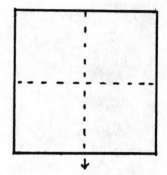

fold

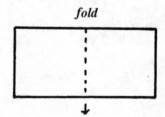

fold

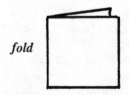

Snowflake pattern,
two lines of symmetry

Two lines of symmetry,
vertical and horizontal

Next move to four lines of symmetry.

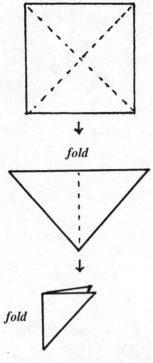

fold

fold

Two diagonal lines of symmetry

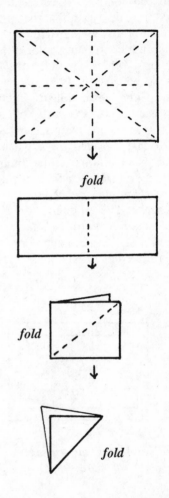

fold

fold

fold

Four lines of symmetry

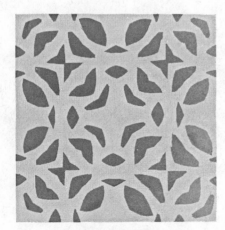

Snowflake pattern, four lines of symmetry

It is helpful to have the students draw in each line of symmetry with a different color of crayon. This makes it easier to determine which lines of symmetry have already been counted.

239

After this initial directed exploration, the students can continue investigating on their own. You might suggest that they select their favorite cut-out symmetrical pattern, and mount it on a contrasting color of paper.

Rotational symmetry and translation can be introduced effectively at the same time, since each involves a transformation of the original shape. In the case of rotational symmetry, the shape is turned or rotated. A tagboard shape placed on a piece of construction paper, (both are then thumbtacked onto a piece of cardboard) can be used. The tagboard shape can be traced, rotated and traced again. The student should continue with the rotations until the shape returns to its original position. The number of times the shape is moved and traced may vary considerably.

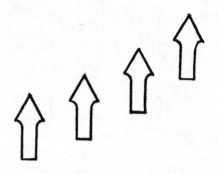

Translation

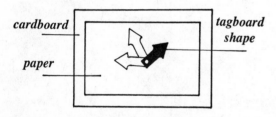

cardboard   *tagboard shape*

paper

Rotating and tracing tagboard shape

Students can also use potato prints to explore both rotational symmetry and translation. Some interesting pictures and patterns result.

Translation involves moving a shape to the side and/or upward or downward, without turning or rotating it.

Rotational symmetry

240

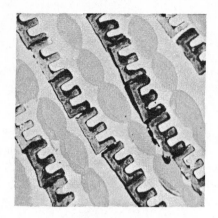

Translation

Often they will find both are included in the same pattern or design.

This is a good time to return to the letters of the alphabet. Have the students search for letters which previously would not fit the category of "mirror symmetry," but which do have rotational symmetry (N, S, and Z). They also should be encouraged to discover which letters have both mirror symmetry and rotational symmetry (X, H, I, and O).

While working with the letters of the alphabet, it is best to have students write the letter, or trace around a template. Cut the letter in half at the point of rotation, hold the papers to the light, making them somewhat transparent, and rotate them.

Translation and mirror symmetry

If possible have wallpaper pattern books, fabrics, trims for fabric, and floor tiles available. Have the students look through these for rotational symmetry and/or translation.

N S Z

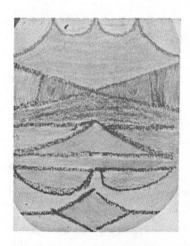

*Symmetrical mask made
from student's name*

241

Masks made from the students' names are a good symmetry/art project. By writing their name in a different position on the paper and/or combining upper and lower-case letters, or all upper-case letters, a variety of effects can be achieved.

The above photograph was made in the following manner.

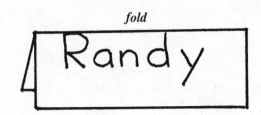

fold

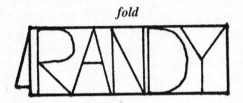

fold

Step 1, "Name mask"

Other ways which could have been used to create a different outline include:

Variations, Step 1, "Name mask"

fold

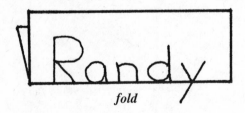

fold

Students can also write their names in connecting block letters, cut these out, mount them on a contrasting color, and add details to turn them into interesting creatures!

fold

Step 1, Symmetrical name creatures

Completed name creature

242

2. Fold the triangle two additional times.

Kaleidoscope design

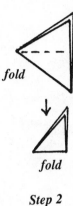

fold

fold

Step 2

Students of all ages (kindergarten to adult!) enjoy making kaleidoscope designs. The step by step procedure follows:

1. Fold 12″×18″ paper to form a square. Cut off and discard the extra part of the paper. Put an "X" on the outside corner.

3. Hold the point in your hand. (The corner with the "X" should be at the top. —You'll need to look inside to find the "X.")

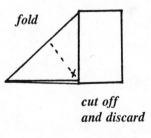

fold

*cut off
and discard*

Step 1

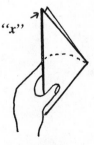

"x"

Step 3

4. Round off the upper edge if you want a circular shape. Or you may prefer to scallop the upper edge.

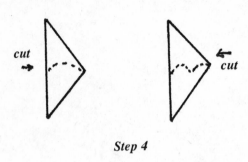

Step 4

6. Fold the paper, so the design you have drawn is face down on the adjacent wedge.

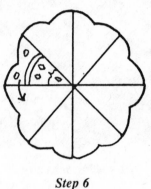

Step 6

5. Open the paper and you should have eight wedge shapes. Using a soft lead pencil, draw a design in one of the wedges. Do not use extremely tiny shapes or very intricate designs.

7. Color the back side of the design with a pencil, thus transferring the design to the adjacent wedge.

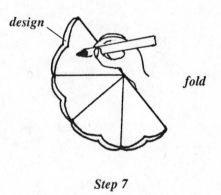

Step 7

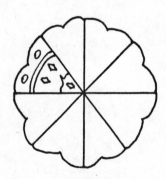

Step 5

8. Open the paper. The design should faintly appear on the adjacent wedge.

Trace over it with a soft lead pencil. Then fold it onto the adjacent section and color on the back of the design to transfer it.

When you introduce this process, be certain to have kaleidoscopes available for student exploration. Some students may be interested in investigating how a kaleidoscope works by standing two hinged mirrors upright on a sheet of paper and experimenting with drawn lines and shapes, as well as objects.

This background unit on symmetry forms the basis for many other experiences. For upper-grade students the principle can be applied to palindromes (numbers which are the same whether read forward or backward—23732). Palindromic exercises provide excellent drill in addition.

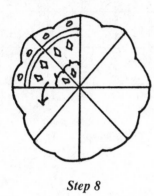

Step 8

PALINDROMES

9. Continue in this manner, always making certain that the design you have just traced is folded against the adjacent wedge. When the design has been transferred around the entire circle, it should be colored. Use colored pencils, crayons, or felt pens. Students should be encouraged to repeat the pattern with identical colors. I.e., if a triangle is colored yellow, wherever it reappears, it should also be colored yellow.

These kaleidoscope designs are especially attractive when they are mounted on contrasting colored paper.

$$\begin{array}{r} 158 \\ +851 \\ \hline 1009 \\ +9001 \\ \hline 10010 \\ +01001 \\ \hline 11011 \end{array}$$

Three steps

The number of steps needed to arrive at a palindromic number varies according to the initial number.

$$
\begin{array}{r}
182 \\
+281 \\
\hline
463 \\
+364 \\
\hline
827 \\
+728 \\
\hline
1555 \\
+5551 \\
\hline
7106 \\
+6017 \\
\hline
13123 \\
+32131 \\
\hline
45254
\end{array}
$$

Six steps

+	1	2	3	4	5
1	2	3	4	5	6
2	3	4	5	6	7
3	4	5	6	7	8
4	5	6	7	8	9
5	6	7	8	9	10

*Symmetry in an
addition chart*

X	1	2	3	4	5
1	1	2	3	4	5
2	2	4	6	8	10
3	3	6	9	12	15
4	4	8	12	16	20
5	5	10	15	20	25

*Symmetry in a
multiplication chart*

Addition and multiplication tables also reveal signs of symmetry. Ask students to try to discover the reason for the symmetry and what the implications are in relation to learning facts.

Extensions of symmetry can be found in

Freedom to Learn (2). In addition, *Symmetry,* by Arthur G. Razzell and K. G. O. Watts, has background information and many experiments that older students enjoy (3).

Notes

---

1. Education Development Center (ESS), *Mirror Cards,* McGraw-Hill Publishing Company, New York City, 1968.
2. Edith E. Biggs and James R. MacLean, *Freedom to Learn,* Addison-Wesley, Menlo Park, California, 1969.
3. Arthur G. Razzell and K. G. O. Watts, Symmetry, Double-day and Company, Garden City, New York, 1964.

CHAPTER XIII

Centers Which Require Minimal Teacher Supervision

Activities for Unsupervised Centers

As teachers begin learning centers, the question always arises, "But what am I going to have the students *do* at the centers which are unsupervised?" Often that word "do" becomes the primary concern. The teacher searches for something, anything, to keep the children occupied. Students spend hours coloring dittos of people from other countries in native costumes (which in reality they seldom if ever wear), and this is then called a Social-Studies Center! Or the children fill in dot-to-dot puzzles, day after day, at a "Numbers Center."

Dot-to-dot puzzles are not necessarily a waste of student time. For instance, if a teacher had worked with the children on number sequence and then reinforced this concept with several dot-to-dot pictures, this could be considered a valid activity. The key word is valid—is it a worthwhile activity at

this time for these children? An activity which is valid this week may be inappropriate several weeks or months from now. Short-term activities often are appropriate for unsupervised centers. They can be useful provided that the program for basic skills is set, and the short-term activities are augmenting the basic program. However, the teacher should be extremely cautious about attempting to build the entire program around short-term centers.

If children are to work successfully at an unsupervised center, it is important that they thoroughly understand what they are to do at that center. Be certain you have explained the activity or assignment and have then had them explain it to you. "What are you going to do when you get to the center? Then what? Where are you going to put your paper when you are finished?" This will save you innumerable interuptions during the actual centers time.

Explain the directions and provide sufficient background information and instruction so that the students will be able to complete the activity or assignment independently. Without thorough student preparation, unsupervised centers will not succeed.

Even with a thorough introduction and instructions, students must be assured that, if they have difficulty with the assignment, they should come to you for help. If you anticipate that several students are going to need help with a particular activity, plan it for a day when you are working at a center where you can easily handle interruptions, perhaps when you are helping students on a one-to-one basis at the math or writing center.

Choices can often be included as part of an unsupervised center. Once again, student preparation is essential. If students are to have a choice of activities at an unsupervised Writing Center, the teacher should explain that they are going to be on their own and therefore should choose an activity for which they will need little or no assistance. Give examples. For a Writing Center you might state that if creative writing is quite easy for them, this would then be a good choice. If they need help with spelling or the mechanics of writing a story, copy work or recopying and illustrating one of their stories into a

The following ditto was used to introduce a group of young students to the television section of the newspaper.

TV Newspaper Guide

_____
Name

If you could watch two TV programs each night, which two would you choose?

	Time	Channel	Program
Monday			
Tuesday			
Wednesday			
Thursday			
Friday			

If you have extra time, you may turn your paper over and write which programs, times, and channels you'd like to watch on Saturday and Sunday.

---

book format, would be a wiser choice.

Some of the regularly scheduled centers require little teacher supervision: (1) Individualized Spelling, when the students make their weekly lists of individualized spelling words; (2) The Individualized Spelling Center when they practice their words; (3) Independent Centers; and (4) many of the Discovery Centers.

When last-minute changes in planned centers need to be made, it is helpful to have several activities completely organized and ready. Several dittos duplicated on capitalization and punctuation, or all of the materials needed for an art project can be collected and stored in a box. All that is then needed is an explanation, and your center is ready.

Other ready-to-go centers can be built around newspapers. Copies of your local newspaper will generally be delivered free of charge if you contact your local newspaper service. If you periodically have them deliver 30 or more copies of an issue, you can prepare a list of questions which pertain to the newspaper. This is an excellent activity at any grade level.

The following questions were given to a class of second-graders.

Name _____

Date _____   *Newspaper*

1. The picture of people skiing on Mount Tamalpais is on page _____ .

2. Find the picture of London Bridge and a double decker bus. It is on page _____ .

3. Some first-graders wrote how to fix turkey and cake. Find their recipes on the bottom of page 13. What do you think about their recipes? _____

_____

4. The picture of an explorer scout putting string on his bow is on page _____ .

5. Look at the bottom of page 15. What day does the movie WONDER OF IT ALL start?

6. Is it at the Novato Theater? _____

7. What time will it be shown on Saturday and Sunday? _____

Questions for upper-grade students can require analyzing a story for statements of fact, statements of opinion, and other interpretative questions, as well as questions which cover comprehension, location of information, use of index, etc.

Commercial task cards for both primary and upper-grade students which require the use of newspapers are also available (1).

In addition to having several ready-to-go centers, make a list of possible unsupervised assignments and activities for each of the centers. This list is a marvelous tool when making lesson plans, or when you suddenly find yourself faced with setting up an unsupervised center because an aide is unable to help in the classroom that day.

You will find that many of the activities which are successful in a traditional classroom can also be used for centers. The key word again is "valid". At any given time, you must decide if the activity is being assigned just to keep the students busy, or whether it is a worthwhile activity for the children.

These activities (some ideas follow) do not have to be terribly exciting. But they should be assignments which you think will help the students.

Writing and Language Arts Activities Requiring Minimal Supervision

1. Copy work booklets: poems, riddles, tongue-twisters, etc.
2. Copy and illustrate original story into a book format.
3. Copy a story or poem from the chalkboard (handwriting).
4. Copy a story and add punctuation and capitalization.
5. Answer questions with a complete sentence. (This can correlate with science, social studies, etc., for upper-grade students, or can be simple questions for primary grades. A list of words may need to be written on the chalkboard.)
6. Copy words and categorize.

Primary Grades	*Upper Grades*
A. real/unreal	A. states/cities
B. large/small	B. parts of speech
C. heavy/light	C. plurals
D. homonyms	D. prefixes/suffixes
E. contractions	E. synonyms/antonyms
F. phonics: words which start with sh, ch, wh, etc.	F. homonyms

7. Copy sentence and replace word.

Primary grades: Jane $\boxed{\text{cannot}}$ see me.
(contractions)

Upper grades: He $\boxed{\text{said,}}$ "Let's meet after school at the football field."
(synonyms)

8. Copy and follow directions written on the chalkboard.

Primary grades: Make one brown house.
Now make two trees and six red flowers . . .

Upper grades: Make a list of all the New England states.
Circle the states which border the Atlantic Ocean . . .

9. Dictionary skills: Look up the following words and
   A. Copy definition
   B. List guide words
   C. Divide into syllables . . .
10. Introductory dictionary skills:
    A. Where would you find these words: front, middle or the back section of the dictionary?
    B. Alphabetize the following words . . .
11. Addressing envelopes:
    Make a ditto with outlines of envelopes.
    Students "address" the envelopes.
12. Task cards made from old readers with words crossed out:
    Students write missing words.
       (context clues and synonyms)
13. Local newspapers:
    Students answer questions.
14. Check available commercial English textbooks or writing textbooks for assignments which the students could complete at an unsupervised center.

Computational Math Activities Requiring Minimal Supervision

1. "How many ways can you make 14?"
      (9+5=14, 4+10=14, etc.)
2. "Choose something from your math folder that you can do without help, or work with math games. (If you insist that everyone work with math games, some children may be disruptive. It is generally better to give them the choice of playing a game, working with flash cards, or working on their math folder.)

3. Review drill sheets.
4. Color ditto: "Color all the combinations which equal seven green, the sixes blue, etc." (This can be a pleasant change of pace once in a while.)
5. "Think and Do" Booklets—A colleague, Blair Gamble (2), saves all of the leftover math drill sheets. Periodically she staples together assortments of these dittos and makes thirty "Think and Do" Booklets which automatically provide drill on previous concepts and skills!
6. Illustrate sets: addition, subtraction, multiplication, fractions (draw pictures).
7. Roll two or more dice and record the problems and answers: addition, subtraction, multiplication.
8. Catalogues or menus: "You have $5.00 to spend. . . ."

Discovery-Center Activities
Which Require Minimal Supervision

This list should include specific activities, task cards, worksheets, etc., which you feel the students could handle independently, as long as you provide sufficient background information. Include specific activities for topics similar to those which follow:

1. science units
2. telling time
3. ordinal numbers
4. fractions
5. odd/even experiments
6. place value
7. more than/less than
8. money
9. estimation
10. symmetry
11. map making
12. linear measurement
13. volume (sand and water measurement)
14. area and shapes
15. geoboards
16. classification
17. attribute blocks
18. balance scales
19. mobiles
20. building structures (straws, toothpicks, bridges, etc.)
21. co-ordinates
22. working with various size scales: 1 inch, ½ inch, ¼ inch, etc.
23. tangrams
24. geometry concepts (line segments, points, "closed and not closed")
25. solid shapes

Independent Center Activities

wood-working   film strips
puppet-making   games
working with clay   flash cards
writing on the chalkboard   library privileges
listening posts   games
painting   puzzles
reading   animals
reference books   blocks
science experiments

Other lists which can provide helpful information include:
1. *Directed Centers with Teacher (18-20 minutes)* instructional groups, telling time, money, fractions, co-ordinates, geometry concepts, place value, grammar, parts of speech, etc.
2. *Centers with Aide (18-20 minutes)* discussion groups, instructional games, science experiments, etc.
3. *Centers without Aide (18-20 minutes)* secret codes, listening-post activities, number sequence activities, manipulative math experiences, etc.
4. *Art Activities with Aide (30 minutes)*
5. *Art Activities without Aide (30 minutes)* There are many appropriate art activities for unsupervised centers. One such activity which is always successful is a center which helps students learn to draw people, animals, and cartoon characters. In addition to the center itself being successful, the skills the children develop are greatly appreciated when it comes time to illustrate stories they have written. (Commercial materials which can be used for this type of center, with either primary or upper-grade students, are listed in the chapter notes, 3-7.)

Lists of this type help clarify your thinking and organize potential activities into specific categories. They are then readily available as needed.

Obviously the lists will vary according to the activities and assignments which a teacher feels are important, as well as the availability of materials.

Adapting Commercial Task Cards

In the last few years there has been a tremendous influx of commercially prepared task cards in almost all subjects. These are often misused because teachers think that "individualizing" and "task cards" are synonymous. However, most task cards are nothing more than the equivalent of a textbook or workbook torn apart and cleverly illustrated.

If teachers buy task cards and all the students work the entire set, then the purpose of the task cards is defeated.

Task cards may be designated for third grade. But, after careful examination of the cards, you may find a span from low second grade to fourth or early-fifth grade. For the task cards to be used effectively then, it becomes necessary to adapt them. This can be done in one of two ways. The cards can be grouped according to specific skills and assigned to students on that basis. In contrast, the task cards can be adapted in a way which is less individualized, but allows you to provide individual students with a series of cards which are at an appropriate level.

Sort the cards according to the approximate level of each word. For example, a set of language-arts task cards might be divided into three levels, each level containing twelve task cards. (The original set may contain forty to forty-five cards, but some may be discarded if you feel that they would confuse the students more than help them.)

Level 1

a, an
is, are
final punctuation marks
easy homonyms
alphabetizing by first letter
contractions
ran, run; came, come, etc.
beginning capitalization
compound words

Level 2

me, I
who, when, what, where, why
capitalization of names of people, places and titles
complete sentences
commas in dates and addresses
alphabetizing by second letter
go, went, gone; do, did, done
abbreviations
suffixes

Level 3

reading a newspaper article and answering who, what, when, where and why questions
synonyms
writing and punctuating complete sentences
capital letters: states, book titles, names of streets, etc.
apostrophes
abbreviations for months
word sequence
antonyms
writing a letter
prefixes
correcting misspelled words

To keep the three levels separate, a different color should be assigned to each level. Each card is then identified by an adhesive circle (available at stationery stores) in the color of that level. The cards in each set should be numbered from one to twelve, enabling a student to keep track of which cards have been completed.

Once the sets of cards are prepared, determine in which level each student should work. Duplicate a record sheet for each student. (The record sheet which comes with the task cards will need to be adapted.)

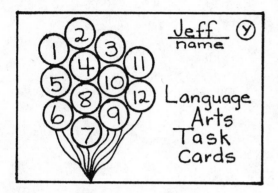

Student record sheet for task cards

Fill in a student's name on each record sheet and indicate which color the child should work: "r" indicates red-dot cards, "o" indicates orange-dot cards, and "y" the yellow cards.

Have lined paper available the same size as the record sheet. The students should first color in the "r," "y," or "o" circle. This will serve as a visual reminder of which set of cards they have been assigned. Each student should then count out twelve answer sheets and staple these to the record sheet. It thus becomes a record booklet for this specific set of cards.

The twelve cards can be worked in any sequence and marked off in the corresponding number on the record sheet as each card is completed. When all twelve cards are

completed, the booklet is turned in for correction.

The attractiveness and durability of task cards can be increased by coloring the drawings on the cards, mounting them on colored railroad board or tagboard, and laminating or covering the cards with contact paper.

By adapting commercial task cards or other materials that you already have, and by taking time to think about traditional classroom assignments which can be equally valid in a centers program, it is possible to develop a list of worthwhile activities which are appropriate for centers requiring minimal teacher supervision. But don't forget that word "valid!"

Notes

1. Ethel McCullough and James Robson, *Newspaper Task Cards*, The Detroit News, Educational Services, Detroit, 1972.

    This set of 275 task cards is printed with large type. The directions are given with a minimum amount of words. Approximately half the set is designed for primary grades, the remaining cards for upper grades. Cards are divided into the following areas: Science, Social Studies, Math, Language Arts, and Introducing the Newspaper.

2. Blair Gamble, Teacher, Novato Unified School District, Novato, California.

3. Ed Emberley, *Ed Emberley's Drawing Book of Animals*, Little, Brown and Company, Boston, 1970.

This book gives simple step-by-step illustrations on how to draw a wide variety of animals.

4. James Dickie, *I Can Draw*, Fearon Publishers, Belmont, California, 1968.

   Contents include: cartooning, heads, stick figures, hats, hands, feet, figures, animals, automobiles, and boats.

5. Frank Webb, *Time to Draw*, Teachers Exchange of San Francisco, San Francisco, 1974.

   Task cards of amusing cartoon figures which start out as a letter of the alphabet or a number. Simple step-by-step illustrations indicate the process of converting the original letter into a delightful cartoon figure.

6. Frank Webb, *Let's Draw: Quick and Easy Steps to Cartooning*, Golden Press, Racine, Wisconsin, 1975.

   More cartoon characters from letters and numbers, in an inexpensive book format.

7. J. Risk, *Face Make 1*, Teachers Exchange of San Francisco, San Francisco, 1974.

   This is composed of three wheels: one with mouths and chins; a middle wheel with noses, eyes, eyebrows, and ears; and an outer wheel with the top portion of heads. By placing the wheels in various positions, a wide variety of faces can be made.

CHAPTER XIV

Scheduling a Reading Program in a Learning Centers Environment

Introduction

In Chapter I reference was made to the advantages of providing a separate time block for reading instruction and related skills.

Many schools, in the primary grades, utilize a split-reading session. Only half the students are in the classroom for the first and last hours of the day. If this is the case, when a teacher first begins learning centers, the reading program can remain the same. At a later time a learning centers format can be applied to the reading time block.

However, if all of the students are scheduled to arrive and leave at the same time, a reading centers time block needs to be established. This chapter describes such a schedule (with and without aides) for primary grades. With minor adaptations, the ideas are also applicable for split session reading schedules, or for upper grades.

Mechanics of Organizing Reading Learning Centers

Instead of grouping the students sociometrically for reading centers, they should be re-grouped according to reading skills. The groups may vary tremendously in size. One group may consist of only one child unable to work with other students, or whose needs are vastly different from others. There may be a few groups of six or seven students, primarily comprised of the more capable readers who are on individualized reading programs. Most of the groups will consist of three or four students.

The groups whose programs are structured on a basal reading series, meet daily with either an aide or the teacher to work

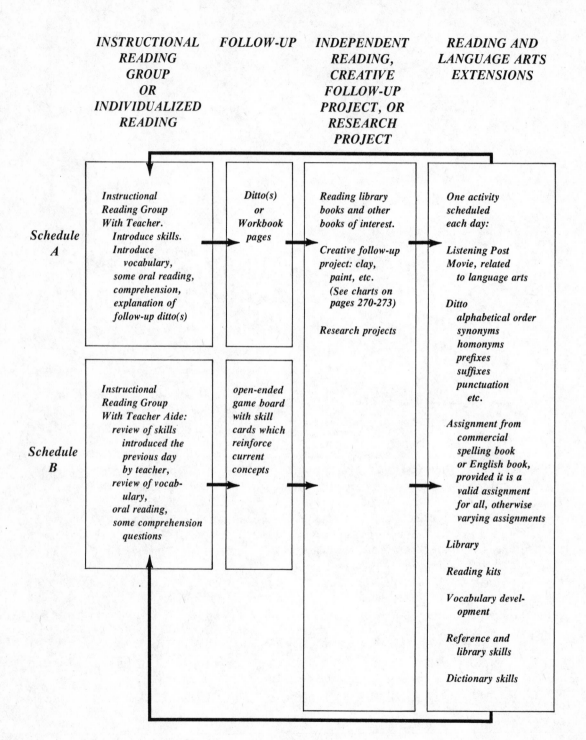

INSTRUCTIONAL READING GROUP OR INDIVIDUALIZED READING	FOLLOW-UP	INDEPENDENT READING, CREATIVE FOLLOW-UP PROJECT, OR RESEARCH PROJECT	READING AND LANGUAGE ARTS EXTENSIONS
Schedule A *Instructional Reading Group With Teacher.* *Introduce skills.* *Introduce vocabulary, some oral reading, comprehension, explanation of follow-up ditto(s)*	*Ditto(s) or Workbook pages*	*Reading library books and other books of interest.* *Creative follow-up project: clay, paint, etc. (See charts on pages 270-273)* *Research projects*	*One activity scheduled each day:* *Listening Post Movie, related to language arts* *Ditto alphabetical order synonyms homonyms prefixes suffixes punctuation etc.* *Assignment from commercial spelling book or English book, provided it is a valid assignment for all, otherwise varying assignments* *Library* *Reading kits* *Vocabulary development* *Reference and library skills* *Dictionary skills*
Schedule B *Instructional Reading Group With Teacher Aide:* *review of skills introduced the previous day by teacher, review of vocab-ulary, oral reading, some comprehension questions*	*open-ended game board with skill cards which reinforce current concepts*		

260

Typical Two-Day Schedule
for a Reading Group

CENTER	ASSIGNMENT/ACTIVITY

Monday (Schedule A)

Reading and Language Arts Extensions:	Reference skills Assignment
Instructional Reading Group:	Teacher introduces new vocabulary, and presents a lesson on prefixes
Follow-up:	Workbook pages on prefixes, and a ditto on comprehension
Independent Reading Creative Follow-up Project or Research Project:	Read library book, or work on creative follow-up project

Tuesday (Schedule B)

Reading and Language Arts Extension:	Dictionary skills assignment
Instructional Reading Group:	Aide reviews prefixes and vocabulary introduced previous day, then listens to oral reading
Follow-up:	Skill game works on prefixes
Independent Reading Creative Follow-up Project or Research Project:	Research Project

Wednesday (Schedule A)

on decoding skills, oral reading, and comprehension.

Students who are competent in decoding skills (short vowels, long vowels, blends, digraphs, diphthongs, etc.), oral reading and comprehension, are placed on individualized reading programs. In addition, they meet in groups of six to eight students once or twice a week for group reading and discussions. On the days that they do not meet as a group, they confer on a one-to-one basis with either the teacher or an aide regarding their individualized program. During the conference the student reads aloud from the current book; comprehension questions are asked; skills are diagnosed. (The actual process of instituting an individualized reading program, diagnosing, and record-keeping, will not be discussed in this chapter. There are many books on the market which describe the topic in detail. See Chapter Notes 1-4.)

The schedules on pages 260-261 were designed to accommodate eight reading groups of varying sizes, some using basal reading programs and others on individual reading programs. If you have fewer reading groups, the scheduling problems are lessened, and this schedule can be adapted accordingly.

Eight activities take place in the classroom simultaneously. Each child takes part in four activities on one day, and the other four the following day. Twenty to thirty minutes are allotted for each center, resulting in one and a half to two hours of reading instruction daily. Each day a student is involved in: (1) an instructional reading group with the aide or teacher, or a reading conference with either; (2) follow-up work: dittos, workbook pages, or instructional games; (3) independent reading, creative follow-up projects, or research projects; and (4) reading or language-arts extensions.

Instructional Reading Center

The emphasis at the Instructional Reading Center varies. It depends on whether the students are working with the aide or the teacher. The teacher's time is spent introducing new skills and vocabulary, and working on comprehension. The aide reviews these skills, perhaps with flash cards or by going over work the teacher has written on the chalkboard for the students. The aide also spends more time listening to oral reading.

When students who are on individualized reading programs rotate to the Instructional Reading Center, they may be scheduled to meet as a group with the teacher or aide. Or they may be assigned to continue with their individualized reading program, and to confer with the aide or teacher during this time block.

At the beginning of reading centers, the teacher may need to explain briefly the assignment at the Reading and Language Arts Extension Center. After this, each of the groups should be able to begin work at their assigned center. The only exception is the group scheduled to start at the Follow-up Center. The teacher should briefly meet with these students, explain their assignment, and give them the necessary workbook pages or dittos. Then the teacher can work with the group at the Instructional Reading Center.

This first group, called to the Instructional Reading Center, should be composed of no more than the four students with the shortest attention spans (those whose concentration decreases as the day progresses), and those who need a great deal of reading-vocabulary review. While they wait for the teacher to finish explaining the assignment to the group at the Follow-up Center, the Instructional Group can become constructively involved in word review. Reading words from the day before can be listed on the chalkboard. One student, using a pointer, points to each word in turn. A second student reads each word. A third student writes the reader's initials by any word that he or she misses. Roles are then reversed. This keeps several children actively involved in word drill. By the time the teacher gets to the center, they will have checked each other on the reading vocabulary. The teacher can either quickly go over the words with the group as a whole, or can have the individual students read their initialed words. As soon as the child says the word correctly, the initials are erased. The teacher then proceeds with that day's lesson.

Follow-up Center

The activities planned for the Follow-up Center also vary. The teacher explains the workbook or ditto pages to the group, when it is time for the students to rotate to the Follow-up Center. However, a teacher aide, who is in the classroom only once a week, cannot be expected to remember all the directions and explanations for four different sets of dittos. Therefore, an open-ended game is scheduled to follow the aide's center. (For information on open-ended games, see Appendix III.)

One gameboard, with four sets of different skill cards, can be placed at the Follow-up Center. There is one set for each group. The cards for one group may provide drill on current reading vocabulary. The cards for another group might require the student to apply a new phonetic rule, one just learned, in order to decode the words. Still another set of cards for a different group may present contractions, prefixes, or suffixes. Although different skills are reinforced, the game format remains the same. Therefore, the aide needs only to understand the one game, and to make certain each group is given the correct set of cards.

The students are asked to play each game at least once. They may then continue to play, change to a different skill game, work with flash cards, or rotate to the Independent Reading Center, without waiting for the end of the time block.

Since some students will rotate to the Independent Reading Center ahead of time, the area designated for this center needs to be larger than the other areas.

If you have the same aide each day during reading centers, or even several days a week, this person can introduce the dittos or workbook pages because of the opportunity to become familiar with the material and the process of introducing the pages.

When students finish their workbook pages, they may rotate immediately to the next center, Independent Reading.

Independent Reading Center

Since two groups are scheduled simultaneously at the Independent Reading Center, (those rotating from workbook pages, and those rotating from the open-ended game), some careful calculating is needed when scheduling groups, to make certain that this center does not become overcrowded. Figure the number of students in the group working with the teacher, and the number working with the aide. The total should approximate one-fourth of the class enrollment. If the teacher is working with a large group, a small group must be scheduled to work with the aide during that time block, and visa versa.

The Independent Reading Center should be well stocked with books children will *want* to read: books you have purchased, public and school library books (which should be changed frequently), and books students have brought from home.

Research is also an excellent project at this center. Time should be allotted every week or every other week in order to discuss research projects and/or follow-up projects with students. This can be facilitated by scheduling one day when both you and your aide confer individually with students. During the time block which would normally be used for instructional groups, assign independent work. This could be reading a story silently or with a partner, and answering comprehension questions. Conferences can

BOOKS I HAVE READ

BOOK TITLE	DATE I FINISHED BOOK/ FOLLOW-UP PROJECT	(circle one) COMMENTS (circle one)
		very good too easy good just right not very good too hard
		very good too easy good just right not very good too hard
		very good too easy good just right not very good too hard
		very good too easy good just right not very good too hard
		very good too easy good just right not very good too hard
		very good too easy good just right not very good too hard

then take place at the Independent Reading Center.

Each student should keep a record of all the books read, so you will know how the time was spent at the Independent Reading Center. Ten or more of the record sheets on page 264 should be duplicated for each student. These should then be stapled together with front and back covers, made from 9"×12" construction paper. As a student finishes reading a book, the information is recorded in this stapled record booklet.

When you confer with a student concerning creative follow-up projects, ascertain whether the previous follow-up project has been completed and discuss this. Examine the stapled record booklet to determine how much the child has read since your last conference. (One long book is just as valid as eight short books!) If the student has read very little, suggest that he or she continue to use the Independent Reading Center to read library books. At the next conference, the child can select a creative follow-up project for one of the recently completed books.

If the student has read an appropriate amount since the last conference, say "How would you like to do a follow-up project on one of the books you read?" If the child does not wish to, discuss the current book being read. Then, let the student return to reading.

If the child is interested in a follow-up project, discuss alternative projects. When the student has made a selection, record it and the date in the middle column on the stapled record book, opposite the title of the book. The student then spends the next scheduled time, or several times, at the Independent Reading Center working on the creative follow-up project. When it is completed, the child returns to independent reading.

If, one day during the week, you have two aides during the reading time block, either you or one of the aides can hold conferences at the Independent Reading Center. The regular schedule for the rest of the students can be maintained.

Creative Follow-up Projects

Creative follow-up projects should not be introduced until reading centers are well underway. Several examples of initial choices for such projects follow:

1. BOX MOBILE

Have available white drawing paper cut to 6"×8", on which students draw pictures or make cut and paste pictures about books they have read. These are attached with paper clips to each of the four sides of a hanging box mobile.

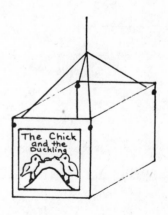

Box mobile

A box mobile can be made from a piece of 9"×29" tagboard.

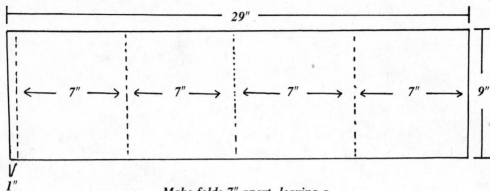

*Make folds 7" apart, leaving a
1" flap at the opposite end.*

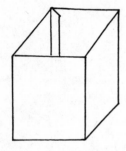

*Fold into a box shape. Glue
the flap to the box.*

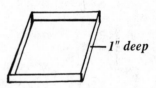

1" deep

*Fold the edges to make a shallow box. Secure
the corners with tape.*

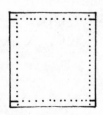

*To reinforce the box, cut a piece of tagboard
9"×9". Fold one inch on all sides. Cut each
corner as illustrated.*

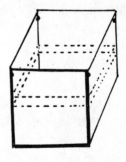

*Insert the shallow box in the
larger box. Secure with tape.*

*Punch holes in each of the
corners, one inch below the top.*

266

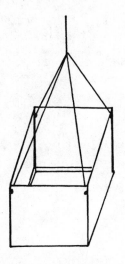

Attach yarn to each of the corners to make a hanging "box mobile."

Suspend from light fixtures, or from string which is stretched between light fixtures.

A strip of shelving paper 8″ wide is then cut. The length of the strip will vary, depending on the number of events to be depicted. Eight inches need be allowed for each event, plus an additional sixteen inches: eight inches for the title of the book and four-inch margins at both the top and bottom.

A line four inches from the bottom is drawn first, then every eight inches, with four inches remaining for the top margin. The title of the book and a picture depicting the story are drawn in the bottom eight-inch square.

2. CLAY MODELS

A clay model can be made of a character or object in the book.

3. PAINTING

A picture depicting the book can be painted.

4. STORY STRIPS

To make a story strip (1), the student first writes five to eight sequential events in the story and has these approved by the teacher.

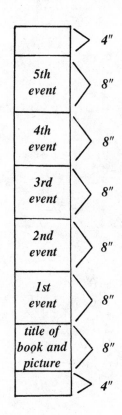

Story strip

A sentence about the first event is written on the next line. The second event goes on the line above that, etc. Pictures are drawn to illustrate each of the events.

To present the story to the class, the student places the story strip in a holder, and then gradually pulls the strip downward, revealing one scene at a time.

The holder for the story strip is made from a piece of 12″×18″ tagboard.

CONSTRUCTING A STORY STRIP HOLDER

Presentation of story strip

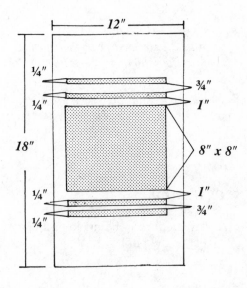

Step 1:
Cut out the center 8″×8″ square (shaded), leaving a 5″ margin at top and bottom, and a 2″ margin on each side.

Step 2:
   Cut out and discard the ¼″ slits (shaded), as diagrammed.

glue

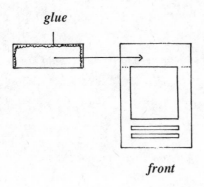

front

Step 3:
   Cut two 5″×12″ pieces of tagboard. Put glue along the top and side edges of one of the pieces. Attach this piece horizontally to the front of the holder, covering the top slits.

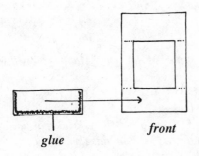

glue   *front*

Step 4:
   Put glue along the bottom and side edges of the other piece of tagboard. Attach this piece horizontally to the bottom of the holder, covering the bottom slits.

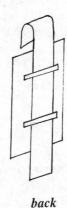

back

Step 5:
   The story strip is then threaded through the slits on the back of the holder.

   Additional choices for follow-up projects can be introduced gradually.
   Charts on writing, art, and group follow-up projects can be posted for student reference. Some of the ideas listed on the following charts were developed by the Davis Joint Unified School District (California) (2), and by Amy Elizabeth Jensen (3).

269

READING FOLLOW-UP PROJECTS
TO DO BY YOURSELF

$$\boxed{WRITE}$$

1. Write two questions that you think someone else who has read this book could answer.

2. Write a letter to the author.
     What did you like best?
     What would you change?
     Questions . . .

3. Write a different ending for the story.

4. Write a radio commercial for the book.

5. Write a letter to a friend, and tell your friend about the book you read.

6. Write about the main problem in this story and what the character, or characters, do to solve it.

7. Write a poem about something in the story that gave you a feeling.

8. Write about a character in the story that you liked or didn't like. Tell some things that made you like or not like this character.

9. Write about the funniest, most exciting, or saddest part of the story. Maybe you will want to send it to "Kids" magazine.

10. Make a bingo game of sixteen interesting words from your story. Make a card with sixteen squares, and write one word in each square. Be sure to make cards for the caller also.

READING FOLLOW-UP PROJECTS
TO DO BY YOURSELF

ART

1. COLOR a picture for a box mobile

2. CUT and PASTE a picture for a box mobile

3. CLAY—Make a model of something or someone in the book.

4. PAINT a picture about the book.

5. DIORAMA—Make a scene in a box.

6. WIRE FIGURES—Make a wire figure or pipe cleaner figure of one of the characters in the book.

7. DRAW four important things that happened in the story. Fold and make it into a book.

8. CARTOONS—Draw a series of cartoons showing a part of the story you enjoyed.

9. BOOK COVER—Make a book cover.

10. TORN PICTURE—Make a torn paper picture of your story

11. WATER COLOR or COLORED CHALK—Write some descriptive words from your story that made a picture in your mind. Then paint that picture with watercolors or colored chalk and starch.

12. STORY STRIP—Make a story strip.

READING FOLLOW-UP

GROUP PROJECTS

1. *Give a PLAY about your favorite part.*

2. *FLANNEL BOARD—Use paper or fabric to make the characters for a flannel-board story about the book.*

3. *PUPPET SHOW—Make puppets for a puppet show about the story.*

4. *VISIT another classroom—WRITE a letter to another teacher to see if you can show your play, flannel-board story, or puppet show to that class.*

5. *DIORAMA—Make a scene in a box.*

6. *MURAL—Make a mural showing a scene from the book.*

7. *MOBILE—Make a mobile of characters in the story.*

8. *MOBILE—Make a mobile showing different parts of the story.*

9. *TAPE a dramatization. Make it sound like you are listening to a play.*

You also may want to post a sign-up sheet for special reading follow-up projects. By having sign-ups, you can limit the number of students involved in the special project at any given time. The special projects should be written on separate cards so they can frequently be changed.

```
SPECIAL   READING
    FOLLOW-UP
      PROJECTS
  ┌ ─ ─ ─ ─ ─ ─ ─ ─ ┐
  │ Sign up to...   │
  └ ─ ─ ─ ─ ─ ─ ─ ─ ┘
```

This sign remains up at all times.

A special project card is thumb-tacked here.

```
┌──────────────────────┐
│ 1. _____   │
│ 2. _____   │
│ 3. _____   │
│ 4. _____   │
└──────────────────────┘
```

Students sign up on this paper. When the paper is filled, they must wait for a new piece to be posted.

Special project sign-up chart

Special project cards include:

> ### READ
> *to younger children*

> ### READ
> *a favorite part of the story to our class or your group.*

> ### TAPE RECORD
> *what happened in the story. Tell it in your own words.*

> ### HOW TO
> *do it at home and bring it in and show the class. Tell, step by step, how to do it.*

> ### TELL
> *the class about the funniest, the saddest, or the most exciting part of the story.*

Reading and Language Arts Extensions

Generally one activity each day is scheduled for the Reading and Language Arts Extension Center. To simplify planning, it is often helpful to develop a master schedule, showing which day will be scheduled for each type of activity. The specific assignment can then be determined each week.

Occasionally, you may plan an activity at the Reading and Language-Arts Extension Center for half the group. It could be that a listening-post activity may accommodate only half the students, in which case the other half can have a different assignment. On the following day, the assignments are reversed.

Communicating Directions to Teacher Aides

Since a teacher aide supervises four different groups during reading centers time, a set of directions for each group is necessary. A copy of each group's basal reader can be kept at a specific location in the room. A record page is kept in each of the books, indicating previous assignments for that specific group and their assignment for the following day. The record page needs be nothing more than a piece of 9″×12″ construction paper folded in half. It is best if the paper is a pastel color, as it is more noticeable if one page is left out of a book.

When the front page of the folder is filled in, it is turned over. The daily assignments are continued on the back page.

The inside of the folder is used to list the specific words with which students are having problems. These are noted as the students read orally. In addition, every two weeks or so, each student is checked on the current reading-vocabulary words listed in back of the reading book.

Any words the child does not know are listed inside the folder. At the beginning of the Instructional Reading Center, the teacher or aide takes a few moments with each student to have the words read aloud which are listed under the child's name. This provides daily drill on words which are difficult for each student. As a child masters the listed words, they are crossed off.

students in group —— Sammy, Scott, Jane

book they are —— Around the Corner
reading

date and person working with group	11/10 — mrs.Q	Intro. words #112-134 —— *reading vocabulary words (listed by page numbers in the back of the reading book)*
		Discuss compound words
		Read p. 103 - 107
	11/11 mrs.fred	Drill on words on Chalkboard (#112-134)
		Use flash cards to review compound words
		Read p. 107- 114
	11/12 mrs.Q	Intro words #134-149
		Review words #112-134 and compound words
		Read 114-118
	11/13 Debbie	Check each student on words #94-134
		(List missed words inside this folder)
		Review words #134-149
		Read p. 118-121
	11/14 mrs.Q	Words inside this
		Intro words #150-166
		Review words #134-149 and compound words
		Read p. 121-

This reminds the person working with the group to have each student work on the words listed inside the folder. (See below.)

This is always left open. The person who reads with the group fills in the page number to indicate how far they read.

Comments can be written in the space below the assignment.

Inside of folder

When the teacher or aide finishes reading with a group, this person fills in the page number, indicating how far they read. If necessary, the teacher or aide writes a comment. The folder is then placed inside the book, so that it protrudes beyond the top of the book, revealing the names of the students in that group.

At the completion of reading centers, all of these books are put in one specific place. At the end of the day, the teacher takes the books, and, by referring to the folder in each book, determines the assignment for the next day, and writes it on the folder.

The following day, the teacher and aide each take the four books, with folders inside, for the groups they will supervise.

Utilizing Upper-Grade Students As Aides During Reading Centers

Upper-grade students can be used effectively during reading centers, provided that they are not put in charge of a large group of students. As mentioned in Chapter VII, they are most successful working on a one-to-one basis, or with a small group of two or three students. They can be used to: (1) Confer with students who are on individualized reading programs, spending most of the time listening to each student read orally. (This necessitates that you concentrate on comprehension and diagnosis when you work with the students on the following day.) (2) Supervise review of skills and/or vocabulary drill with groups of two or three students. (3) Supervise open-ended games at the Follow-up Center.

Reading Centers Without Teacher Aides

If there are no teacher aides available during reading, the same basic program can still be utilized. At the center where an aide was assigned, students work independently, in silent reading, or reading with a partner, and answering comprehension questions. The students work with you one day at the Instructional Group Center, and independently at that same center on the following day.

One other option, for classrooms without teacher aides, is to arrange the students into four groups, instead of eight, and follow only Schedule A. Although the groups are larger, the students still have a reading group each day, follow-up dittos or workbook pages, independent reading, creative follow-up projects or research projects, and a reading and language-arts extension center.

Upper-Grade Reading Centers

An upper-grade reading program is similar to the program previously described for the

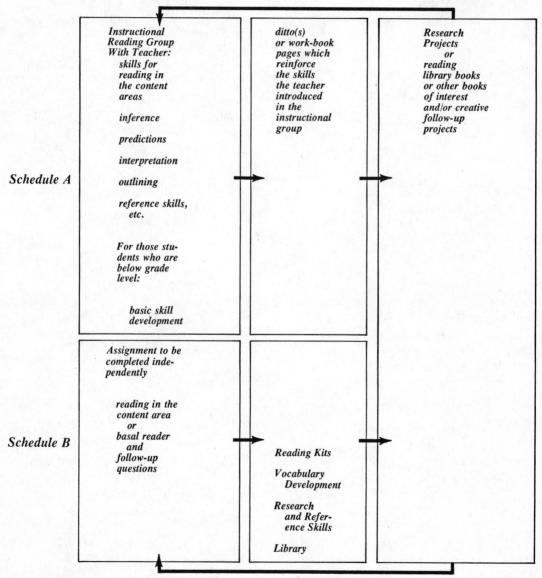

INSTRUCTIONAL
READING
GROUP
OR
INDIVIDUALIZED
READING

FOLLOW-UP

INDEPENDENT
READING,
CREATIVE
FOLLOW-UP
PROJECT,OR
RESEARCH
PROJECT

Schedule A

*Instructional
Reading Group
With Teacher:*
    *skills for
    reading in
    the content
    areas*

    inference

    predictions

    interpretation

    outlining

    *reference skills,
        etc.*

    *For those stu-
    dents who are
    below grade
    level:*

    *basic skill
    development*

*ditto(s)
or work-book
pages which
reinforce
the skills
the teacher
introduced
in the
instructional
group*

*Research
Projects
    or
reading
library books
or other books
of interest
and/or creative
follow-up
projects*

Schedule B

*Assignment to be
completed inde-
pendently*

*reading in the
content area
    or
basal reader
    and
follow-up
questions*

Reading Kits

*Vocabulary
    Development*

*Research
    and Refer-
    ence Skills*

Library

primary. However, instead of eight groups, it is possible to divide the students into six groups of varying levels and varying sizes.

The schedule on page 277 allows for six groups with the teacher working in the classroom without a teacher aide. The aspects discussed earlier in this chapter apply to these centers, with the exception that the students go to three centers daily instead of four.

Notes

1. Peggy Brogan and Lorene K. Fox, *Helping Children Read*, Holt, Rinehart and Winston, New York, 1961.

2. Jeannette Veatch, *Individualizing Your Reading Program*, G. P. Putnam's Sons, New York, 1959.

3. Jeannette Veatch, *Reading in the Elementary School*, Ronald Press Company, New York, 1966.

4. Roland West, *Individualized Reading Instruction*, Kennikat Press, Port Washington, New York, 1964.

5. Alma Briggs, Teacher, Sausalito School District, Sausalito, California.

6. Davis Joint Unified School District, *Davis Oral Reading Test (DORT)*, Davis, California, 1969.

7. Amy Elizabeth Jensen, "Attracting Children to Books," *Elementary English*, p. 335, October 1956.

CHAPTER XV

Adaptations for Kindergarten Learning Centers

Keeping Track of Students When Centers Are Free-Flowing

Many basic procedures and strategies apply equally well to kindergarten as to the other grades. My preference is to begin the year in kindergarten with free-flowing centers, and then to group the children and move into formalized rotating centers in the spring.

During the free-flow period, it is much easier to adjust to the tremendous difference in the children's attention spans, length of time they can sit, etc.

Centers during this time consist of typical kindergarten activities: (1) play house, (2) easels, (3) art projects which require cutting, pasting, etc., (4) small muscle activities such as puzzles, legoes, tinker toys, peg sets, (5) math center, (6) writing-readiness center (working on printing their name, tracing lines, writing numbers), (7) listening post, (8) game center, (9) blocks.

The children are free to stay at a center as long as they like, or to move to a different center. The exception is the child who is in perpetual motion. This child is asked to choose a center, and is then shown the clock on the wall and directed to stay at the center until the big hand is on the _____ , perhaps a grand total of five minutes! The student then reports back to the teacher and chooses a next center and stays at that center until the hand is on the _____ , or longer if able. Gradually the time can be lengthened.

The number of students at any one center is limited by the number of chairs at that center. The teacher starts center time by asking students where they wish to go.

It is helpful to keep check lists for any of the popular activities: block building, play house, easels . . . to insure that each of the students has an equal number of turns. A separate check sheet is needed for each of these activities. As you call off volunteers to go to the blocks, put a check by each of their names on the "Block List." The following day remind them that, if they were at the blocks the day before, it is someone else's turn today. Continue this procedure each day, explaining that everyone has a chance for a "first turn" before the class starts on second turns. When most of the children have had first turns, simply call off each of the remaining names. If they choose not to

MATH-CENTER RECORD

Math Center - stapled booklets	5/2	5/3	5/4	5/5	5/6	5/9	5/10	5/11	5/12	5/13	5/16	5/17	5/18
Alice	X	X	X		X	X	X	X		X	X	X	X
Betty	X		X		X	X		X	X		X		
Carl	X				X			\	✓		X		
Dan		\		✓		✓			X				
Ellen		X			⊗		X			X			⊗
Fred		X	X	X		X	X	X	X	X		X	X
Greg	✓		✓	\	X		X	X	X			X	X

Code meanings: "X" indicates that the child worked at the Center; " ⊗ " shows that child needs assistance; " / " that he did an inadequate amount of work; "✓," that it was necessary to ask the child to come to the Center.

play with the blocks, put a dash on the check sheet to indicate they had an opportunity but did not choose to work there.

Other check lists are used at each of the centers, which are supervised by an aide or the teacher. The date is written at the top of the column. As a child comes to the center, an "x" is placed next to his or her name, denoting that this student worked there. If the child spends only a few minutes at the center and then leaves, instead of an "x," a slash mark is placed next to the name. This indicates that the student was there, but did not get very involved. A check indicates that the child did not come voluntarily, but had to be recruited. A circle around an "x" or check denotes the child had problems and needs help.

Before long, a definite pattern evolves. You discover those students who consistently work at certain centers, those who have never gone to a center, still others who come to a center but consistently leave before getting much accomplished.

The above chart indicates that Alice and Fred consistently work at the Math Center on stapled booklets, whereas Carl, Dan and Ellen do not come to the Math Center nearly as often. In addition, Dan is consistently recruited for this center, which may indicate a need for a different type of activity in math. Ellen's pattern indicates a need for help every so often. Greg had to be recruited to the Math Center the first two times, but once started, has continued to come on a regular basis.

Check lists of this type should be kept for all supervised centers: manipulative math, writing, fingerpainting, directed art projects, games, oral language, etc. The check list is particularly valuable for teacher aides, so that they can alert the teacher when a child needs help. (In addition to circling the check or "x," encourage them either to talk with you about the problem, or attach a brief explanatory note to the check list.)

Although the basic structure is free-flow, there should be required centers which are supervised by the teacher or an aide. If a child has not once come to these centers under personal volition after several days, the teacher or aide can say, "I'd like you to come to my center and do some work with us." If the child is at a well-liked center, perhaps blocks, ask one of the children to keep a place for the departing one. Assure the student that the place will be waiting as soon as some work has been completed at your center.

There actually are few children who will need to be recruited. Most kindergarten children are anxious to work with the teacher, especially if the work is one-to-one or in a small group.

The responsibility of getting to the required center(s) gradually can be shifted to the children by announcing the required center(s) for the week. Remind them each day at the beginning of centers time that it is their responsibility to be certain to do some work at this center before the week is over. On Thursday, write on the chalkboard and announce the names of those who have not yet attended the required center. Tell them that you would like them to come today, then recruit them if necessary.

Later, instead of recruiting on Thursday, erase the names of those who do remember to come to the center. On Friday, any names left must go to that specific center first.

These are the beginning steps in training the students to assume responsibility.

Individualizing the Work and Introducing New Centers

Just as in other grades, the work in kindergarten should be planned on an individualized basis. It is ridiculous to require number pages to be filled in, if the child already knows numbers, or to drill on colors, when the student can easily identify them.

The first step in implementing an individualized classroom in kindergarten is to design and administer a brief diagnostic inventory in order to determine basic information about the child. This can easily be accomplished by asking the child a few questions: "Can you write your name?" (If "Yes," the student should do it.) "Do you know your telephone number?" . . . Ask the child to identify various colored objects (blocks, crayons, etc). Similarly, have the child identify shapes, numbers, etc. Record this information on a form similar to the one on page 286.

The next step is to initiate centers which will allow you to plan work appropriate for each child. On-going centers provide an ideal structure for work of this type. However, with kindergarten centers, the on-going activities change more frequently than in the other grades. Therefore, the organizational procedure is somewhat different. This involves the establishment of a center by the teacher (introduction of the appropriate materials, coupled with successful experiences for the children). Then, it can, in a few days or a week, be placed under the supervision of an aide.

The teacher is now free to introduce a new center which requires initial instruction. Later, one of the supervised centers is temporarily eliminated. This procedure allows a variety of centers and skills to be introduced and later reinforced. Generally, there are two or more supervised centers: one new center which the teacher supervises and gets firmly established, and one or more supervised by an aide, which provide on-going reinforcement activities.

A typical schedule for supervised centers at the beginning of the year follows.

Step One
Teacher introduces Writing Center, helping students learn correctly to print their names.

Step Two
Aide continues this center.
Teacher introduces Math Center and Individualized Number Books. (See below.)

Step Three
Aide continues this center.
Teacher introduces writing patterns (see pages 112-116) and continues helping students write their names.

Step Four
Aide continues this center.
Teacher introduces rhyme books. (See pages 119-124.)

In addition to the supervised centers, there are a variety of unsupervised centers and activities: blocks, painting, doll house, etc.

Example of Supervised On-going Center
(Individualized Number Books)

Have available a stapled blank book for each child (fifteen or more pages of ditto paper or white construction paper). Write the child's name and the results of the diagnostic survey on the cover. E.g., if Jimmy knew all of his numbers from one to ten except seven, eight and nine, then these three numbers would be written under his name, indicating where work is needed. However, if Sally only knew the number one, you might code the front of her book "2, 3, 4, 5," which would provide ample work for her.

Another child might know numbers through ten, but need to work on numbers in their teens. Under that child's name you would write "teen numbers." Still another student might be ready to work on numbers in the twenties.

In addition to the stapled blank books for each child, have available several illustrated number strips. (Use felt pens to illustrate each number with a variety of brightly colored dots on a piece of 3″ by 12″ tagboard.)

1	2	3	4	5	6	7	8	9	10
*	*	*	**	**	**	***	****	****	****
	*	*	**	*	**	*	****	*	**
		*		**	**	***		****	****

Illustrated number strip

Write one of the numbers the child needs to work on, at the bottom of the first page in the Number Book. Have this student find the corresponding number on the illustrated number strip. Together, count the dots below that number, so the child can determine what the number "says." The student can then draw pictures to illustrate that number. The child completes the illustration, comes to the person supervising the center and reads the number at the bottom of the page, and counts the drawings submitted.

A new number is then written for this student on the next page, etc. This center can easily accommodate eight children. As you work with one child, the others are making their illustrations.

When the novelty of drawing pictures wears off, you can introduce other variations. Pre-cut construction paper shapes can be pasted on the page to illustrate the number. Or an ink pad can be used for the student to illustrate the number with thumbprints, or commercial stamps (cartoon characters, animals). Or place a stack of cards in the middle of the center, each with a simple drawing (dog, cat, house, tree, owl, frog, etc). After you have written the number on the student's page, the child draws one of the cards. If you had written a seven, and the card drawn was an owl, the child would then draw seven owls.

You should use a somewhat different procedure for children who are working with numbers in the teens and twenties. Instead of having them draw that number of pictures (horror!), use two boxes of 1" square graph paper which you have cut in two sizes. One box has strips 1" by 10" (ten squares long). Another box has 1" square pieces. Students who are working on their teens begin with a ten-strip, and then add as many squares as are needed to make their number. If you wrote seventeen at the bottom of a child's page, the student would paste one ten-strip and seven one-inch squares on the page. Before long, the child discovers that the teen numbers always have one ten. Children working in their twenties start with two ten-strips and then add as many 1" squares as necessary to make their number.

Thus, the work at the numbers center is planned according to individual needs of the students.

For other appropriate center activities, see the beginning of each subject chapter.

Providing for Students Who Need Special Help

The results of the diagnostic survey always indicate some children who seem to need a great deal of help on all the basic kindergarten skills: counting, numbers, colors, shapes, etc. Generally, these children are not attracted to centers which require concentration, sitting still, and use of small muscles. You may recruit them for short intervals to this type of center. (Two ten-minute sessions are much more profitable than one twenty-minute session.) But if you are to teach the skills they need, you will have much better luck if you involve them in active experiences. Two examples follow.

Numbers

Use pieces of wallpaper, writing a number on each one and placing these randomly on the floor. Then have a student do a two-foot jump from 1 to 2 to 3, etc. Several of the other children who need special help can stand at the side waiting their turn and call out the number as the child makes each jump.

Colors

Pompoms from crepe paper can be made by cutting lots of 1" strips and tieing them together. Several pompoms of each color should be made. Have the students who need work on colors sit in a circle. Give each of them the color pompoms on which they need reinforcement. As you hand each of them a pompom, be certain to tell them the color.

Call out a color, hold up a piece of paper of the same color, and ask everyone to throw the pompom of the same color into the center of the circle. The child both hears the word and sees a splash of the color sail through the air, landing mid-circle. Call out all of the colors, re-distribute the pompoms and repeat the process. Gradually omit holding up the colored paper.

The experiences may be of a physical nature as the two described above, or they may involve the physical manipulation of objects. The important ingredient is active involve-ment, rather than having the student sit and color, or sit and write.

To insure that you work daily with the students who need extra help, you should plan a short activity (ten to fifteen minutes) each day on one of the basic concepts. At the beginning of the centers time, before pro-ceeding to the center you intend to super-vise, call off the names of the students who need work on the specific skill you plan to reinforce. Designate a place in the room for them to wait for you.

The other students should be told that, as soon as they see you at your regular center, they may come to that center and begin their work. Then call off volunteers to go to each of the other centers.

After working with the special-activity group for ten to fifteen minutes, you may want to continue the activity for a short while and let some of the other children join in. When you are ready to go to your regular center, put the special materials away, or, if you prefer, leave the materials at hand, and let the interested students continue playing with them on their own.

Kindergarten-Student Conferences

Frequent days for holding one-to-one con-ferences with students should be planned. The children love these days when they each get a special time to work with the teacher alone. You should again go over the diagnos-tic inventory with each child, recording the results on a check sheet. A check is made for each skill in which the child needs work.

It is important to point out to the student all that has been learned since your last spe-cial time together. (They love to see the checks on their card diminish.) The confer-ence not only provides a time for evaluating, but can also be used for special help and in-struction, if needed. It also gives you an op-portunity to discuss what they should now be working on.

Several things result from this type of con-ference: the child (1) no longer feels the need to compete with everyone in the classroom,

Kindergarten Beginning Inventory
(page 1)

Peggy
name

date	red	blue	white	purple	yellow	green	brown	black	orange		□	o	△	▭	O
9/15		✓	✓	✓	✓	✓					✓		✓	✓	✓
10/5															✓
10/22															
10/26															

date	writes name		0	1	2	3	4	5	6	7	8	9	10	teens	20's
9/5	✓		✓		✓	✓	✓	✓	✓	✓	✓	✓	✓	{~	{~
10/5	✓		✓				✓		✓	✓	✓	✓		{~	{~
10/22							✓			✓	✓	✓	✓	{~	{~
10/26										✓	✓	✓		{~	{~

*Student record for
kindergarten inventory*

(2) becomes aware of the progress being made, (3) has increased positive feelings about school and self.

In addition, the student is more willing to become involved when you suggest a specific activity, since both of you know the goal.

Changing the Materials

The materials at the various centers (peg sets, clay, special art projects, puzzles, etc.), should be changed frequently. It is helpful to have them disappear for awhile, and then later reappear. The children feel as if they are meeting an old friend when one of their favorite activities reappears at a center after an absence.

A good general rule is to watch how much the center is used. If it is a popular activity, assure the children that, if they don't get a chance to use the materials one day, they will still be there the next day and for as long as there is interest. Then, as interest wanes, forwarn them when the last day of that specific activity is scheduled, so that they will still have a chance to go to the center.

Starting Formalized Rotating Centers

As the year progresses, you may want to group the students and start formalized rotating centers. (See Chapter III.) In this case be certain that you start with short centers, no more than ten to fifteen minutes. The time can be increased if the children's attention-spans warrant. (Twenty minutes can be eternity to a kindergartener!)

If you begin formalized learning centers in kindergarten, it is especially important that you do not rely on "busy work" at the cen-ters. The materials, discussed at the beginning of each of the subject chapters, are appropriate for kindergarten centers, and should help you initiate on-going activities.

Teacher aides and upper-grade students are particularly helpful at kindergarten learning centers and are effective superivsors for both long and short-term centers. (See Chapter VII, "Recruiting and Training Teacher Aides.")

CHAPTER XVI

Developing Your Own Basic Learning-Centers Lesson-Plan

Introduction

Now that you are ready to set up your own learning centers, a written basic lesson-plan, listing the activities you plan to schedule each week, is one of the best ways to organize your thoughts. This basic plan is designed with blanks for any of the activities that vary from week to week. These blanks are filled in each week as you determine the specific activities for that period.

Once you have determined the contents of your own Basic Learning-Centers Lesson-Plan, write it on a ditto master and make dittoed copies. Staple these copies together and then all that is necessary is to fill in the blanks each week. This is a real time saving device. Your entire weekly lesson plan can be completed in twenty to thirty minutes!

The Basic Learning-Centers Lesson-Plan is also helpful to substitute teachers. It provides details of the activities you have planned. The substitute can easily see which activities are new (requiring more detailed instructions and supervision), and which are continuations of on-going centers.

Preliminary Plans

On page 291 a sample of a Basic Learning-Centers Lesson-Plan is illustrated. A plan of your own can be constructed by following the directions in this chapter, and using the sample as a guide.

One of the first things you need to consider is how well your students work independently. This will have a great effect on how you plan your centers. If they are basically independent workers, there are many centers you can plan which will be successful without supervision.

If, however, your students are not yet able to assume the responsibility of working independently, you will need to plan a different type of unsupervised center—ones which require less movement, mess, and ingredients for catastrophies! For instance, unsupervised finger-painting would be an unwise choice for children who were unable to assume responsibility!

As the year progresses, your students will become more independent and self-reliant. You will then be able to provide additional unsupervised centers which require these abilities. In the beginning for both your sanity and the children's, plan your centers according to what you know about your students' present level of independence.

Another factor, that you will want to consider before constructing your plan, is which areas of the curriculum you want to handle yourself, and which areas of the curriculum you will feel comfortable assigning to teacher aides. (Throughout the book, various aspects of the curriculum which aides can handle effectively, have been discussed. Have you made certain that they are comfortable, working in their assigned subjects? Have you taken the time to train them adequately?)

Your Basic Learning-Centers Lesson-Plan should reflect the thinking you have done about learning centers and classroom organization, observations about your aide(s) and yourself, plus your knowledge of situations in which the children work well as well as situations which are difficult for them to handle.

You will need to determine which subject areas you want the children to be involved in daily, such as Math and Language Arts, and what other activities you want to incorporate on a weekly basis. But at this stage in the development of the Basic Learning-Centers Lesson-Plan, you are only considering activities which you want the children to do *every* week all year. For example, every Monday you may want the children to select their individualized spelling words, every Thursday to practice them, and every Friday take a spelling test. Once a basic plan such as this is established do not waste time writing the same thing down each week. This is the purpose of the dittoed Basic Learning-Centers Lesson-Plan—the permanent activities are already on the ditto. Only the variables need be filled in weekly.

Analyzing the Basic Learning-Centers Lesson-Plan

One of the first things you will notice about the sample Basic Learning Centers Lesson Plan on page 291, is that there are only three centers planned on some days. On other days four centers have been scheduled. Whole-group activities, such as tumbling and movement exploration, are planned once a week (Mondays). On Thursdays the class goes to the library. Therefore, on Monday and Thursday there is not enough time for the children to complete four centers and still have a sufficient period for their special activities. As a result, only three centers are scheduled. This necessitates regrouping the children, as explained on page 23.

Writing and Math centers are planned four days a week, Spelling three days a week. The specific activity for each day is written in, since it remains unchanged from week to week. A Discovery center is planned for two days each week. Follow-up on Science or Social Studies projects is included as a center one day a week. In addition, some of the more routine assignments have been listed as possibilities for the third center on

LESSON PLANS FOR WEEK OF _____

Centers run approximately 30 minutes each Monday through Thursday

M O N D A Y	*WRITING*	*a.m. – Mrs. McDonald* *p.m. – Mrs. Antoine*
	MATH	*Mrs. P. – Choice: computation games or math folder*
	SPELLING	*Choose 10 to 20 words. Make list in blue book and list to take home. Bring to me to initial, then select a quiet activity to do.*

T U E S D A Y	*WRITING*	*Mrs. P.*
	DISCOVERY	*Mrs. Wilson, Art or cooking*
	MATH	*Mrs. Estournes – Corrections and 2nd grade math book*
	SCIENCE/SOCIAL STUDIES, STRATEGY GAMES, ETC.	*a.m. – Mrs. Schwab* *p.m. – Mrs. Smyth*

W E D N E S D A Y	*WRITING*	*Mrs. O'Keefe*
	DISCOVERY	*Investigation task cards, art or listening post*
	MATH	*Mrs. P. – Stapled books (basic computation practice)*
	SPELLING	*Practice individual spelling words. Check the chart for various ways. If you finish, practice them a different way.*

T H U R S D A Y	*WRITING*	*Mrs. Gregory*
	MATH	*Mrs. P. – Diene's Blocks (place value, carrying, borrowing)*
	Write 1-100 by 1's, 2's, 5's, 10's – number before and after, alphabetizing, dictionary skills, follow-up for social studies/science unit, etc.	

F R I D A Y	*INDIVIDUALIZED SPELLING TEST*	*Mrs. Smyth* ⟨*4 short centers, 18-20 minutes each*⟩
		Mrs. Wright
		Mrs. P. – Instructional group (place value, area, fractions, etc.)

Independent . . . choose what you would like to do.

Thursday. At a glance, the teacher is reminded of some of the possible choices that might be included in Thursday's schedule.

Friday's format is considerably different from the other days of the week. Since the Individualized Spelling Test takes only 18 to 20 minutes to administer and correct (see Chapter VIII, "Individualized Spelling"), it works well to plan four short centers on Friday.

This allows one day during the week to plan activities which do not require a full 30 minutes. Instructional groups (fractions, telling time, place value, etc.), are ideal for 20-minute centers. Likewise, many manipulative math experiences are well suited for a 20-minute center (attribute blocks, geoboards, tangrams, pattern blocks, etc.).

Instructional games, and those which review skills, are much more effective if planned for short centers. The students generally get restless if they are expected to continue playing a game for 30 minutes (unless it is a game which requires a great deal of thinking, planning, and involvement). Many art projects are also ideally suited for 20-minute centers. Scheduling one short-centers day each week enables the teacher to incorporate into the plan many activities which would not be suitable for 30-minute centers.

Volunteer aides who work in the classroom, and their assigned centers, are also clearly indicated.

When filling in the Basic Learning-Centers Lesson-Plan it is generally easier to consider one subject area for the entire week, rather than attempting to fill in an entire day.

The following step-by-step explanation of the process of filling in the blanks of the basic plan demonstrates the time-saving usefulness of this tool.

Filling in a Basic Learning-Centers Lesson-Plan

Sample 1 *(page 293)*

WRITING CENTER

Several days during the week the children will be divided into two sub-groups at the writing center. For convenience we will call them #1 and #2. Ways of clearly indicating these sub-groups to the children, and the reasons for them, were discussed on pages 185-186.

1. Monday: Sub-group #1 will continue writing stories, or if they have finished their previous story, they will choose a new story-starter ditto. (See pages 178-179.) Sub-group #2 is scheduled to work on the mechanics of printing or cursive, using their copy-work books. (See pages 140-142.)

2. Tuesday: Monday's schedule is reversed. #1's are to work on mechanics of writing. #2's are to work on creative writing.

3. Wednesday: The children will use the weekly TV section from the local newspaper, filling in a ditto requiring the use of the TV section as a reference.

4. Thursday: The students may choose their own activity. Some will concentrate on their copy-work books. Others may continue stories. Still others may work on writing and illustrating a book.

LESSON PLANS FOR WEEK OF_____ SAMPLE 1

Centers run approximately 30 minutes each Monday through Thursday

MONDAY

WRITING	a.m.-Mrs. McDonald p.m.-Mrs. Antoine	#1's Continue old story or start new story starter ditto. #2's Copy work books
MATH	Mrs. P – Choice: computation games or math folder	
SPELLING	Choose 10 to 20 words. Make list in blue book and list to take home. Bring to me to initial, then select a quiet activity to do.	

TUESDAY

WRITING	Mrs. P.	Reverse Monday #1's Copy-work books #2's Write stories
DISCOVERY	Mrs. Wilson – Art or cooking	Clothes pin dolls
MATH	Mrs. Estournes – corrections and 2nd grade math book	
SCIENCE/SOCIAL STUDIES, STRATEGY GAMES, ETC.	a.m. – Mrs. Schwab p.m. – Mrs. Smyth	ecology: kit from library, classify animal pictures

WEDNESDAY

WRITING	Mrs. O'Keefe	TV section from newspaper with ditto to fill in
DISCOVERY	Investigation task cards, art or listening post	#1's Measure table with 3 different things and record #2's Trace foot, cut out, measure things in room and record
MATH	Mrs. P. – Stapled books (basic computation practice)	
SPELLING	Practice individual spelling words. Check the chart for various ways. If you finish, practice them a different way.	

THURSDAY

WRITING	Mrs. Gregory	Choice
MATH	Mrs. P. – Diene's Blocks (place value, carrying, borrowing)	

Write 1-100 by 1's, 2's, 5', 10's – number before and after, alphabetizing, dictionary skills, follow-up for social studies/science unit, etc.

FRIDAY

INDIVIDUALIZED SPELLING TEST	Mrs. Smyth	4 short centers, 18-20 minutes each
QUIZMO	Mrs. Wright	
CLOCKS: Diagnostic work to determine various skill levels of telling time	Mrs. P. – instructional group (place value, area, fractions, etc.)	

Independent . . . choose what you would like to do.

DISCOVERY CENTER

1. Tuesday: With the help of an aide, the children will make clothes-pin dolls.

2. Wednesday: The students will use task cards which require that they work on linear measurement, using non-standard units of measurement. Sub-group #1 is scheduled to measure the long work-table with three different things (scissors, pencils, crayons, etc.). They then write a description of what they did and of their discoveries. In sub-group #2 each child will trace around one of his or her feet, cut out the tracing, and then use the "foot" to measure various things in the room. They too will write about their findings.

REMAINING CENTERS (Monday through Thursday)

1. Tuesday: An activity which involves classifying various animal pictures is scheduled. (This is part of a kit on ecology from the school library. It correlates well with a unit in science which the entire class has been studying.)

2. Thursday: The students will write to one hundred by 1's, 2's, 5's, and 10's.

FRIDAY'S FOUR SHORT CENTERS

1. An aide will help the children play Quizmo, a commercial game which reviews basic math combinations.

2. The teacher will do diagnostic work on telling time.

This completes the thinking process for filling in one week's Basic Learning-Centers Lesson-Plan.

Sample 2   (page 295)

WRITING CENTERS

1. Monday: #2's are continuing old stories or starting a new story. (The teacher has added a collection of mounted pictures as a tool to stimulate creative writing.) #1's are working on the mechanics of printing or cursive and writing in their copy work books.

2. Tuesday: The children will fill in a ditto, describing the things they like best and least, or would like to change, in the classroom. This has been scheduled for a day when the teacher will be at the writing center. Then the children can freely discuss with the teacher some of their thoughts about the classroom.

3. Wednesday: The students will make a Class Booklet. (See pages 166-175.)

4. Thursday: Monday's schedule is reversed.

DISCOVERY CENTER

1. Tuesday: With the help of an aide, the children will be making individual servings of Granola.

LESSON PLANS FOR WEEK OF_____ SAMPLE 2

Centers run approximately 30 minutes each Monday through Thursday

MONDAY	WRITING	a.m. – Mrs. McDonald p.m. – Mrs. Antoine	#2's Continue old story, or select a mounted picture #1's Copy work books
	MATH	Mrs. P. – Choice: computation games or math folder	
	SPELLING	Choose 10 to 20 words. Make list in blue book and list to take home. Bring to me to initial, then select a quiet activity to do.	

TUESDAY	WRITING	Mrs. P.	All: ditto – What do you like best/least in the classroom, etc.
	DISCOVERY	Mrs. Wilson – Art or cooking	Granola (individualized recipe)
	MATH	Mrs. Estournes – Corrections and 2nd grade math book	
	SCIENCE/SOCIAL STUDIES, STRATEGY GAMES, ETC.	a.m. – Mrs. Schwab p.m. – Mrs. Smyth	Ecology: library kit animal survival game

WEDNESDAY	WRITING	Mrs. O'Keefe	Class book: A good thing to be . . . A good thing not to be . . .
	DISCOVERY	Investigation task cards, art or listening post	Reverse last week: #1's trace foot. #2's Measure table with 3 different things
	MATH	Mrs. P. – Stapled books (basic computation practice)	
	SPELLING	Practice individual spelling words. Check the chart for various ways. If you finish, practice them a different way.	

THURSDAY	WRITING	Mrs. Gregory	Reverse Monday: #2's Copy-work books #1's Write stories
	MATH	Mrs. P. – Diene's Blocks (place value, carrying, borrowing)	
	Write 1-100 by 1's, 2's, 5's, 10's – number before and after, alphabetizing, ditto, dictionary skills, follow-up for social studies/science unit, etc.		

FRIDAY	INDIVIDUALIZED SPELLING TEST	Mrs. Smyth	*(4 short centers, 18-20 minutes each)*
	TANGRAMS	Mrs. Wright	
	CLOCKS: Re-group according to skill levels on telling time. Provide instruction using individual clocks	Mrs. P. – instructional group (place value, area, fractions, etc.)	

Independent . . . choose what you would like to do.

The aide will be instructed to stress skills in reading, volume, fractions, and sequencing.

2. *Thursday:* Last week's schedule for the Discovery Center is reversed. (See page 293.) #1's are each using a "foot" tracing to measure things. #2's are measuring the table with three different things.

REMAINING CENTERS (Monday through Friday)

1. *Tuesday:* The children will work with an aide, playing an ecology animal-survival game.
2. *Thursday:* A ditto which reinforces alphabetizing skills will be assigned.

FRIDAY'S FOUR SHORT CENTERS

1. An aide will work with the children on Tangrams (an ideal twenty-minute activity).
2. The teacher will have re-grouped the children before the start of centers, according to their various skill levels in telling time. Teacher will then work with each group on appropriate activities when they come to his or her center. The children will remain in these groups for all of today's centers. They will return to their regular groups on Monday.

Determining A Basic Weekly Schedule For Learning Centers

Use a pencil to fill in the Basic Weekly Schedule on page 297. You will fill in the blanks with the centers that remain the same each week. Do not fill in the specific tasks that vary from week to week. When you have completed filling in your Basic Weekly Schedule, it should resemble the sample on page 291.

1. If you plan on having an Individualized-Spelling program, decide which day the children will be taking their spelling test. On your Basic Plan make a note that there will be four short centers (18-20 minutes each) on the day you have chosen as Spelling Test day. Fill in one of the blanks on your Basic Plan for that day | *Spelling Test* |

Choose which day you want the children to select their Individualized Spelling words. Fill in a blank on your Basic Plan for that day, | *Spelling* | —choose words.

Determine which day you want the children to practice their spelling words. Fill in a blank for that day | *Spelling* | — practice words.

If there is any other spelling activity that you want the children to do each week during their centers time, such as alphabetizing their spelling words, using them in sentences, working in a commercial spelling work book, etc., choose a day and fill in the blank in your Basic Plan.

2. Determine which subject areas you want the children to have daily, such as Math, Writing, etc. Fill in blanks in your Basic Plan. (Do not fill in the specific assignment if it will vary from week to week.)
3. If you have aides in your room, fill in your Basic Plan with the aides' names next to the activity that each will supervise. Write your name on your Basic Plan next to the activity that you will supervise each day.

BASIC WEEKLY SCHEDULE

MONDAY

- [ ]
- [ ]
- [ ]
- [ ]

TUESDAY

- [ ]
- [ ]
- [ ]
- [ ]

WEDNESDAY

- [ ]
- [ ]
- [ ]
- [ ]

THURSDAY

- [ ]
- [ ]
- [ ]
- [ ]

FRIDAY

- [ ]
- [ ]
- [ ]
- [ ]

4. Are there any other activities you feel are crucial for the children to have every week during centers time? If so, fill in the blanks accordingly. Be certain to take into consideration which activities will need to have an aide or the teacher available, and which activities can run independently.

5. Determine which days you want to have 3 centers and on which you would prefer to hold four centers. Cross off the extra blank on your Basic Plan for any days in which you are planning to have only three centers.

6. Now look at your plan and consider filling in blanks for art, listening post, etc. (Don't forget to think about whether the activity will need supervision, and whether you will have an aide available.) Try to balance each day. Consider such things as noisy and quiet activities, centers which demand concentration and/or staying seated versus centers where the child is free to move around, etc.

7. You may want to consider scheduling an Independent Center daily, or several times during the week. As described on page 5, it is an excellent way for helping children become independent. It assures that every child is provided with time to make choices, interact with peers, and engage in fun activities. It provides a place for you to use many of the materials you already have: games, puzzles, etc. Therefore, it will not require a great deal of teacher planning time. The choices may be completely left up to the student, or you can structure the choices. (See pages 9 and 255.)

8. Your Basic Plan should resemble the sample on page 291. You could transfer the information to a ditto master and run off copies to provide your own basic Learning-Centers Lesson-Plan. You would then need to fill in only those activities which vary from week to week.

Developing Lesson Plans For One Week

You are now ready to schedule your actual lesson plan for one week. (Good luck!)

1. Use a felt pen or ball-point pen to copy your Basic Weekly Schedule, (page 297), on to page 299. When you are finished copying it, pretend that you had run all that information off on a ditto master and you are now ready to fill in specific lesson plans for one week. (Copying the permanent schedule in ball-point or felt pen helps to separate the Basic Plan visually from the specific tasks, which you will write in pencil.)

2. Take one subject area, such as Writing (refer to Chapters IX and X for ideas), and fill in with pencil the specific task for each day, in that subject area.

3. Continue filling in your Sample Lesson Plan this way until it is complete. Don't forget, if you are planning on having one day when the centers will all be short, 18-20 minutes each, (Spelling-Test Day), that the activities you plan for that day must also be short. Consider instructional games, short art activities, and teacher-directed instruc-

LESSON PLANS FOR WEEK OF _____

MONDAY

TUESDAY

WEDNESDAY

THURSDAY

FRIDAY

tional groups. A shortened centers day can be used to provide the children with independent time for them to choose activities they would like to do. . . painting, blocks, checkers, continuing with writing or math activities, reading, etc.

As you fill in your Sample Lesson Plan, keep the balance between active and non-active, noisy and quiet activities in mind. If you plan several noisy activities on the same day you will have problems. Also, think about the activity that you will be involved with that day. Is it an activity in which interruptions will be difficult to handle? If so, do not plan on having other activities going on that day that will necesitate having the children come to you. Instead, plan activities that can be carried out independently and/or with the help of an aide.

Always look over each day's plans for potential problems. . . noise, the teacher being needed in too many places at one time, children finishing early (what are they to do?), etc. Make changes accordingly. Remember, with only three centers, there will be more children at each center. You will discover that some activities work better with smaller groups of children, and, therefore, should be planned on days when you have four centers. Other activities are suited to a larger number of children at the center. These are obviously the activities to plan on three-center days.

APPENDIX I

Smock Pattern

MATERIALS:

Terry cloth, 1 yard at least 36″ wide.
Elastic, approximately 18″
Binding tape

Step 1: Hem the top and bottom. Do not hem selvages.

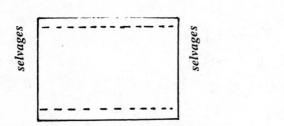

Step 2: Fold in half.

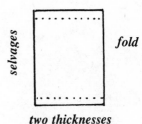

two thicknesses

Step 3: Fold in half again.

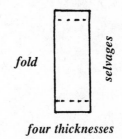

four thicknesses

Step 4: Cut armholes from folded edge, 4″ from top. Bind armholes.

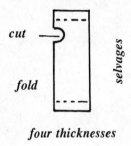

cut — *fold* — *selvages*

four thicknesses

Step 5: Run elastic through top hem at neck and tack at the back about 2″ from the top.

back

APPENDIX II

Cloth-covered Folders for Individualized Spelling (1)

MATERIALS:

9½"×12" corrugated cardboard . . . two per folder, cut from grocery boxes. Make sure the weight of cardboard in any one set is the same, and that the corrugation runs in the same direction. Cutting the cardboard on a paper cutter is the best way. It takes about two hours to do sixty boards (thirty books).

Two pieces medium-weight cloth material per folder, cut 11½"×14" each. (This allows a margin of ¾"–1" on each edge.) Have students bring fabric from home, pre-cut to proper size for younger students . . . use as a measurement experience for older students.

Piece of cord, approximately 28" per folder.

(Seine #35 macrame cord works well.)

1 piece of construction paper 9"×11½" for inside back cover

1 piece of construction paper 7½"×11½" for inside front cover

White glue, slightly thinned with water

Brushes for white glue (1"–2" wide work well)

Gauze (2" wide). . . one strip cut 26" long per folder

Newspapers to cover table

Waxed paper . . . to place between folders after gluing

METHOD:

After cardboards are cut to size, one side

(the front) must be hinged to open easily. Cut off 1¼" on the long side. Then cut off ⅓" from the small strip and discard. Lay the 1" strip and the remaining large piece next to each other, leaving a ⅓" hinge-space between them. (See below.)

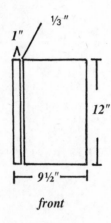

front

Hinge front cover

To create the hinge it is necessary to cover the open space with gauze. Brush white glue along the edges adjacent to the hinge space. Cover with a 26" strip of gauze, and wait a few minutes for it to adhere. Turn front cover over. On the other side, brush on glue. Wrap gauze around the overlap 1"-2".

Place the cardboard so advertising side is down. (It may show through the fabric otherwise.) Have child brush glue on the front of the cardboard. (Caution the student not to saturate the cardboard, or the folder will warp during the drying process.) Cover

with fabric. Center. Turn cover over and miter corners.

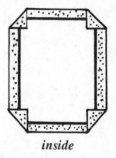

inside

Miter corners.

Glue down the turned-over corners. Fold in sides of fabric. (Make certain the fabric does not cover the hinge-space.) Reinforce the turned-in edges with pieces of masking tape.

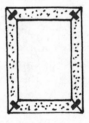

**Reinforce mitered corners
with masking tape.**

Repeat same process for back cover.

Have student round corners of pre-cut construction paper. Glue construction paper to inside of front and back covers. (Trim, if necessary, to make certain it does not cover hinge in front.)

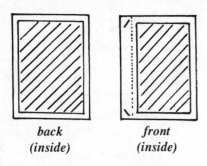

back
(inside)   *front*
                          (inside)

Glue construction paper
to inside of front and back covers.

When dry, two holes may be punched in front and back covers by hammering a nail through the folders to a board underneath. Fill with two-hole punched paper (spelling lists). Bind book by tying a 28" piece of macrame cord through the punched holes.

**** *IMPORTANT:* Before you begin folder construction, check contents so the folder can be made (1) with ample margin space on the left for holes, (2) so that no writing will be obscured, (3) so pages will not extend beyond covers on the right.

APPENDIX III

Open-ended Games

Open-ended games designed to reinforce many skills and to be used in many subjects, are far more useful than instructional games constructed for only one skill. For example, a game board which has long vowels written on each space is a "closed game," and can only be used to reinforce long vowels. But a series of open-ended game boards and sets of cards can be constructed so that any set of cards can be used with any game board. The cards can range from long vowel words or blends, to math facts, money, telling time, history, geography, or science.

*Set of cards to accompany
an open-ended game board*

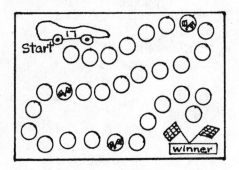

Open-ended game board

Use binder rings to keep the various sets of cards separate. The top card should be slightly larger than the other cards, so the set can be easily located. Label it to indicate which skill it reinforces, or which book and unit it parallels. These ringed sets of cards can then be stored in shoe boxes, near the open-ended game boards.

RULES:

Player one takes the top flash card· If the

307

correct answer is given, player one spins a spinner or rolls a die, and moves the marker the number of spaces indicated. Player two does likewise. If a student doesn't know the answer, or answers incorrectly, he or she doesn't spin/roll, and cannot move ahead.

A problem which frequently occurs with games is that the smartest child wins, while the child who most needs the added practice loses. Soon the child who needs to play the reinforcement game the most says, "I don't want to play." If you ask why, the student will usually say something like, "I don't feel like it," or "I don't like to play games." In truth, the child does not want to risk losing again. The student knows before even starting, that failure is likely. Therefore, it is easier just to avoid playing the game.

To eliminate this type of problem, it is of utmost importance to structure the situation so that both players have an equal chance of winning. The winner should be determined by luck, not ability. Indicate on the spinner or die some sections which send the player ahead on the game board, and some sections which send the child back.

Spinner

When you introduce the game to the students, you can tell them honestly that the person who wins the game will not necessarily be the smartest but, instead, the luckiest. Explain that, even if they knew all of the correct answers, but rolled/spun 1's and 2's or got sent back many times, they might lose. On the other hand, a student could give incorrect answers for several cards, and still win, if he or she landed on lots of 2's and 3's, and on very few "go-back" sections. This removes the threat of failure for the child with less ability. This student can say, "Boy, was I unlucky today. . . ." Similarly, a child who is very capable also has an excuse for losing. In addition, the intelligent child experiences losing, an important social-growth factor. Many bright students have a difficult time coping with losing, as they are seldom faced with this situation.

The answer can be written on the back of each card for math, social studies, or science questions, but not for reading vocabulary words. Therefore, it is extremely important that there is a person available to make certain the words are read correctly, and appropriate responses are reinforced. If a "referee" is not available, two students who are weak in reading may give incorrect responses, and agree that they are correct! This can be handled in one of the following ways:

1. An upper-grade student, or one of the students in the class who has already mastered the words, acts as referee. Students from the Independent Reading Center can take turns in this function. This also allows students at different levels to play an open-ended game together, each using an appropriate set of word cards, with a referee who has previously mastered both sets of words.
2. Three or four students at approximately the same level play a game. When there is doubt about the answer,

two of them will gang up against the more forceful students and insist the word be verified. In this case, be certain to specify to whom they should come in the event of disputes (you, the aide, or another student). Be certain to encourage them always to check if there is any doubt. They are usually anxious to make certain that no one moves ahead on the game board unless he or she is deserving!

Open-ended games are easy to make. Use tagboard or colored railroad board. Draw a picture in the middle of the game board and a road or path around the picture. Lick-on or self-sticking dots make a convenient and colorful path. If you have difficulty drawing, cut pictures from greeting cards, party invitations, or gift-wrapping paper. Punch-out bulletin board decorations (Snoopy and friends are great for all ages), bridge tallies, and paper coasters, also make good decorations for game boards. You can even cut pictures from party table cloths and/or party napkins!

To add elements of chance, place special spots on the game board: dots of different color, small pictures, or seals.

For instance, small Snoopy seals designed to go on the back of envelopes, can be used as the special spots on a Snoopy game board.

To stimulate interest, the children can make their own rule on what happens when they land on a special spot, such as an extra turn, loss of a turn, or double the amount shown on the die or spinner. (The "special rule" should, of course, be agreed upon before the game starts.) Children will often play a game one time, with one rule for the special spots, and then immediately play it again, with a completely different special-spot rule.

For upper-grade students, special directions can be added: lose one turn, go back to the red circle (to the flower, etc.) back to go, etc.

Notes

1. Helen Joseph, Teacher, Novato Unified School District, Novato, California.

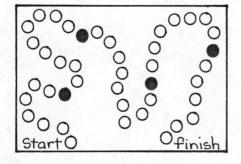

Game board with special spots

DATE DUE

DE 1 '82	DEC 5 '82		
AP 10 '83	APR 8 '83		
AP 16 '84	APR 16 '84		
FE 06 '91	JAN 22 '91		